YANKEE Magazine's

Now That's Ingenious!

Everyday Experts Reveal Their
Secrets for Handling More Than
1,200 Common Cleanups,
Fix-Its, and Other Tasks around
the House and Garden

From the Editors of

YANKEE Magazine

Printed in the United States of America on acid-free ∞, recycled ♻ paper

Library of Congress Cataloging-in-Publication Data

Yankee magazine's now that's ingenious! : everyday experts reveal their secrets for handling more than 1,200 common cleanups, fix-its, and other tasks around the house and garden / from the editors of Yankee magazine.

     p.   cm.

Includes index.

   ISBN 0–89909–383–3 hardcover

   ISBN 0–89909–387–6 paperback

   1. Home economics.   2. Dwellings—Maintenance and repair.   I. Title: Now that's ingenious!.   II. Yankee (Dublin, N.H.)

   TX158 .Y353   2002

   640'.41—dc21   2001008451

Distributed to the book trade by St. Martin's Press

2 4 6 8 10 9 7 5 3 1 hardcover

2 4 6 8 10 9 7 5 3 1 paperback

YANKEE *Magazine's*

Now That's Ingenious!

YANKEE BOOKS STAFF

EDITOR: Ellen Phillips

COVER DESIGNER: Christopher Rhoads

YANKEE PUBLISHING STAFF

PRESIDENT: Jamie Trowbridge

BOOK EDITOR: Lori Baird

CONTRIBUTING WRITERS: Linda Buchanan Allen, Larry Bean, Tom Cavalieri, Sally Cunningham, Bill Keller, Rose Kennedy, Arden Moore, Lynn Naliboff, Michelle Seaton

BOOK DESIGNER: Eugenie S. Delaney

ILLUSTRATOR: Kirk Caldwell

PHOTOGRAPHER: Tom Cavalieri

INDEXER: Barbara Long

FACT-CHECKERS: Mary Johnson, Trish Johnson

COPY-EDITOR: Barbara Jatkola

PROOFREADERS: Marina Maina, Robert Potterton, Deri Reed

contents

PART 1

ALL AROUND THE house

Kitchen Clutter • Bedroom Stuff • Clearing Out
the Bathroom • Family Room • Kid Clutter • Unexpected
Storage

Kitchen • Bathroom • Living Room and Dining Room •
Bedroom • Mudroom • Windows

PART 3

yard AND garden

introduction

I WAS READING THROUGH THE NEWSPAPER a few years back when I saw something that made me shake my head. A fellow had written to an advice columnist with a problem. A friend of his accidentally fired a basketball right into the letter writer's car door, leaving a dent. The fellow wanted to know whether he should make his friend pay the insurance deductible to have the door repaired.

"You, my friend, are asking the wrong question," I said aloud. I was cheered considerably a week or two later when another letter appeared in the same newspaper. A retired body shop owner wrote that these friends wouldn't need to worry about car insurance deductibles if they would try a simple technique to take the dent out of the door (which is just what I'd been thinking). He suggested sucking the dent out with a toilet plunger.

Now *that's* the kind of everyday ingenuity you'll find in this book. All the folks you'll meet in the following pages are "everyday" experts on their topics. They're real folks who have learned the ropes from years of real-life experience, whether it's a policeman explaining how to use timed lights to protect your home or a professional antiques restorer sharing his ways to get the best deals on antiques.

Bob Grimac of Knoxville, Tennessee, is just one of those experts. He's a passionate environmentalist who runs a recycling consulting operation and writes and edits a statewide environmental newsletter. Before I read his advice, I had no idea you could lure flies from the house by turning out the lights or that the local school might be a good place to borrow mousetraps.

Another of our ingenious experts is building inspector Michael

Melchiorri of Natick, Massachusetts. He knows the ins and outs of protecting homes from structural damage. But he's just as knowledgeable about preventing accidental fires, because his father was a firefighter who saw firsthand the destruction fires can cause.

They're only two of the folks you'll meet. Among the others are master gardeners, professional chefs, and doctors. It's true, these experts come from widely different backgrounds, but they have two things in common: They're passionate about what they do, and they know what they're talking about, whether it's protecting your home from fire or protecting your hair from split ends.

Do you know the best part about all this advice? The editors of *Yankee* Magazine have analyzed the information for you and laid it out in an easy-to-read format, with lots of tips and lists. I've even tossed in a few tidbits that I've learned in my 30-year association with these ingenious folks, including two of my favorites: a fitting way to preserve the garage door and a quirky way to keep lipstick on your lips indefinitely. (If you want to know what a guy like me knows about lipstick, turn to page 222 for the full story!)

This is all advice you can use right away in the living room, at the store, or on the phone with your contractor. Before long, you'll be adopting habits such as using 2-by-6s instead of 2-by-3s to halve the cost of privacy fence stringers, or taking a battery-operated smoke detector on vacation with you for safety's sake, or using an empty tuna can to gauge how much water the trees in your yard need. That's right, an empty tuna can. Like some of the other tips in this book, they may sound a bit quirky, but they're right on the mark if you want to do more with what you have.

Thomas Edison said, "Genius is 1 percent inspiration and 99 percent perspiration." Our ingenious experts have done the sweating. You're holding the book that will take care of the other 1 percent. Could you become a genius in everyday living? I like the odds.

— *Earl Proulx*

PART 1

ALL AROUND THE

house

Whether you own your home or rent it, whether it's a two-story Federal-style or a two-room apartment, whether it's 100 years or only 100 days old, your home really is your castle. And wouldn't you like to know how to give that castle the best care you can?

You've come to the right place. In this section, our everyday experts offer ingenious tips for handing cleanups and fix-its in every room of your house—and its exterior, too. Here you'll find clever ways to organize your home, including a way to clear space in your freezer— just by wearing mittens! (It's on page 8.) We also show you how to rid your home of pests such as ants without using harmful chemicals. In fact, our experts recommend using cucumber peels in some instances. (That one's on page 51) There's more, too, including hints about getting the best deals on furniture and fixing that refrigerator door that won't quite close. Finally, we offer a whole chapter about turning your home sweet home into a home *safe* home.

clearing out
c l u t t e r

MAYBE YOU'VE SEEN THAT DESKTOP MOTTO, "If a cluttered desk is the sign of a cluttered mind, what's an empty desk the sign of?" The idea is funny, but clutter isn't. It muddles your mind, saps your energy, and often wastes time and money.

So what's the answer? Well, this chapter will get you off to a fine start. In the following pages, you'll learn to master some of the clutter-cutting essentials that apply to nearly every room inside the house. And along the way, you'll meet our everyday experts—folks like executive chef Rob Stanford of Tampa, Florida, and food editor Lynn Naliboff of Stamford, Connecticut, who share their tried-and-true tips for keeping kitchen clutter under control. Nancy Byrd, a chronically organized marketing pro who lives in Indianapolis, cut her teeth as a facilities planner at Virginia Commonwealth University in Richmond. In that job, she organized classrooms for all the evening and summer classes—in the days *before* computers. She offers tips for cutting clutter in closets, bathrooms, and family rooms. Joanne Kennedy of Toano, Virginia, suggests some clever ways to clean out clothes closets, and she's had lots of practice: Joanne organized a home—with eight children—for more than two decades, then went on to a second career organizing books as a librarian. There are other experts, too, with different backgrounds, different lifestyles, and different jobs, but they all have one thing in common: a knack for solving household organizing dilemmas in wonderfully ingenious ways.

Are you worried that our experts will suggest unreasonable plans tailored for some clean freak with unlimited time and zeal? Don't be! Our experts are real people who will show you how to organize your household in a way that suits your real-world lifestyle. So read on for a sampling of ways to tame the clutter that reigns in the kitchen, bathroom, bedroom, and other areas of your home. (For tips on cutting the clutter in your garage, basement, and attic, see Chapter 7.)

Kitchen Clutter

Even the most functional kitchen tends to be a clutter magnet. That's because every member of the family uses it and it's the one room chock-full of the kinds of stuff that goes bad, takes up space, and hangs around in the sink waiting to be washed.

But a cluttered kitchen can set back the entire household routine. Most people, such as kindergarten teacher Keyne Stanford of Tampa, just "can't think when there's a lot of clutter." And you

MAKE it **LAST**

Maintain your clutter-free kitchen

WE KNOW, you're trying to keep your counters free of clutter. Here's an idea that might sound counterproductive but will ultimately help make your kitchen organizing plan last longer.

Sacrifice one kitchen counter to clutter. That's right. Have an agreement with other members of your household that most of your kitchen counters will stay pristine but one will act like a junk drawer: It will be the repository for the paper towel holder, the coffee machine, the school calendar, and all the other stuff that regularly gets deposited there. To prevent all your counters from overflowing, try designating one as "junk counter." It just might work.

need to have a clear head when you're gulping down breakfast while trying to get out the door and to the office on time, planning a nice meal with friends in the evening, or even just sitting down to pay bills once a month or sign a report card.

So how do you do away with kitchen clutter or keep it at bay before it becomes a major problem? Constant vigilance is the key, says Keyne, particularly if you live with a chef, as she does. Her husband, Rob, an executive chef at a yacht club, is always bringing home food samples. He's also "a sucker for weird condiments" and has lots of pots and pans to stow. "Luckily, we're both really neat people," Keyne says, "so there's not a lot of stuff on the counters."

Besides keeping watch over your counters, Keyne offers two more tips to prevent clutter: Systematically weed through your kitchen stuff fairly often, and buy only what you need, rotating your stock often. Read on for more clutter-cutting ideas.

PERFECTING YOUR PANTRY TECHNIQUE

What is in your pantry, anyway? Tomato soup circa 1957? Or maybe there's some bomb-shelter-vintage chipped beef. If you can't bear to look inside your pantry, maybe you should heed the advice of our seasoned experts.

Put the squeeze on squeeze bottles. Sure, the kids in the television commercials squeal with delight when they decorate a burger with squeezable mustard, but is it really all that great to be able to squeeze mustard (or mayonnaise or relish) from a bottle instead of using a knife or spoon to spread it? Not if you consider that you can halve the storage space such products require by buying these condiments in glass or plastic jars rather than squeeze bottles. The flat-topped jars allow you to stack them in the pantry or fridge, and they fit on much shorter shelves. Jars also tend to be cheaper, they're reusable and recyclable, and it's much easier to scrape the bottom of a jar with a spoon or small spatula than to squeeze the remains out of a squeeze bottle.

Give up your extras. Scour the pantry for food bank donations on the last Saturday of every month with 31 days. People who live on fixed incomes or who receive federal checks or food stamps are paid only once a month, so food banks tend to have a greater number of people coming in during the longer months. If you clean out your pantry during those months, you'll be doing yourself—and someone else—a big favor.

THE INS AND OUTS OF POTS AND PANS

Even if you're striving to be a gourmet chef, Rob Stanford recommends keeping the number of kitchen gadgets down to a very valuable few. He believes that people buy more of these items than they need or can comfortably store—particularly these days,

STOCK UP FOR ONLY ONE STORM

Ever heard these comments at the grocery store? "Oh, look! Tomato soup's on sale—let's buy a case!" or "Never can get too many dill pickles. Let's buy this three-gallon jar!" Keyne Stanford thinks that people go way overboard stocking up on provisions. Instead of saving money, they end up wasting space and collecting food they'll never cook. "We keep just enough extra stuff around—beyond what we'll eat each week—to make chili if we get snow," she says.

when home cooks want to fix restaurant-quality meals in their own kitchens. What's Rob's advice to reduce pot clutter? Just wok away.

"I gave my woks away years ago," he says. "You see, the woks in professional kitchens get hotter than we can imagine, and that's why they make such great Asian foods. The green vegetables turn vibrant before our very eyes! There's no way to achieve those temperatures at home. You'll get the hottest surface using a heavy skillet over a gas flame."

Here are two more ways to organize your pots and pans.

Peg down your clutter. As a food editor who works in New York City, Lynn Naliboff spends a lot of time in test kitchens, so she knows a thing or two about managing her own kitchen. Lynn's tool for keeping her pots and pans (and her whisks, eggbeater, corkscrew, bottle opener, rolling pin, box grater, and cookie cutters—of which she owns about 200) organized? A Peg-Board. It hangs on one wall in her kitchen and keeps all of those tools within reach.

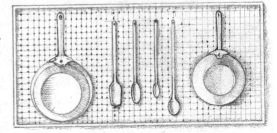

put your mittens on

WEARING MITTENS can help you cut clutter. When you wear mittens or gloves as you unpack frozen foods from the grocery store, you won't have to hurry the job because your hands are cold. And that means you'll be able to take time to rotate foods that have been in the freezer awhile to the front or to the top of the stack—where you're more likely to see them, use them, and free up some space.

Stick with the basics. Don't curse your cabinets if they're large enough only for a few pots and pans. They're really doing you a favor, says Rob Stanford. That's because a pan you use all the time will turn out the best food. You'll learn its idiosyncrasies and know how to get good results from it. "Chef friends almost always rave about a pot, and it will be the same one their mother used," Rob says. "That makes sense, because you know how to cook your family's recipes in a pot that's just like your mother's."

FREEING UP THE FRIDGE

It's too easy to let your refrigerator become a repository for unrecognizable leftovers and your freezer become a museum for UFOs (unidentified frozen objects). But uncluttering your refrigerator and freezer is not the impossible dream. Just follow these simple tips.

Don't freeze home-cooked foods. What's the best way to save space in your freezer? Don't store your home-cooked foods there, says Rob Stanford. "Home-cooked foods don't come out of the freezer with the same quality they had when they went in," he says. "They're spoiling by the second."

Save the freezer for frozen foods. So what *can* you store in your freezer? Rob Stanford recommends that you use it for previously flash-frozen foods such as frozen corn or broccoli—the kind you buy at the grocery store. "A home freezer can keep a solidly frozen food frozen without compromising the quality," he notes.

SHHH: TAKE ADVANTAGE OF SECRET STORAGE

The kitchen—maybe more than any other room in the house—is chock-full of hidden storage areas. "You can't take a lid off a pot in my kitchen without finding something stored inside," says Lynn Naliboff. Here are six of her favorite "secret" hiding spots in the kitchen.

1. Check the cupboards. We mean *underneath* your upper cupboards. Insert screw-in hooks to hang your coffee mugs.

2. Deposit it in the dishwasher. Okay, this works only if you use yours infrequently, but the dishwasher has the perfect design to hold lots of dishes, pots and pans, and extra utensils.

3. Put 'em in pitchers. Large decorative pitchers are perfect for storing your wooden spoons, potato masher, chopsticks, hand graters, and spatulas, freeing up space in your drawers.

4. Move it to the microwave. You'll never start the microwave without opening it first, and that makes it a handy and safe storage place. Bread and other baked goods fit nicely inside, as do extra plates or even your toaster or electric mixer.

5. Don't forget the oven. Store ovenproof dishes, cookie sheets, pots and pans, skillets, or your Dutch oven there. Why only ovenproof items? If someone turns on the oven without checking inside first, those items won't burn, melt, or otherwise be ruined.

6. Place it in a picnic cooler. If you keep your picnic cooler tucked away in the kitchen closet, put it to work. Picnic items are a natural fit: tablecloth, small cutting board, plastic utensils, and the like.

Move the snack foods to the back. One good way to cut freezer clutter is to store the sweets and fast foods in the back and the vegetables and meats in the front. That way, anybody looking for a snack will touch and move all the food in the freezer. Why is this good? It means nothing can hide in the back, taking up space when it's outdated or unlikely to be used. And you won't inadvertently waste expensive food because no one realized there was, say, a king's ransom of pesto tucked back there.

Bedroom Stuff

Sure, it's the bedroom. But it's also the reading room, the dressing room, the sickroom, the television room, the hiding-presents room, the dog's room, the makeup room . . . In other words, the bedroom is a natural repository for a lot of stuff. But that doesn't mean it has to be marred by disorganized, dusty heaps. In fact, clutter in a bedroom is positively unhealthy, because seeing all the chaos makes it hard to relax and fall asleep. And it wastes time, since it takes longer to find your clothes for work in the morning. There are two clutter-cutting approaches to creating a tidier, more serene bedroom for yourself or other members of your family. You can pare down the functions your bedroom is supposed to fill—and the clutter that goes with them—or you can toss a few items out and organize the rest of the objects in a more efficient, eye-pleasing way. With either method, strive to prevent more clutter from creeping in. Here are some ideas to get you started.

Wash out bedroom clutter. The key to ultraorganized sociologist Judy Van Wyk's exquisitely simplified bedroom is in her basement. That's where she keeps her washer. "I cut down on having lots of clothes lying around or having to store lots of clothes and linens by keeping up with the wash," says Judy, who lives in Narragansett, Rhode Island. In fact, when Judy or her

SAGE ADVICE ABOUT CONTROLLING CLUTTER

Judy Van Wyk, an assistant professor of sociology and criminology at the University of Rhode Island in Kingston, has moved seven or eight times since her childhood, and has never taken more than 2 days to unpack. What's her secret? The right attitude. Here's Judy's anticlutter philosophy: "I have a place for everything, and that's just where it goes. I never lose my keys, because I always put them in the front pocket of my purse. The remote control for the TV is always on the coffee table. Even my office is neat." But this isn't just neatness for neatness' sake. "I can't think well if things are cluttered," she says.

Judy can't abide wasting time either. "I don't want to deal with things several times," she says. "I don't hang on to cardboard boxes just in case I might need them. I break them down, fold them up, and take them to the recycling center."

All this purging doesn't mean that Judy isn't sentimental. She has every birthday candle her 12-year-old daughter, Allyson, has ever blown out. "And I can tell you where each one is, too," she says. "Right in the flat storage box I keep for each year of Allyson's life, labeled on the outside and stacked in the basement."

Lots of those birthday candles were lighted in a house that Judy considers her greatest clutter-cutting success. "For six years, when I was working on my master's degree and then my doctorate, Allyson and I lived in a tiny two-bedroom house with three cats and two dogs. The center of one room was the dining room, and all around it was my office. But I managed to keep things organized enough that I could write my entire dissertation in the middle of all that."

daughter, Allyson, changes clothes, she usually takes the soiled laundry right down to the basement, where two laundry baskets wait—one for light-colored clothing, one for dark. The minute either basket is full enough, Judy runs a load. So that they don't have to traipse downstairs in the dark of night, they put soiled clothes in a laundry basket in the hall between their rooms. "But first thing in the morning, as soon as I wake up, I take those clothes to the basement," Judy says.

Add to your underbed space . . . The problem at Wade Slate's Knoxville, Tennessee, home is that all the available closets are full of decades' worth of previous owners' junk. While his family works on the tremendous task of cleaning out the heir-loom-packed closets, his stepdaughters still need somewhere to store things. One solution Wade hit on was to add much-needed storage beneath a wood-framed futon bed that's low to the ground. He used flat drawers from an old changing table that the family didn't want to throw away but wouldn't use again for years. Two of the 6-inch drawers fit easily below the frame, which is 8 inches off the floor. So that his stepdaughters can slide them out easily, Wade used bolts to attach 1-inch rollers to the four corners.

. . . Or eliminate it altogether. If your bedroom is like most, the clutter under the bed is much more fearsome than any monster could ever be. That space is just irresistible, whether you're an adult who's too tired to put away a book after you're through reading in bed or a teenager trying to pass room inspection without actually picking anything up. And we all know that there's a magnetic force under beds that sucks in shoes, socks, dust, and pet toys, some never to return.

One solution to below-bed clutter is almost painfully obvious, says Jim Slate of Winnsboro, South Carolina. Retired long ago from the Navy, Jim knows how to keep a bedroom shipshape. "But I didn't realize how much a platform bed would help until my wife bought one," he says. "Nothing can get under the bed, accidentally or on purpose. And this particular model has two drawers underneath the bed where we store blankets, and that really freed up space in our hall closet."

Make your bed some saddlebags. You do need a place near the bed for your current reading material, but who says it should be in a cluttered heap on the floor or nightstand? Instead, lose the nightstand and sew a book-size drawstring bag for each side of the bed. Using Velcro®, connect the two bags to a strip of cloth or canvas that's long enough to span the width of the bed between the mattress and box spring, with a little left over so the bags will be at arm's length when you're lying in bed. With a pouch instead of a flat surface, you'll have to make an effort to store each book, and you won't be tempted to cram a lot of books in there—just your current reading. If you sew the pouch from some nice scraps, it will be a lot prettier than an ungainly stack of magazines.

With just a few supplies, you can make clutter-cutting saddlebags for your bed.

Store sheets safari style. If you already have more sheets than you can comfortably store in your linen closet, consider rigging a type of hammock below your bed. Double over a sheet made of a substantial fabric, such as flannel, and sew small Velcro® squares to the four corners. Use wood glue to attach corresponding Velcro® squares to the bottom of your bed frame at the foot of the bed. Attach the folded sheet to the frame, letting it hang down a few inches, like a hammock. This is a great place to stash a few sets of sheets. Also, having the hammock draping down will keep you from stashing clutter under the bed. Make sure to cut an extra

Sew Velcro® squares to the corners of a sheet and glue four more to the bottom of your bedframe to make a hammock where you can store your bed linens.

13

set of Velcro® squares that match the set on the sheet. Should you want to use that sheet, you can pop the extra squares over those on the sheet to protect the Velcro® from undue wear.

CLOSETS AND DRAWERS

We call them the "eyes-closed" closets. You know, you ease the door open with your right hand just wide enough to cram something inside with your left hand. Then, eyes closed and fingers crossed, you slam the door shut and lean on it a little to make sure it doesn't burst open and spew forth years of accumulated stuff. Disorganized closets can undermine your entire de-cluttering effort. When the closets contain junk, where do you put the carefully culled items that deserve space in your home but that you don't want to see every day—such as neckties, the plunger, the checkerboard? They end up hanging from the curtain rod, piled up on the floor, in the dog's bed—you get the idea.

So stop the madness. Make your household closets and dresser drawers functional and cut down on clutter in other places at the same time. How can you achieve a closet that you can approach with your eyes open? Take some of these ingenious tips to heart.

Hang 'em high, hang 'em low—just hang 'em. Nancy Byrd, a marketing professional from Indianapolis, has an ingenious way to avoid stacks in her closet. "I know it's a little weird, but I hang up everything, even T-shirts," she says. "I fold sweaters in two and then drape them over hangers. Stacks of clothes are so easy to upset and so hard to sort through without having to refold everything. Hangers are much easier—you just slide them from side to side." So that she has space for all these hangers, Nancy installed two rods in each closet, one high and one about halfway down. She also has one closet with space for extra-long items such as dress coats and long skirts.

Limit clothes to close the closet. Scrupulously neat Judy Van Wyk doesn't worry about cleaning out a cedar chest to store her winter clothes when spring arrives or where to stash her bathing suits in the summer. "I use only one closet and one dresser for all my clothes, all year round," she says. "If I don't have any room in the closet or dresser, I don't buy anything new." Judy acknowledges that this sounds like a harsh approach, but she also contends that she enjoys her clothing as much as anyone. "I buy things I really like, because I'm going to wear them often," she says. "And I don't miss all the dry cleaning bills, the time it takes to match outfits, and the constant moving of clothes to find my wardrobe."

Downsize upscale clothes. You wouldn't be caught dead in that hot pink bridesmaid's dress, so why let it take up space in your closet, even if it cost you half a month's salary? Joanne Kennedy has purchased a lot of formal wear over the years as the mother of eight, with five mother-of-the-bride (or groom) dresses among it. But Joanne doesn't keep these bulky, dust-catching dresses around, particularly since she and her husband retired to a new, low-maintenance home. Here's how she redirects upscale clothing to those who need it as much as she needs the space.

WHATSIT?

Q: This wooden object, which belonged to the great-great-great-grandfather of one of our readers, looks like a miniature wooden temple. It's constructed from a rough grade of walnut. The front and sides are varnished, and the back is unfinished. The front section, between the two front columns, slides up. It's similar in design to an old-fashioned rolltop desk, but with a hole at the peak. Can you guess what it is?

A: This ingenious contraption, circa the eighteenth century, was probably made by a man handy with tools to sit on a nightstand. He could keep his bottle and a small glass in the base for a nip in the wee hours, and his pocket watch was lowered into the top, with the chain left hanging to hold the watch against the front, so he could read the time during the night while he was nipping.

THE PERPETUAL
SELF-PURGING WARDROBE

Who hasn't resolved to do away with clothes they simply don't (or can't) wear anymore? And who doesn't have at least one closet or set of drawers brimming with the evidence that they haven't kept up with the resolution?

Nancy Byrd, for one. She needs an executive wardrobe and loves to dress well. But that doesn't mean she has crammed closets. "I may sound like some Howard Hughes obsessive-compulsive type, but I have this great method for keeping my wardrobe current—and it gives me plenty of room in my clothes closet," she says. "I pull outfits to wear from the right side of the closet. I put outfits I've worn once or outfits I've recently laundered on the left. That way, if an outfit comes up on the right and I don't like it or wear it anymore, I give it away. Eventually, all the outfits show up on the right!"

Nancy's method not only saves her space, but it also keeps her from buying clothes she doesn't need (while a similar item languishes in the back of the closet). But Nancy's husband, Bob, would never dream of doing the same with his clothes; he's just not wired that way. Her solution? "I read about this in a magazine, and it really works. I hang his clean clothes with the tops of the hangers backward, facing out. Once he's worn clothes, he hangs them the way anyone would. I can go through his closet and tell what's getting worn and what's not just by looking at the tops of the hangers."

1. Take a picture. "I remind myself that I have photos of all these dresses, so I don't need the dress itself."

2. Keep the best; toss the rest. "Instead of a whole collection of, say, cocktail dresses, I keep my favorite."

3. Hold the bag. If you want to remember a special outfit, keep a small reminder of it, such as the beaded handbag, not the bulky skirt.

4. Consign away. "It's no use turning suits or dressy dresses over to places that serve people who are down-and-out," Joanne says. "Instead, I take them to a consignment store." She collects a percentage of the sale, and the store she favors won't accept clothes it doesn't feel it can sell. One tip on consignment stores: Deal only with a store that doesn't require you to take back unsold items.

5. Get in on the act. If you have vintage formal wear that a consignment store won't accept, consider donating it to the drama department at the local high school or university.

Clearing Out the Bathroom

If you do an honest overview of your house, you'll almost certainly agree that the bathroom is the major clutter disaster area. Bottles heaped on every surface, combs, brushes, makeup, soaps, lotions, hair dryers, toothpaste—the list is endless. And we're not even talking about the medicine cabinet or the space (shudder) under the sink. If you can't solve the problem by adding more bathrooms, try these ingenious tips.

Move toward minimal. Buy fewer towels and wash them more often. Buy towels in solid colors that you can mix and match. That way, you won't have to store an entire set at once, and you'll still have some backups if you give the dog a bath or have an unexpected overnight guest.

Try a (n)ice way to organize. Pieces of jewelry, cotton swabs, lip balm, and the like scattered around your bathroom drawers virtually guarantee that you won't be able to find what you want when you need it. Nancy Byrd puts small stuff at her fingertips and avoids clutter by stocking one bathroom drawer with plastic ice cube trays. "They're inexpensive and washable,"

SAY NO TO SHAMPOO SALES

Especially when you're talking about a room as small as most people's bathrooms, it's vital not to automatically buy products on sale. At a certain point, the savings in cash just aren't worth the space you have to give up to store the extra items.

Judy Van Wyk is still paying back student loans, but she doesn't ordinarily bother to buy shampoos and toiletries on sale. "If it's saving me only fifty cents or so, I'd rather have the space in the bathroom closet," she says. Judy will buy extras of pricey products when they're on sale, as long as she's saving at least $2 on each.

---

she says. "I put a pair of earrings in each space, or a lapel pin, or some twist ties—whatever." The smooth plastic trays also keep her from scraping a finger or breaking a nail, which is easy to do when you're trying to pick up small objects from a flat particleboard surface.

De-counter your clutter. Wade Slate discovered a way to keep his bathroom counter clear. He made it nearly impossible to rest anything on top. Before he took this drastic measure, the counter was a jumble of toothbrushes, cups, cleaning supplies, facecloths, bath toys, shaving supplies, and even homework papers and spare change.

Wade replaced the standard cabinet with plastic-coated wire cage boxes—the type discount stores sell for stashing kids' toys in. This particular product is configured in a six-cubbyhole unit. Wade puts towels in each of the top three units and cleaning supplies and such in the bottom three. But because the wire mesh openings are almost 2 inches wide, anything that someone sets on top will fall right through the opening, or at least teeter dangerously.

"It's nice, because the kids don't have to think about whether it's okay to put something down. They literally can't set things on the countertop," he says. Wade did install a wall holder for the family toothbrushes and a gadget that temporarily converts the faucet to a "water fountain" to eliminate the need for a collection of cups for after-brushing rinsing.

Family Room

As the old joke goes, if it's your possessions that are lying around, it's valuable stuff; but if it's someone else's, it's junk. Nowhere is this more applicable than in the family room. So how can you regain the upper hand on family room clutter—yours, mine, and ours? Make your family room a clutter-free zone by employing some of these ingenious ideas.

Make your clutter commute. Nancy Byrd admits that her family room is often a complete mess. But it's only temporary. "All we keep in the family room is a comfortable sofa, a chair, an end table with a telephone, and a console with the TV, VCR, and stereo system." Everything else actually "lives" somewhere else, and various family members bring their items to the family room only while those items are being used. After the family member is finished with them, back they go to the owner's bedroom closet, the kitchen drawer, or the garage. There are two advantages to this approach, Nancy says. "We can clean the family room very quickly when it does get cluttered, and we have a space available when my husband or the kids or I want to do a big project, such as beads or the photo albums. We don't have to spend time finding a space and clearing it."

Rotate your recreation. Only a truly gifted few can listen to a compact disc (CD), watch television or a videotape, play a

annals of ingenuity

HAIL THE PAPER CLIP!

how on earth did people organize papers and clip them together before paper clips were invented? Imagine the mess!

Well, up until the early nineteenth century, folks coped by threading papers together with string and ribbon. Sure, it looked nice, but it wasn't really practical. A slightly more dangerous option became available in 1835, when a New Yorker named John Ireland Howe invented a machine for mass-producing straight pins. Yes, the pins were designed for use in sewing, but desperate organizers, tired of the twine method, bought the pins, which became popular for fastening papers together. Ouch.

Although it's not completely clear who actually invented the paper clip, it was probably a Norwegian gentleman named Johann Vaaler. His paper clip design received a patent in 1899—much to the delight of bloody-fingered consumers everywhere.

video game, and listen to an old record album at the same time. So why clutter up the family room with everything you'd ever need to do all these things?

Here's an idea: Display accessories for only one or two of these pastimes at a time and give the others a rest in the attic or garage. If it's too hard to move the electronics, at least stash some of the myriad accessories: cassette tapes, video games, and so forth. In a few weeks, rotate, say, the CDs for the videotapes. Not only will you cut down on clutter and dust, but you may find that you enjoy each pastime more when you're not distracted by a multitude of options.

Make a game of it. Board games are indeed the stuff of the wholesome family room, just waiting to be pulled out and played during family time. Have yours just been taking up space that you could use for potted plants or framed photos? Find out by starting a family game night. Even if it's just the two of you—children at heart, squinting over cribbage or Scrabble®—make it a point to play board games at a designated time once a week.

Playing games regularly may not sound like a way to reduce clutter, but it is. That's because you'll quickly notice which of the games aren't getting into the rotation—something that's not evident when they're all collecting dust on the shelves. It's also much easier to part with a game when it's fresh in your mind how much you despise Uncle Wiggly or the way only obnoxious Aunt Mabel knows any of the MGM trivia answers. And last, if you never open the boxes, you'll never discover missing pieces or that the entire Yahtzee game (save for a pencil stub) is gone. Best of all, if you find out that you want to keep all your games, that will be because they're all still fun—and no one can have too much fun.

Can the paperboy hit the recycling bin? Home delivery of the newspaper is a civilized luxury. But here's something that's neither civilized nor luxurious: last Thursday's sports section draped over the armchair, while Tuesday's and Wednesday's classifieds lay bunched up behind the end table and the unopened Sunday paper dominates the hearth. Of course, the newspaper belongs in the family room, but only while you're reading it. So try this: Skip the fancy shelf or basket intended to store the newspaper (probably no one uses it anyway). Instead, store the paper in the recycling bin. No, not later, now—before you or anyone else reads it. Then, if no one opens it, it's already where it belongs. If someone does read a section, he can go get it, take it to the family room to peruse in comfort, and then take it back to the bin. There'll be no papers cluttering up the family room and no extra trips around the house to collect them on recycling day.

Kid Clutter

Sure, a baby is a bundle of joy, but he or she is also a bundle of clutter, from the first bottle to the last piece of trendy clothing at age 18. Some of it is inevitable. Face it, you'd be criticized if your child had only cold cream lids to play with. You need to tote a certain number of diapers for a day on the town, and even the neatest child might be expected to make an occasional mess in the house with, say, a plaster of paris volcano for a winning science fair project. But the other sources of clutter—too many toys, too-small clothes, endless baseball gloves and bats strewn about the garage? Those you can fight, first tooth to last purple-painted fingernail. Here are some day care providers and working moms to tell you how.

TOYING WITH TOSSING TOYS?

Sure, we all talk about American kids having way too many toys, but does anyone do anything about it? Nancy Byrd, a marketing executive who serves on the advisory board for a working mothers' magazine, certainly does. Taking her cue from her own childhood, she rotates toys and games for her son, Ryan, who's 8, and her daughter, Brook, who's 6, periodically storing all but a few. "That cuts down on the chaos around here," she says, "and the kids also enjoy the toys more, because they seem new after a few months in storage." Her tactic also forces her to go through the toys frequently, which means that she quickly gets rid of any toys the children have outgrown or are no longer interested in. Here are some more ingenious ways to cut down on toy clutter.

Ditch broken toys. Teresa Black operates a 52-child learning center in Seymour, Tennessee. Her experience has given her something of a hard heart, but only when it comes to tossing out toys. "You're kidding yourself if you think children will ever again play with toys that are broken or have missing pieces," she says. "I throw them out the second they break, the second I can find only a few of the pieces." Not only does that give her more space for toys that are in good working order, but it reduces the danger that a very small child will get injured by a broken toy.

TAMING THE BIRTHDAY BARRAGE

Sort of the way conservative parents sometimes end up with liberal offspring ("You voted for whom?"), the most clutter-conscious families often have relatives and friends who are overconsumers. Ordinarily, this matters not one whit—until a child's birthday or a holiday, when those folks inundate you with presents.

Teresa Black has an ingenious way to deal with the issue. "I know it sounds harsh, but even with birthday presents, I think, 'If you're not going to use it, why have it?' So here's what I do. I put the gifts in my children's bedrooms, somewhere obvious, and wait three days. Then I check. If the wrapping on the toy hasn't been opened by that time, I know that my child's not that interested. So I take the gift and put it in a big box. Then, when it comes time for my kids to go to someone else's birthday party, I wrap the gift for them to take." Teresa also gives the unopened presents to some of the children at her day care center who "don't get nearly so many gifts as my children. That makes me feel better."

She also holds herself and her husband to a similar standard. "Unless it's an item for another season, I can tell I'm not going to use it if I haven't even broken the packaging within a few days," she says. "So I save it for gifts for teachers or people at the retirement home."

Ask for cash. Teresa Black tries to avoid having lots of plastic or trendy toys in her household, but it's difficult when her kids receive them as gifts. "Here's how I cut down on toys that my kids aren't interested in and that only clutter up the house," she says. "When a person calls and asks what to bring Josh or Sarah for a birthday, I politely say that the child is saving up for something special (this is always true, and it's usually a high-priced clothing item) and that he or she would probably most appreciate a little money toward the purchase. Of course, I'd never make the suggestion unless someone asked!"

MARK MERIT WITH MEDALS, NOT TROPHIES

I t used to be that a kid had to be the champ to get a trophy. These days, mantels are littered with trophies awarded to every child who made it through the soccer or swim season—or who attended two practices before she was grounded for bad grades. These trophies are too light to serve as doorstops, are odd shapes and sizes, and are most definitely going to attract dust. But are *you* going to be the one to tell little Jimmy that your family doesn't "do" trophies?

Heavens, no! But try this: Ask Jimmy's coach or team mom if the team could award medals instead of trophies. They're handsome, they cost less, and they usually come draped on an Olympic-style ribbon. They're also much easier to dust and to store (in a drawer, on a peg, or even on a doorknob).

MANAGING OTHER KID CLUTTER

It's not just toys you're tripping over—it's homework assignments, clothes, even trophies! Is it a lost cause? Not with our ingenious clutter-cutting advice.

Cut storage down to size. Little children are no better than the rest of us when it comes to wadding up clothing and stuffing too much of it into drawers. But marketing executive Nancy Byrd has an ingenious way to make sure her kids can't stuff too much into their dressers: shoebox-sized drawers. "I buy the inexpensive cardboard drawers from the discount store, and stack two in their closets," she says. "One advantage to this technique is that the cardboard drawers open and close much more easily than nice wooden dressers. The other advantage is that each drawer isn't large enough to hold much—maybe several pairs of socks, or at most, one outfit. So you don't have big piles of things to sort through every time the kid gets dressed."

Give kids a clutter rule. It's one thing to keep yourself organized, and quite another to have a child in the household keep things neat. To keep from picking up her own stuff—and then picking up after her child—Judy Van Wyk has a rule: "If Allyson doesn't put something back, she can't use it the next time. She'll say, 'Mom, I have to have the tape for school. It's homework!' But I tell her forget it—if she wants tape, I'll take her out and she can buy herself some with her own money. Of course she doesn't want to spend her money that way, so she usually follows the rules."

Unexpected Storage

You can never be too rich or too thin—or have too much space. Have you considered these ingenious storage opportunities?

Take a page from photocopiers. Let heat or humidity reach your cherished classics (or even sci-fi paperbacks), and they're ruined. If you can't afford climate-controlled vaults for your beloved books, bring home photocopy paper boxes from work, says Amy Witsil, a mechanical engineer in Chapel Hill, North Carolina. "I've learned that the paper manufacturers pay a premium to design boxes to keep moisture out, so the paper won't be ruined," she says. "If it's good enough for Xerox's paper, it's good enough for my old receipts and my husband's old books from law school that he doesn't look at anymore."

Change the litter, load the washer. If you are of the scoop-and-flush school of kitty litter management, consider storing your bag of *clean* kitty litter (always a bulky, messy item) in the bottom of your bathroom hamper. With any luck, you'll need to do laundry on about the same schedule that you clean the litter box.

clever cleaning
ideas

TOOTHPASTE. BAKING SODA. LEMON RINDS. What do these ordinary items have in common? They all make nifty homemade household cleaners.

In this chapter, our experts will show you how to keep your kitchen spotless, your nooks and crannies looking neat, and your entire home in tip-top shape. For instance, Marcie Ness, owner of Marcie's Housecleaning Service in Tulsa, Oklahoma, reveals a finishing touch that will keep your brass bed shiny and new. And Donna Liangis, who owns the House Ka-Teers cleaning company in Dearborn, Michigan, shares her surefire tips for making toilet bowls sparkle and removing wax from carpeting. Todd Graham offers his ways for deporting dust bunnies—and as the owner of Totally Clean! housekeeping service in San Francisco, he knows a thing or two about dust.

If you follow the advice of these and our other experts, your friends and neighbors will think you spend hours keeping your place looking its tidiest. Let them think it! Only *you* will know all the minutes and hours you've saved by incorporating these tricks, tips, and techniques into your cleaning regimen.

Kitchen

Who doesn't love the aroma of fresh-baked bread or the wonderful fragrance of homemade pasta sauce bubbling in a saucepan? What no ones likes is the cleanup. But you can keep your kitchen looking its very best with these handy, helpful tips.

SINKS AND DRAINS

Pity the poor kitchen sink. It works so hard, but how often do you show it the appreciation it deserves? Here are some gentle and all-natural ways to keep your drain smelling fresh, flowing freely, and as clean as a whistle.

Dispose of drain odors. In your search for the source of that unpleasant kitchen odor, your nose may lead you directly to the garbage disposal. Here are two can't-miss ways to keep those odors at bay.

1. Stamp out smells with citrus. "Whenever you use lemons or limes during cooking, save the rinds, then put them in the garbage disposal," says Donna Liangis. "Run the disposal for a few seconds with the water running, and you'll get rid of fish and garlic odors and be left with a nice citrus smell."

2. Freeze out odors with vinegar. Fill an ice cube tray or two

TAKE CARE OF THE TARNISH

The best thing about copper cookware, besides conducting heat well, is how shiny it looks—until it tarnishes. Well, you can keep your copper pots shiny and stain-free with ingredients from your kitchen. Here are two ingenious (and chemical-free) secrets recommended by Donna Liangis.

1. Lay on the sauce. Rub Worcestershire sauce on the copper surface with a sponge. Let it sit for a minute or so, and then wipe clean.

2. Try an old standby. Fill a spray bottle with vinegar and add 3 tablespoons salt. Put the top on the bottle and shake it up. Give the copper a few squirts with the solution, let it work for a few minutes, and then wipe clean with a damp sponge.

with vinegar and freeze. Once a month or so, toss a few of the vinegar cubes into your garbage disposal. As the disposal grinds and crunches the ice, it gets a good cleaning, and the vinegar eliminates unpleasant odors. Don't forget to keep a steady stream of cold water flowing into the drain while the disposal is running.

Keep it flowing. For those occasions when cooking grease holds your kitchen drain hostage, fight back with this homegrown solution. Pour 1 cup warm salt water and 1 cup carbonated soft drink (such as Coca-Cola®) into the drain. Follow that with 1 quart boiling water. This 1-2-3 solution works wonders for minor grease plugs, says Karl Smith, a retired U.S. Navy warrant officer and stay-at-home dad who regularly wows his Newark, Delaware, neighbors with his clever housecleaning tips.

Rub out germs. Of course you know that rubbing alcohol kills germs. That's why you store it in your bathroom medicine cabinet. But did you know that it can keep your kitchen germ-free, too? Donna Liangis advises filling an empty spray bottle with rubbing alcohol and keeping it under your kitchen sink. After you finish the dishes, spray a little alcohol on the faucet and other sink fixtures, then rub everything down with a clean cotton dish towel. You'll win the war on food-borne germs pronto!

LARGE APPLIANCES

The only way to guarantee that large appliances such as refrigerators, ovens, and dishwashers stay clean is not to use them. Alas, that's a bit impractical. But never fear—our experts have come to the rescue with easy and ingenious ways to keep your appliances sparkling.

Eliminate refrigerator odors. Is your refrigerator a bit, um, fragrant? Here are two ways to beat the odors—one to help you stop them and another to mask them (until you have time to give your fridge a good cleaning).

1. Charcoal in, odors out. You can eliminate most refrigerator odors by filling a small bowl with charcoal (the kind you use in

---

ODOR-B-GONE

Love to cook with garlic, but don't relish the pungent odor it leaves on your hands? Well, help is on the way. Our ingenious expert, Donna Liangis, suggests these three ways to get rid of garlic odor.

1. Reach into the utensil drawer and grab a stainless steel spoon. Rub the back of the spoon on your fingers and hands to make the garlic smell disappear.

2. Rub fresh rosemary leaves on your hands.

3. Wet your hands with water, then rub them with a spoonful of salt. Rinse and dry your hands with a cloth towel.

---

potted plants; it's available at your local nursery or garden store) and placing it on a lower shelf without a lid. Tuck the bowl in the back or behind yesterday's leftovers so it's not so obvious. The charcoal will absorb odors quickly and effectively. Replace it monthly.

2. Reach for vanilla. If you don't have any charcoal on hand and you want to get rid of refrigerator odors right away, dab a little vanilla extract on a cotton ball and tuck it inside the refrigerator.

Let your racks soak. Oven racks are difficult to clean because most sinks are too small to accommodate them. What's the answer? While you're cleaning your oven, soak your racks in the bathtub.

Wash your dishwasher. Sure, dishwashers clean your pots, pans, dishes, glasses, and utensils, but don't be fooled into thinking that this cleaning machine doesn't need a little TLC, too. Once a month, pour a cup of white vinegar into your empty dishwasher and let it run through its entire cycle. This solution will keep soap film from forming, and that means spotless glasses and utensils.

WHATSIT?

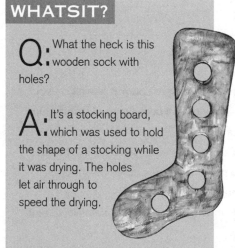

Q: What the heck is this wooden sock with holes?

A: It's a stocking board, which was used to hold the shape of a stocking while it was drying. The holes let air through to speed the drying.

SMALL APPLIANCES

Toasters, can openers, and other small appliances—with all those nooks and crannies and teeny-weeny gears—can make for big headaches when cleaning day rolls around. It's almost enough to make you skip cleaning them at all. But here's good news: Our experts have discovered some ingenious ways to shrink the job down to size.

Brush up on blender-cleaning techniques. Milkshakes, smoothies, and frozen drinks. In some households, the blender is always on, and that means there's practically no time to clean it. Well, do yourself and your blender a favor and give it a good cleaning with these ingenious tips.

1. Blend away food residue. Fill the blender less than halfway with warm (not hot) water, add a few drops of dishwashing liquid, slap on the lid, and blend the soapy mixture for about 30 seconds. Rinse well with hot water.

2. Clean those hard-to-reach spots. Here's an easy way to remove that guck that gets stuck where the motor meets the pitcher. Grab a new or, better yet, old stiff-bristled toothbrush. Dip the brush in vinegar and scrub away.

Don't have a meltdown. Have a melt-off. Uh-oh, you left the English muffin bag a little too close to the toaster oven and now there's melted plastic all over it. Not a problem. Just dab some nail polish remover on the plastic, and it'll come right off. No nail polish remover? Petroleum jelly will work just as well.

Gear up to clean your can opener. Have you looked at your electric can opener lately? Specifically, have you inspected the gear and the blade that cuts the can? If you're like most folks, yours probably needs a good cleaning. Try this surefire technique. First, give the blade and gear a shot of WD-40® and clean it up with an old toothbrush. Next, rinse it well with hot soapy water. Not only will the WD-40® clean the blade and the gear, but it will prevent more gunky buildup and inhibit rust, too.

COUNTERS AND CUTTING BOARDS
Want to keep your counters and cutting boards clean and fresh? Look no further than your kitchen cupboards.

annals of ingenuity

THE IMPOSSIBLE DREAM?

Close your eyes and imagine a house that cleans itself. The ceiling of each room is outfitted with a cleaning/drying/heating/cooling unit. At the touch of a button, the unit sprays the room with soapy water, rinses it, and then blows it dry. Kitchen cupboards double as dishwashers. After dinner, you put your dishes away, and the next time you open the door, they're clean. Laundry is a snap, because clothing is cleaned and dried in the closets. Not only that, but all the sinks, tubs, and toilets in this fantasy home are self-cleaning, too.

This dream house is a reality. Unfortunately, it's currently occupied by its inventor, Frances Gabe, who lives in Newberg, Oregon. Born in 1915, Frances became interested in home design as a child hanging out at construction sites with her father, an architect. She entered college at age 14 and finished 2 years later. This was a woman who obviously had more to do with her time than dust bookshelves and who called housework a "thankless, unending job." Shortly after World War II, she set to work on her invention. Unfortunately, the house, which includes nearly 70 patented inventions (including self-dusting bookshelves), is not for sale.

Keep your cutting boards lemon fresh. Here's a nifty use for a lemon wedge. Rub this all-natural cleaner back and forth over your cutting board after you've chopped onions, garlic, or any other pungent food to curb odors.

Add vinegar and subtract ants. Sponge your counters with white vinegar. Not only will the vinegar cut grease and eliminate odors, but it also will repel those pesky ants that seem to visit the kitchen every summer.

Bathroom

Ever wonder why there's no room under your bathroom sink? Probably because it's stuffed with oodles of pricey store-bought cleaning products. Your stash may include one product for cleaning the bathtub, another for cleaning the sink, another for the fixtures, and yet another to get rid of the mildew growing on your shower curtain. All these products can add up, both dollar- and space-wise.

The solution? Make your own cleaners. Homemade cleaners cost only pennies and perform many cleaning chores better and faster than store-bought ones. Read on to learn what a little Kool-Aid®, fabric softener, and furniture cleaner can do to make the smallest room in your house a source of pride.

TOILET

Never mind the potty talk. Try these simply ingenious ways to make your toilet bowl clean enough to please even your picky mother-in-law.

Flush away toilet stains. Struggling with toilet stains? Our experts have uncovered some truly ingenious solutions.

1. Have some Kool-Aid®. This thirst quencher works wonders on stubborn toilet bowl stains, says Donna Liangis. Head for the

---

KIDS: THE CLEANING DREAM TEAM?

Enlisting your children to help out with the cleaning can take some doing, but it's worth the effort. The secret is to turn housecleaning into a game. For instance, arm your children with old toothbrushes, boxes of baking soda, and vinegar, then march them to the bathroom sink. Have them sprinkle a little baking soda onto the sides of the sink, plug the drain, and then pour a capful or two of vinegar on the baking soda. "Your kids will love the fizzing action, and you'll love how sparkling clean your sink gets," Donna Liangis says.

POOL CHLORINE IS A COOL CLEANER

Penny Bosch must have clean genes. Even as a little girl, she kept her bedroom spotless and her school desk neat and orderly. "I used to arrange my schoolbooks by subject and size," she says with a laugh. Today this grandmother's three-bedroom home is a picture of perfection. And one of her favorite household cleaners is pool chlorine powder. She mixes ¼ cup pool chlorine into a 1-gallon bucket of warm water. The batch is enough to restore sparkle to the inside of her refrigerator, shower, and bathtub. "A little goes a long way, and it is much more economical than household bleach or expensive kitchen-cleaning products," says Penny, known affectionately by her family and friends as the "Queen of Neatness and Tidiness."

kitchen, grab a packet of the unsweetened beverage powder, and sprinkle it in the bowl. Let it sit for a few minutes, swish it around with your bathroom brush, and flush.

2. Keep your bowl tidy. The secret to keeping toilet bowls clean and their working parts from wearing out prematurely is knowing how to clean porcelain, says Robert Maiolo (aka The Friendly Plumber) of San Francisco. He advises against putting commercial drop-in toilet cleaners inside the tank, where the chemicals can erode the rubber gaskets and other parts. Instead, hang the cleaner inside the bowl, which is 100 percent porcelain and tough enough to handle these chemicals. "Try it, and you'll flush away your worries," Robert says.

MISCELLANEOUS BATHROOM-CLEANING IDEAS

Here's a hodgepodge of bathroom tips to help you clean your shower curtain liner, remove hair spray from walls and mirrors, and more!

Launder your liner. There's no need to toss out your shower curtain liner just because of mildew and dirt buildup. You can extend its life span by tossing it in your washer. Set the machine for warm water and the gentle cycle. Add the liner and 1 cup detergent. Throw it in the dryer on low heat or fluff for about 20 minutes, and voila! Your liner will emerge clean and wrinkle-free.

Make hair spray go away. Is the wall directly behind where you stand when you spray your hair covered with a glossy buildup? Just pour a capful of fabric softener in a small bowl of room temperature water. Moisten a clean cloth with the solution, then gently rub it on the wall. Watch the hair spray disappear without harming the paint finish.

Wax on, fog off. Fed up with a bathroom mirror that fogs up during a hot shower? Donna Liangis has a simple solution: Apply a light coat of a wood furniture cleaner that contains lemon oil to the mirror or a glass shower door once a month. Look for

---

SWIRL AWAY SPA DIRT

Plumber Robert Maiolo knows a thing or two about bathtub spas. If you're fortunate to have a whirlpool tub or spa that offers bubbling magic to ease muscle aches and pains, you can keep it clean without a lot of elbow grease.

Every 3 months, fill your spa with warm water, then add 2 to 3 teaspoons dishwasher detergent and ½ cup household bleach. Turn on the spa for 2 to 3 minutes and watch this bubbling cleaner kick into gear. Drain and refill the tub with cold water. Let the cold water swirl and bubble for 5 minutes, then drain again. Finish the job with a manufacturer-recommended wax, and you'll keep your spa looking clean and working at its finest for a long time. You'll also save money and aggravation in dirt-related repairs.

SERVE UP SOME COFFEE FILTERS

That box of paper coffee filters can deliver more than a fine cup of java. They also make dandy cleaners for glass surfaces and mirrors in any room of the house. And here's the best news: They remove streaks and smudges without leaving any lint behind.

---

this product on the same supermarket shelf where you find other cleaners that moisturize woods.

Fight cavities—and rust stains, too. If your house has hard water and you're frustrated by those unsightly rust-colored water stains in your sink, fight back with a little dab of toothpaste. "It works great," says Donna Liangis. "Put a little toothpaste on an old toothbrush and gently scrub the rust stain. It will disappear like magic."

Living Room and Dining Room

When it comes to size, the living room and dining room usually reign in most homes. But those heavily trafficked rooms double as dust magnets and soil collectors. And although you can shut the door on a messy bedroom or den, you can't hide a living room or dining room from view. This section offers solutions for everyday cleaning jobs, from removing wax from the carpet to capturing cobwebs without any muss or fuss.

CEILINGS, WALLS, AND FLOORS

There's no getting away from ceilings, walls, and floors—they have you surrounded. But there are some ingenious ways to obliterate the dust and dirt they can accumulate.

Rub away pencil marks with rye. Did your budding young artist draw on your wallpaper? The best way to get rid of the marks is to rub them with a slice of fresh rye bread. You'll remove the pencil marks without marring your wallpaper.

Curtail cobwebs. Remove cobwebs from ceiling corners easily by wrapping an old sock, dish towel, or T-shirt around a broom, then securing it with rubber bands or string. Mist your "mop" with a little water, and you have an instant magnet for cobwebs and an easy way to reach them.

Slip a sock over a broomstick, and you have one ingenious cleaning device.

Don't be taxed by wax. The aroma of a scented candle can make a living room smell and feel cozy. Unfortunately, a minor bump on a coffee table can send hot candle wax flying onto the carpet. Put a chill on the spill, says Donna Liangis. Put a couple of ice cubes in a resealable plastic bag and hold it directly on the wax until it hardens. Then gently lift the wax with a butter knife or metal spatula.

DON'T CRY OVER SPILLED WINE

When the holidays arrive, Donna Liangis becomes the champion rescuer of carpets. "We get lots of calls from frantic folks around the holidays," she says. "They call in a panic: 'Help! Someone just spilled red wine on the carpet. What do we do?'" Donna offers this simple solution: Sprinkle some salt right on the wet spot. Wait 10 to 15 minutes, then vacuum up the salt. "Salt crystals attract and absorb wine," she explains. "This tip works for cotton or linen tablecloths, too."

Make your ceramic sparkle. Save yourself some money and keep your ceramic tile looking its best, says Karl Smith, who makes his own floor cleaner for just a few pennies. Fill a small plastic bucket with warm water. Add ¼ cup baking soda, 1 cup ammonia, and ½ cup white vinegar. Vacuum the floor, then wash with this solution—no need to rinse. *Note:* If you use a sponge rather than a mop to apply the solution, wear rubber gloves to protect your hands.

MORE LIVING ROOM CLEANING IDEAS

From dusting your ceiling fans to showering with your house-plants, here are some ingenious tips to help you keep your living room spotless.

Rule your louvered doors. Louvered doors can be tricky to dust. Try wrapping a clean cloth around a ruler. Spray it with a dusting spray and carefully run the ruler across each louver. This nifty trick is quick and easy, says Jonni McCoy, of Colorado Springs, Colorado, and author of *Miserly Moms: Living on One Income in a Two Income Economy.*

Sing (and dust) in the shower. Clever cleaner Karl Smith has been known to bring a couple of his extra-dusty living room plants into the shower with him on occasion. A light misting from the showerhead and a gentle scrubbing with his soapy hands are enough to knock off the dust and restore the green luster. He lets them dry in the shower before tucking them back in their designated spots in the living room.

Bust the dust on your ceiling fan. Ceiling fans can make a room breezy and cool, but if you're not vigilant, dust will collect on the blades and fly all over your ceiling and walls. Save yourself

SET ASIDE TIME TO CLEAN THE BLINDS

Window blinds are great inventions. You can open them just a bit to let in a little light or close them tight like clams. Cleaning them, however, is another matter.

Penny Bosch designates a cleaning time for all her window blinds four times a year. That's when she takes them down and out to her backyard, where she sprays them clean with her garden hose. Then she quickly dries them by attaching the hose to her husband's air compressor. "It's the same effect you get from those air dryers in the automatic car washes," she explains. "The window blinds dry in seconds."

from having to scrub or repaint your walls by cleaning the blades once a month. Here's how: Fill a plastic spray bottle with warm water and add a squirt of dishwashing detergent. Slip a cotton sock over your hand and spray the soapy mixture on the sock until it's damp but not soaked. If you're under 6 feet tall, you'll need a sturdy stepladder. Carefully glide your sock-covered hand over the blades. When you're finished, just toss the sock in the wash.

Whisk your way to cleaner lamp shades. Fabric lamp shades pose a cleaning challenge: Should you wash them? Replace them? Or maybe you should have covered your lamp shade with one of those lovely plastic covers. Actually, dusting a cloth lamp shade is easier than you think, as long as you use the right tool. All you need is a clean whisk broom or a stiff paintbrush (buy an inexpensive one just for this purpose to avoid adding more dirt to your shade). Remove the lamp shade and hold it steady with one hand while you use the other to briskly brush the dust away. Work from top to bottom and rotate the shade as you go, then put the shade back on the lamp.

Bedroom

If you get 8 hours of sleep each night (and you should), you'll end up spending a full third of your life in your bedroom. That's something to consider if the dust bunnies under your bed are reproducing like the real things and the top of your dresser hasn't seen daylight since the day you brought it home. Luckily, the room you spend the most time in is also a cinch to clean. Follow these simple tips to tidy up your slumber space and make a clean sleep of it!

Blow your baseboards bare. Baseboard heaters—those long, narrow, metal boxes containing heating registers that run along the edges of the room—are magnets for dust and debris. It's especially true in the winter months, when the heaters are on all or most of the time. Try this ingenious trick to clean your baseboard heaters without even having to bend down. Use your hair dryer like a mini-leaf blower. Just aim in one direction along the top of the baseboard, and the dust will fall to the floor like so many autumn leaves. Of course, this is best done before you sweep or vacuum the floor.

Dust-proof your dreams. Here's an ingenious tip for those prone to allergies, particularly allergies caused by dust mites—microscopic creatures that thrive in dark, warm places, reproduce like mad, and wreak havoc with your sinuses. While you have the bed completely stripped of linens, vacuum the mattress, says Todd Graham. This ritual will take care of dust mites, as well as the dust they feed on, and eliminate any lingering odors at the same time.

Move the bed, beat the mildew. In damp weather, walls sometimes feel clammy, because paint can actually absorb mois-

---

DISMISS THE DUST BUNNIES

When vacuuming your bedroom, how often do you make a point of vacuuming the space under your bed? Not often, if you're like most of us, says Todd Graham. "Getting under the bed can be tough, but you really shouldn't skip it. You'd be surprised what collects under there," he says. So pull out the sweater storage bins, bedroom slippers, and long-lost cat toys. Then use a long-handled vacuum attachment and be sure to reach under as far as possible. There now, don't you feel better?

---

ture from the air. If this wetness can't escape, mold and mildew can take hold. Places where the wall is hidden or covered, such as along one side of your bed, are perfect spots for spore growth, says Todd Graham. But you can kill that mold and mildew with a weak solution of water and bleach.

In a bucket, combine 1 gallon warm water and 2 to 3 tablespoons household bleach. Soak a sponge in the solution, wring it out well to prevent drips, and then wipe the spores away. Be sure to allow the wall to dry completely before you move the bed back, or you'll defeat the purpose by trapping more moisture. This tip will help cut allergy attacks in the bedroom. If you have no allergies, it may help prevent them.

Brighten your brass. Cleaning a brass headboard or lamp base can be tricky. Most brass polishes are messy and end up dripping everywhere you wish they wouldn't (such as on your grandmother's antique chenille bedspread). Combine the goop factor with the amazing amount of elbow grease required, and polishing brass quickly moves to the top of the list of least-loved chores. But there's a better way, says Marcie Ness. "I actually learned this tip from one of my clients, who has a brass banister," Marcie says.

"She told me to use nothing but plain spray-on furniture polish, such as Pledge®. Rub it in with a clean dry cloth, and it works really well."

Sand your cedar closet back to new. Lucky enough to have a cedar chest or closet? Good for you. But if you notice that it hasn't been doing its job lately—if, say, the fresh cedar scent has faded or you've started to notice tiny holes in your favorite sweaters—don't resort to mothballs just yet. Go over the wood with some fine-grade sandpaper (be sure to go *with* the grain) to remove the dry outer layer of the wood and expose the still-moist and fragrant layer underneath.

Mudroom

Think of the mudroom (which might be an actual room or just a foyer, a landing, or a hallway near the entrance you use most often) as a buffer zone between the great outdoors and the interior of your home. Having an area devoted solely to dirty shoes, muddy boots, dripping umbrellas, and damp raincoats can cut your house-cleaning time and give you a place to store seasonal gear.

There's only one drawback to having a room dedicated to dirt: You have to figure out how to keep *that* area as tidy as possible to prevent tracking the mess into the house. With the following tips, that's not a problem.

Use more mats for less mess. They say that 80 percent of household dirt comes from our boots and shoes. You can halve that amount simply by doubling up on the number of mats you use. Place one heavy-duty, nonskid mat outside your front door. This exterior mat should have a rough texture to scrub most of the mud and gravel off boots and shoes. Place another mat just inside the door. The indoor mat should be absorbent (to soak up water

that's · ingenious!

<u>grates</u> are great

AT THE SIERRA CLUB'S Clair Tappaan Lodge in Norden, California, winter skiers—lots of them—routinely track snow indoors. To keep huge puddles from forming, the lodge uses an ingenious system that you may want to adapt to your own mudroom or entryway floor.

"We use grates—actually a grated sort of platform that's placed over the floor itself," says assistant lodge manager Bobby Wright. The grates allow snow and water to fall through and eventually evaporate. In the warmer months, the grates catch mud and rocks from hikers' boots. Staff members regularly lift the grates and sweep the floor. You can try this at home on a smaller scale by purchasing grated wooden tiles, which are available at some garden centers or hardware stores. Or go even simpler and try a rubber doormat that has alternating-height strips. Even this small difference in depth will help trap water and debris.

and collect fine grit) and machine-washable. Use a separate rubber backing under the indoor mat if it has a tendency to slip.

Sequester wet items. Avoid carrying dripping clothes through the house every time you come inside. Make a ventilated laundry hamper or laundry basket a permanent fixture in your mudroom or foyer. When you come in from the great, wet, muddy outdoors, it's a cinch to drop all damp or dirty items right in the basket. Just don't forget to empty the hamper on laundry day, then put it back in the mudroom.

Salt *for* the earth. It's bound to happen. Despite all your efforts to the contrary, a muddy footprint or two will probably find its way inside to your beautiful carpet. Rather than resorting to a

Meet the Expert

*H*ave broom, will travel

SOME PEOPLE get their start in business from a family member. Others do it through their own force of will. Todd Graham got the idea for his housekeeping business when he was still in high school.

"I was one of only two students in my senior class chosen to attend Camp Enterprise, a workshop in which a group of entrepreneurs taught students the basics of starting a business," Todd says. One of the student projects was devising a business plan. Todd's idea was a cleaning company. After graduation he logged 108 hours of training time to receive his janitorial certificate. He then took his high school business idea and made it real, starting out as a one-man janitorial service company.

"In the beginning, I was driving around the city on a motorcycle, with a Tupperware® container of cleaning supplies strapped to the back," Todd recalls. "I had to use my clients' vacuum cleaners." Ten years later, he has 13 employees and has traded in the motorcycle for a couple of cars and a van. He also has switched gears to private housecleaning rather than corporate janitorial work. "The biggest challenge I face now," he says, "is whether to keep on growing my company or let it stay small."

rented rug shampooer, try this low-tech trick first. It works best on fresh mud, so try to act fast. Sprinkle a generous amount of table salt on the stain and rub it into the muddy area. Allow it to sit undisturbed for an hour, then vacuum the spot thoroughly.

If the mud has dried, scrape up as much as you can, then vacuum. Blot any residue with a paper towel and a solution of ¼ teaspoon dishwashing soap (Dawn® and Joy® are best) mixed into 1 quart lukewarm water. Vacuum when it dries.

CLEAN YOUR WINDOWS ON MOVING DAY

Okay. You already know that newsprint is terrific for cleaning windows, but you probably also know that it can leave your hands black with ink—unless you keep it around for several days. If keeping old papers on hand doesn't appeal to you, try Penny Bosch's clever solution. After your or a friend's next move, save the packing paper. Stack it flat and store it neatly in your garage. This paper, which is newsprint without the ink, is terrific for cleaning windows, mirrors, and the glass in picture frames. Penny keeps a tidy stash in her garage for just such projects.

Windows

If you're never quite sure what the weather's like without going outside, maybe it's time to clean those windows. Our experts offer some ingenious ways to make the job nearly effortless.

Try this timely use for yesterday's news. If you've used newspaper to clean your windows and glassware, you know how terrific it is. But timing is everything. The best newspaper to use has been around for 2 days or more. Why? The ink on the pages is completely dry, which means that you'll be less likely to end up with black hands, and the paper will clean much more effectively.

Use the gloved approach. If you can't wait for your newspaper to dry and simply must clean your windows, don some dishwashing or surgical gloves to do the job. Your window will get clean—and your hands will stay clean.

Erase the streaks. If you have a clean blackboard eraser hanging around, rub it over your windows after you clean them for a shiny finish.

controlling indoor
p e s t s

BUGS OUTSIDE ARE ONE THING; some people even like them. But nobody likes bugs and other critters when they invade the house. Besides crawling all over your stuff, they can get in your food, eat your clothes, and destroy your house's foundation—not to mention bite and sting you. There's no question that those pests have to go. But a lot of the treatments that are used to eliminate indoor pests are so toxic that they're worse than the creatures themselves. So here's a whole chapter of effective pest controls that are safe for your home, your family, and your pets.

Among the folks who have contributed their pest-stopping tips are Chad Speerly, a supervisor and buyer for a natural foods cooperative in Knoxville, Tennessee. He offers some ways to rid your home of ants and food moths. Our flea expert, Francie Stull, operates a flea products business in College Station, Texas. She explains why you don't need to buy flea shampoo. And Bob Grimac of Knoxville, Tennessee, offers some ingenious ways to say goodbye to roaches, flies, and mice.

Before you beat yourself up for even having a pest problem, remember that some pests are inevitable. "If you're in an older home, it doesn't matter how clean you keep it or how hard you try to make it airtight," says Robin Woodruff, a Concord, Tennessee, pet lover and graphic designer who has worked for the Environmental Protection Agency and other environmental clients. "As your home ages, there will eventually be old pieces of wood for bugs to eat and nest in. Sooner or later, the moisture in the basement or leaky pipes will create places where bugs will live. Windows and doors will warp, and the seals will start getting little holes where bugs—or even mice—can climb in." That's when you call in an arsenal of tried-and-true, nontoxic pest repellents, traps, and insecticides. To find out which weapons will work best for you, read on.

Answers for Ants

Ants. Watch a television show about them on PBS, and they're marvels of nature. Their ordered colonies work like well-oiled machines, and every member does its job. But once ants enter your house or yard, marvel turns to mayhem. Not only do they feed on and contaminate food, but they can infest your home and build unsightly mounds in your yard. And in some cases, the little buggers bite or sting to boot. If you're battling an army of ants, you'll want to learn about our expert ways to win the war.

WHAT'S PESTERING YOU?

Indoor pests seem to show up out of nowhere, but if you have one (or more), there's probably a reason. It may be something you can correct just by changing a few habits.

If It's This	Try This
Food moths	Store grains and nuts in airtight containers. Keep flour in the freezer. Toss old pasta, grain, and nut products.
Clothes moths	Hang or store only clean clothing. Stop using spray starch—moths eat it.
Roaches	Break the habit of leaving food, beverages, or crumbs out in the open. Keep the toaster oven spotless. Wash the drip pan beneath the refrigerator more often.
Sugar ants	Close all food packages. Store sugary foods in the refrigerator. Don't let fruit ferment in the open. Wipe sticky surfaces to clean up spills. Eat only in the kitchen or dining room.
Cluster flies	Let them have their day and then vacuum them up when they die; they're impossible to keep out of old houses.

Puzzle them with pepper. If your ant problem is still in the early stages—maybe you've just seen a couple of ants in the kitchen—you're in luck, says Chad Speerly. "That's because sugar ants send scouts first," he explains. "If the scout doesn't scent any food, the rest of the colony won't come around." To throw those early ants off the track, sprinkle a little ground red pepper on the shelves or behind the sink—wherever ants are loitering. "That way, the ant will smell the cayenne instead of sugar," Chad says. "The other thing to remember is that ants follow one another. If the lead ant walks through a strong scent like the pepper, it covers up his own scent, and the other ants won't know he's been there. They'll go another way."

A sour solution to a sweet problem. If you have more than a few ants around the kitchen, that means they've hit the mother lode: a sugary food or surface. "Cayenne isn't going to help you much once there's an army of ants in the kitchen," Chad Speerly says. But don't panic yet. You may still be able to convince them to be on their way by doing away with their goodies. Send the sugary item they've discovered outside instead of putting it in the kitchen trash, or they'll make a beeline (or should we say an "antline"?) for the trash.

Get rid of less obvious sugar, too, because now they're onto

NATURALLY ANT-FREE

If you care about the environment, you'll want to use nontoxic methods to repel or destroy the creepy, crawly things that sometimes invade your home. Marie Hofer, a biologist, chemist, and horticulturist in Knoxville, Tennessee, offers a perfect example of this. "I went to dinner at some friends', and they had it all: coffee grounds sprinkled on the countertops, pepper on the windowsills, strips of double-sided tape stuck alongside the baseboards," she recalls. "They politely asked us to ignore these odd little piles because they had ants, and those are all good ways to repel them."

Did Marie's friends best the little beasts? "Yes, all those measures worked in combination," she says. "Plus, they went around and resealed all the cracks in their practically brand-new home."

Of course, this is one of those cases where an ounce of caulk is worth a pound of ground red pepper. Lots of pests can be prevented just by sealing the spaces where they can sneak in, eliminating moisture (where silverfish and the like thrive), and keeping food out of sight and off the counters.

---

your kitchen as a source of sweets. Wipe down the counters with a solution of equal parts vinegar and warm water. Then use the vinegar-water solution on the floor where you spilled a little sugared coffee, the baseboard where your niece flung sugary baby food, and the fruit bowl where those last three bananas lingered for weeks waiting to be made into banana bread. Make sure to toss the used rag in the wash so the ants won't attack it, too.

Blow their house down. When an army of ants is particularly persistent, you may have to resort to finding their residence and destroying it. "Use a pressure washer or a very strong water pressure hose to wash the anthill out," says lawn care professional Wade Slate of Knoxville, Tennessee. "You want to make sure you've eliminated the queen, because the ants can't really function without her. You'll know her because she's larger and usually surrounded by eggs."

Ants often build hills in the yard or garden, usually in a protected place, such as under a broad-leaved plant. "They're not real fond of getting wet, which is why they tend to break into your

---

SCENT-SATIONAL ANTI-ANT SPICES

You're supposed to sprinkle some ground red pepper along baseboards to deter ants, right? So you're off to buy a big container of the stuff, even if it does cost $4. Hold on just a minute. The point of sprinkling the spice is to confuse the ants and make it hard for them to find sugar. There's nothing magical about ground red pepper per se. If you have any of the following pungent ground spices readily available, try them instead.

1. Allspice
2. Black or white pepper
3. Cloves
4. Coriander
5. Nutmeg

house when it's raining," Wade says. They prefer light soil, but don't limit your search to areas with sandy soil. (In fact, that "sand" you see on their hills is usually piled-up dead ants!)

And here's an expert tip you really won't want to overlook if you're overrun by ants: Check your gutters. Wade has uncovered many mounds in the gutters above his kitchen.

Clothes Moth Control

It's hard not to take clothes moths personally. They attack your best, most expensive clothing, chomp holes in your favorite winter coat, and destroy the heirlooms that you've packed away for future generations. But they're not doing it on purpose! It's the moth larvae that eat clothing fibers, and they actually start out by eating the dirt on clothing, then move on to the fibers in their feeding frenzy.

THREE MYTHS THAT MIGHT CAUSE YOU TO MISS PESTS

There's a lot of lore about dealing with pesky bugs, and not all of it's true. Here are just a few of the myths that can keep you from dealing with indoor pests effectively.

1. Food is safe from bugs if the container hasn't been opened. Food moths will eat through paper, flimsy plastic, or even light cardboard containers to get to the chow. Other bugs, such as roaches and silverfish, love glue, which holds together cereal, condiments, and other cardboard boxes. So consider even unopened packages when you're trying to figure out where the bugs are living, breeding, and dining.

2. Moths eat only wool. Moth larvae will chow down on cotton, fur, and feathers and have even happily adapted to eating some manmade fibers on occasion. So protect all your clothing from moths, not just winter sweaters and mittens.

3. All ants are sugar ants. The big black ants known as carpenter ants won't go away just because you got rid of all the sugar. They flock to water, so the way to eliminate them is to get rid of moisture anywhere you've seen them.

Their eating habits indicate precisely how to combat clothes moths: Never store clothes, blankets, or linens that haven't been cleaned. This applies to all clothing, not just wool. Moths will go after cotton, fur, even feathers. And they're resilient. They'll adapt to eating some synthetic fibers if that's where the dirt is.

Skip store-bought cedar. Moths and bluebirds disagree about cedar. Bluebirds love it, because cedar birdhouses last a long time and are waterproof. But moths don't like it one whit. That's good news, because it means that you won't have to spend big bucks to buy those fancy cedar balls or blocks from an upscale catalog to keep moths out of your closet, blanket chest, or underwear drawer. Instead, ask a friend who builds birdhouses for his cedar scraps and use those. If you don't know anyone who builds cedar birdhouses, look in your newspaper's classified ads in the spring to find someone who does.

Give moths motion sickness. Got a clotheshorse in your house? You know, a person who can never decide what to wear and is constantly moving outfits in and out of the closet? If so,

---

MAKE it **LAST**

Spurn those snacks

ALTHOUGH IT'S A MYTH that moths feed only on wool, the myth probably got started because wool coats are expensive to clean—so they're more likely to have the crumbs, dirt, and sweat that moths flock to when you put the coats in storage. If you want your coat to last a long time and don't want moths to feed on it, don't eat in the car in the winter. Really. Here's the logic: If you often eat fast food or drink coffee as you drive, you are much more likely to soil your coat. Not only that, but the food you're most likely to eat in the car is the greasy type that stains clothing.

Not that you'd store a coat with ketchup on it, but if you had to have your coat dry-cleaned a couple of times during the winter, you might be less likely to pay to have it dry-cleaned again at the end of the season for storage—and that encourages moths to make their move. Even if someone else often eats in your car, you're more likely to sit in the crumbs and dirty your coat. So put the kibosh on all car snacks and meals in the cold months.

Can't stop the snacking? Stop wearing your dry-clean-only coat in the car and spill all the fast food you like on your street clothes—as long as they don't require dry cleaning!

---

you've found the place you want to store the clothes you don't want moths to eat. Moths require still, quiet environments to thrive. Lots of movement discourages them from coming around or laying their eggs.

Foiling Food Moths

Food moths, also called grain moths, would be all for the FDA's food pyramid, with its recommended 7 to 11 servings of whole grains and pasta a day. Those are the foods they simply adore. They'll even gnaw through plastic canister lids or unopened pasta boxes to reach them. How do you keep such an aggressive foe from ruining food? With a mixture of vigilance and early detection, says Chad Speerly, whose Knoxville, Tennessee, food cooperative sells tons of bulk flour and nuts each year.

"You want to take steps as soon as you see one moth or one cocoon under a jar lid or on a box," Chad says. "Once food moths get established, they're hard to get rid of. You think you have them licked, but they're laying eggs in other packages, and soon more will hatch."

Here are some preventive techniques and some hard-hitting ways to stop moths that have already (literally) wormed their way into your cupboards.

WREATHED IN MOTH PREVENTION

Certain dried herbs, botanicals, and essential oils naturally repel moths and ants but still smell great. Why not try them next time you make a potpourri or dried herb wreath? Here are a half dozen to choose from.

1. Cedar chips
2. Lavender
3. Pennyroyal oil
4. Rosemary
5. Spearmint oil
6. Wormwood

that's • ingenious!

make your own roach motels

ROACH MOTELS are disgusting little contraptions no matter what. But if you have to use them, you might as well make your own and avoid paying top dollar for the honor of throwing out containers of dead roaches. Here's one way.

First, apply a thick layer of cooking grease (either vegetable shortening such as Crisco® or used and coagulated cooking oil) or petroleum jelly inside the neck of a 1-pint or 1-quart mason jar. Stand the jar upright and put a piece of banana inside. (Or try one of the other baits that roaches find irresistible on page 57.) Next, prop a tongue depressor or Popsicle® Stick on either side of the jar to provide the roaches with a sort of "plank" to walk.

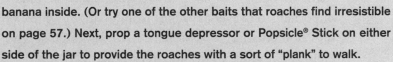

The roaches will walk up and into the jar, and the grease on the rim will keep them from climbing back out again. When you've collected a fair number, screw the lid on the jar and wait for the bugs to suffocate before disposing of them. Scald the jar for another try.

Go for glass. Want to keep food moths at bay? Store all your pasta, popcorn, crackers, flour, raisins, nuts, and breakfast cereals in glass jars. "Moths will eat through paper containers and even plastic bags," Chad Speerly says.

Seize, freeze, and destroy. If you have a food moth infestation, quit bringing pantry staples containing grain or nuts into the house. Okay, bring them into the house, but don't put them in the pantry. Instead, write the date on the packages and put them in the freezer for 2 days. That will kill all stages of food moths in the packages. After the 2-day holding period, empty each package into an airtight container. Then collect the empty packages outside for the next trash pickup or take them to the recycling center.

Rousting Roaches

A college student we used to know would kill a roach in his infested apartment, then pin the carcass above the toaster oven to serve as a warning to the other roaches. This is one of the many roach destruction methods that just do not work. In fact, roaches probably could survive a nuclear holocaust. We already know that the little fiends can survive most insecticides. That's why it's so important to prevent roaches from taking hold in the first place, says Bob Grimac, a passionate environmentalist who writes and edits a statewide environmental newsletter.

Preventing roach infestations is a matter of being ultraconscious about leaving food scraps around and superaware of whether you're bringing in roaches on bags or boxes, says Bob. So he can say with authority that once roaches have a beachhead on your property, you need to act swiftly, holistically, and repetitively to eradicate them. Here are some ingenious ways to do just that.

Help roaches belly up to the bar. There's something roaches have in common with slugs: a love of beer. So a simple way to rid yourself of a few roaches is to soak a rag in beer and place the rag in a shallow dish overnight, right next to the place where the roaches have been spotted most recently. This requires a certain strength of stomach on your part, because the next morning you'll need to dispose of the intoxicated, but still breathing, roaches. Replenish the rag for several days running

---

SIX BAITS ROACHES WILL REACH FOR

Of course, roaches have been known to live on fingernail clippings and soap dish scum. But to increase the chances of luring the pests to the bottom of a homemade roach motel, tempt them with one of these gourmet roach treats.

1. **A little beer mixed with banana and a few drops of almond extract**
2. **Banana peels**
3. **Boiled raisins**
4. **Dry pet food (cat, dog, or rodent)**
5. **Pieces of fresh apple**
6. **Potato peels**

---

until you have 2 days in a row with no victims. Then you'll know you've done in the whole family.

23 (degrees) skiddoo. Each time you bring home a box (any kind of box), you may be toting home roaches or a few roach eggs with your purchase. "Lots of postal warehouses just can't get rid of roaches, and one may jump on a parcel that comes through a warehouse and travel to your house," Bob Grimac says.

Here's a way to foil those crawling nasties in cold weather. When the temperature dips to below freezing, leave boxes outside for a day or two. Roaches and roach eggs will be destroyed when it's colder than 23°F. Of course, do that only if the contents of the box won't be damaged. If the contents aren't cold-hardy, at least unpack the box outdoors so the roaches don't come into the house.

Throw 'em in the drunk tank. Store-bought roach motels present a poisoning threat to pets and children, but they are effective for getting rid of a few roaches—say, a roach family that you accidentally brought in on the bottom of a grocery bag or that fled to your apartment when the neighbors had their place bombed. You can get the benefits of a roach motel without the chemicals by crafting this homemade version. Wrap masking tape around the outside of an empty jam or jelly jar so that the roaches can climb the sides easily. Put about an inch of beer in the jar, then add a few slices of banana and a few drops of almond extract. The roaches should climb up, drop in, get drunk, and drown. Keep the "drunk tank" active for a few days.

So Fleas Will Flee

In the Middle Ages, if your home got infested with fleas, all you could do was set fire to it and move to another house. If you're fighting the flea battle at your home, dropping a match might seem tempting. But we've discovered ways to deal with fleas that our unenlightened ancestors never dreamed of. Read on for some big ideas about getting rid of the tiny pests.

WHATSIT?

Q: This U-shaped hinged item has two springs and what seem like handles. What is it?

A: This appears to be one of those exercise gadgets to build up the muscles of the arms. To use it, you force the handles apart with both hands, then let them close.

Start with the eggs. The reason most people never eradicate fleas is that they try to kill the adult fleas. What you should really go after are the eggs and the larvae, says Francie Stull, who has operated a mail-order flea products business (FLEAS? Never Again!) for more than a decade.

"Fleas spend only 15 percent of their lives as adults," she says. "If you keep using insecticides, which kill only the adults, the eggs will continue hatching on a regular schedule." Although Francie's business, which is now Internet-based, sells insecticides, she heartily recommends another type of product that she peddles, something called insect growth regulator (IGR). "These IGRs are

SIX-STEP FLEA POWDER

You've finally gotten rid of the fleas on Fido, only to find that there are still some lingering in the carpet. You can concoct a homemade flea repellent for your carpet and use up the remains of some potpourri at the same time. Here's how.

1. Grind 1 cup potpourri in a blender or coffee grinder until it is about the consistency of ground coffee.

2. Blend the potpourri thoroughly with ½ cup baking soda and ½ cup cornstarch. You can substitute baking powder for the soda in a pinch.

3. Add 12 drops of one of these essential oils: citronella, pennyroyal, or rosemary. You can purchase essential oils at most crafts stores (for potpourri) or natural food stores.

4. Spread the mixture in a shallow baking pan and allow it to dry completely, which usually takes at least a day, longer in humid weather.

5. Pour the mixture into an empty body powder container or clean Parmesan cheese shaker. Sprinkle the potpourri mixture over the carpet. One cup usually covers 100 square feet. Brush it into the carpet with a dry scrub brush and allow it to sit for a couple of hours.

6. Vacuum up the powder, which will come up easily, bringing the fleas with it. Be sure to replace the vacuum bag, even if it's not full. If you don't, new fleas will hatch there and sneak back into the house.

nontoxic and kill fleas in the immature stages," she says. "They're far more expensive up front than the insecticides, but they take care of the entire environment for a year or more at a time. If you're using those monthly drops that the veterinarian sells, you'll save money in the long run by using IGRs, particularly if you have more than one pet." Insect growth regulators are not widely available, but you can ask your vet about them or request that your exterminator use them instead of insecticides.

Soften your hands while you wash the dog. Once you've treated your home with an IGR, you could just wait 30 days for the adult fleas to croak, says Francie Stull, but most people aren't that patient. Whether you've used an IGR or just want to give your dog a flea bath, there is no need to invest in a special flea shampoo. Instead, says Francie, use any dishwashing liquid. She prefers Ivory liquid because it's mild and nontoxic. "The trick is leaving it on for at least 15 minutes," she says. "That's why the flea shampoos work."

Don't just kill fleas, repel them. Once your home is free and clear of fleas, it's mighty tempting to make your dog live as a hermit so you never import fleas again. But you can create a non-toxic flea repellent instead, says Francie Stull. "This repellent will work if you're going where there might be a couple of fleas that will try to jump on you or your dog from another dog, as in the park or an obedience class," she says. "It's not effective in flea-infested areas, and it doesn't work as an insecticide."

Here's the formula. Into a quart of water, mix 20 drops euca-lyptus, citronella, lemongrass, pennyroyal, or lavender oil. Before you head out where there are other dogs, spray the mixture onto your legs and your dog's. This is not a case where more is better; applying the oil directly to your dog's skin will burn like heck. And never use the mixture on cats. They'll lick it off, which can poison them or at the very least give them stomach problems.

Giving Flies the Boot

What would a barbecue be without houseflies buzzing around? A lot more pleasant, that's what. Flies are even more annoying when they end up inside the house. The good new is that you don't have to resort to toxic chemicals when you have our nontoxic tactics at your disposal.

MAKE YOUR OWN FLYPAPER

Yes, it looks gross flapping in the breeze with scores of flies attached, but flypaper is a nontoxic way to rid your house (or garage or outdoor potluck) of flies. Haven't seen the stuff in the stores? Make your own! It's less expensive than store-bought flypaper, and it's easy to make. Here's how.

1. Cut brown kraft paper or brown paper grocery bags into strips that are 1½ inches wide and 2 to 3 feet long.

2. Using a pin or a hole punch, put a hole in the top of each strip and thread a piece of string through the hole.

3. Combine equal parts sugar, light corn syrup, and water in a heavy 2-quart saucepan. About ⅔ cup each should make enough to start. Bring the mixture to a boil over high heat.

4. Reduce the heat to medium-high and continue cooking the mixture to the softball stage—the point at which a bead of the mixture dropped into a glass of very cold water forms a ball that holds its shape but is mushy, not hard. If you're using a candy thermometer, the temperature should be 234° to 240°F.

5. Paint the mixture evenly onto the paper strips using a small paintbrush or a basting brush.

6. Hang up the strips and start collecting flies.

Flip the switch. Houseflies carry germs, drive you crazy, and fall into food, rendering it inedible. Instead of reaching for an aerosol can, reach for the light switch. "Flies are attracted to light," says environmentalist Bob Grimac. "So if you pull your blinds, open the doors, and turn off the lights, they may go outside. At least, it usually works. Every now and then, they just use the open door to call their friends inside!"

Swat 'em with citrus. Scratch the rind of a lime, lemon, or orange to release a scent that repels flies. Interestingly, cloves also *annals of ingenuity*

HONEY, HAND ME MY FLY BAT

just like the rest of America, Kansas circa 1905 wasn't among the most sanitary spots on earth. Folks just didn't know any better. Items such as common drinking cups at public wells and water fountains were common.

That was before Dr. Samuel J. Crumbine became the state's first full-time public health officer in 1904. Dr. Crumbine was determined to improve public health and sanitation practices. Among his accomplishments was helping the state outlaw those common cups, which led to the invention of the disposable paper cup.

Dr. Crumbine also had it in for another disease spreader, the housefly. The good doctor knew that flies carried typhoid fever, and when the incidence of the disease began to rise, Dr. Crumbine launched an aggressive campaign to wipe out flies in Kansas. The campaign's slogan? "Swat the fly."

Inspired by the campaign, a teacher from Weir City, Kansas, named Frank Rose invented the first flyswatter. He called his invention—a wooden yardstick with a screen tacked to the end—the fly bat. Dr. Crumbine renamed it the flyswatter, and the rest is history.

turn off flies. So if you combine the two—pushing cloves into the rind of an orange—what do you have? A pomander ball. Suspend it from a light fixture, or wall-mounted lamp in the room where the flies are congregating. They'll go away (if you open the door so they'll have somewhere to go), and for many weeks afterward, you'll have a pleasant scent wafting around the house.

Moving Mice Out

Softhearted as she is, animal lover and Humane Society volunteer Robin Woodruff would not hurt a fly, much less a mouse. But she knows that she has to get rid of any mice that take up residence in her home. "They can eat the electrical wires and cause a power outage or even a fire," she says.

There are other reasons even the cutest little mouse has got to go. Mice carry diseases, eat and ruin food, gnaw on books, and have even been known to silence pianos by eating the felt on the keys. Oh, and then there's that little matter of the droppings. And heaven forbid one should meet its Maker inside one of your walls—the stench will make you want to leave home.

But as Robin stresses, there are humane, nontoxic ways to remove mice—even if you're not willing to chase a mouse around the house trying to drop a tiny wastebasket on its head, the way she does. And why should you be nice to rodents that have left only wreckage in your home? If you're not moved by their cute little whiskers, consider that poison will leave you wondering where the corpses are. With traditional traps, you have to listen to those horrible tiny shrieks and ominous "snaps." So what's left, besides the mouse? Keep reading for reasonable, effective alternatives.

First, do no harm. There is absolutely no reason to use a traditional mousetrap anymore, says environmentalist Bob Grimac. "These days, home stores sell humane traps, which catch the mouse so you can release it, still alive, outdoors," he says. One trap he recommends is called the Mouse Master. There are also the Tin Cat, Tru-Catch, and Havahart traps—and those are just the ones Bob knows about. "The way they work is that first, a mouse goes into the opening in the trap," he says. "That springs something that pushes him into a holding chamber." After that, Bob walks the mouse a couple of blocks away and releases it in a park. "They don't come back in if you confuse them enough," he notes.

More is better. You're kidding yourself if you think that only one mouse has invaded your house, says Bob Grimac, who estimates that a mouse family infiltrates his 40-year-old home once every 3 years or so. And because the little rascals breed so rapidly, you have to get as many out at once as you can—before boy meets

---

EIGHT BAITS THAT ARE BETTER THAN CHEESE

Mice may pause at a trap for cheese, but they might prefer a less expensive lure or a food that lasts longer, such as oatmeal, say the folks at Tru-Catch in South Dakota. The company, which manufactures humane mousetraps, recommends the following foods to bait a trap.

1. Bread and butter
2. Cherry pits
3. Flour
4. Gumdrops
5. Oatmeal
6. Oatmeal mixed with peanut butter
7. Small nuts
8. Sunflower seeds, shelled or unshelled

---

girl. That means more traps for fewer days. "It won't work if you have only one trap going at a time," Bob says. "I'd advise more like 10 or 12 for a two-bedroom house. You also won't have to keep the traps around as long if you use more traps at the same time. A week or so should do the trick."

Move them around. Mice can be smart. "So you have to move the traps around every couple of days," says Bob Grimac. "Otherwise, they'll catch on and stop eating at the traps. And then you're back where you started."

Borrow a scholarly mousetrap. If the prospect of buying a bunch of mousetraps is daunting, consider a loan, says Bob Grimac. You can't get mousetraps at the library, but you probably can get them at a local school, which no doubt uses the traps in the cafeteria. If the school uses a lot of mousetraps (as it ought to), it doesn't have to use them constantly any more than you do. So ask if you can borrow the school's traps for a week or so.

making clothes
last

WE DON'T HAVE NATURAL FUR COATS, feathers, or scales to cover us, so we need clothes. Some of us make the most of this by wearing the trendiest garb, while others repair decades-old jackets with duct tape and skirt hems with staples. Most of us fall somewhere in between those two extremes: We want to look good, but we don't want to replace our entire wardrobes every year. When we buy, we want the highest quality for the lowest prices. We want to be able to make our favorites last a long time.

Our panel of Yankee clothing experts will help you do just that. Kate Ross, a professional milliner in Exeter, New Hampshire, will offer ways to distinguish the wheat from the chaff when you're shopping for clothing, and explain how to take care of your hats and shoes. Colleen L. Jones, a technical designer and fitting specialist who owns the Fancy Threads School of Custom Sewing in Newton, New Hampshire, will tell you how to store your sweaters and even how to do your own dry cleaning. Nancy Kimball, a professional seamstress from Exeter, New Hampshire, will explain why seam allowances are important and how to keep your favorite garments in ship-shape. And Mario Ponte, a graduate gemologist also from Exeter, New Hampshire, will offer suggestions on how to keep your fine jewelry sparkling like new. These experts and others you'll meet along the way have plenty of professional tips to help you look like a million without spending more than a few bucks.

Choosing Quality Clothing

You won't waste your clothes budget if you buy quality clothes. But how can you tell? Price and labels don't tell everything, and if you're buying secondhand, the tag may be missing. Fortunately, our everyday experts are on the case. Look for these signs of well-made clothes, and you can't go wrong.

MAKE it LAST
Shop for stability

HATE THE WAY shoulder seams rip out on knitted fabric shirts? Here's how to identify a long-lasting garment. Before you buy a piece of clothing, turn it inside out and look for fabric stabilizer, which can be either elastic or fabric stitched into the seams. You'll also find stabilizer behind embroidery on better-quality garments.

Go for hand-stitching. How can you identify a well-made suit jacket? "Look for hand-stitching on the inside lapels of men's suit jackets," says Kate Ross, co-owner of Head Over Heels, a hat and shoe shop in Exeter, New Hampshire. "A herringbone pattern of stitches stabilizes the lapel and makes it lie flat and smooth." Thus, the lapel is less likely to buckle and lose its shape. Even if you spend a bit more now for a hand-stitched jacket, you'll save in the long run.

Unfortunately, women's suits rarely have this feature. Why? Because patterns for men's clothing usually don't change over the years, explains garment industry veteran Rosella Campion of Medford, Massachusetts. "In women's clothing, you make a pattern, then never make it again," she says.

Ask for a generous allowance. You've found a garment that you absolutely must have: It's in style, it fits, and you like the way the fabric feels. Should you buy it? Not before you check the seam allowances—the fabric along the inside of the seams. A hefty seam allowance adds strength, says professional seamstress Nancy Kimball of Exeter, New Hampshire. It also gives you enough fabric so that you can let the seams out or snip a piece for a repair. If the seam allowances are half an inch or more, the garment will last.

*T*he perfect fit

WHEN YOU SLIP into that favorite jacket or dress, even if it doesn't have a designer label, it has been designed by someone. And after the designer—famous or otherwise—has come up with the general look, a technical designer has to take that look and translate it into real measurements so that it will fit real people. Our expert Colleen L. Jones is a technical fit designer. If your clothes fit, she's the one to thank.

Colleen designs for a clothing manufacturer that supplies garments to clients such as Victoria's Secret, Sears, and Avon Apparel. "We mainly do sleepwear," Colleen says. "Our specialty is silk." But Colleen doesn't stop there. She also owns and runs her own sewing school, called Fancy Threads School of Custom Sewing, in Newton, New Hampshire, where she teaches students how to make their own clothes and accessories. How did she get into this business? She has been sewing all her life, even while making her living in the computer industry. Then, she says, "I had one of those life-changing events. I lost a sister to breast cancer and decided that life is too short not to do something you love." So she fired up her sewing machine full-time and hasn't stopped since.

Select small stitches. Big stitches in clothing are better than small, right? Wrong. Before you purchase a garment, check the seams. If the stitches are small, you're on the right track: Tiny stitches are strong and increase the life of the piece.

Show your shoe smarts. Sore feet can ruin your day, so the next time you shop for shoes, look for these two key elements that identify a good pair.

1. Steel yourself. How can you tell a good shoe from one that's not so great? "A shoe with a small heel should have a steel shank through the arch for support," explains Kate Ross. Kate knows what she's talking about, as she sells high-quality shoes at her hat and shoe shop. You can't see the shank, so you'll have to ask the salesperson if the shoe you're considering has one. One way to tell: If you try to bend a shoe with a shank, you'll feel resistance. Don't look for a steel shank in sneakers, though; they're constructed differently.

2. Count on good heels. A heel counter—a little strip surrounding the inside of a shoe heel—will extend the life of a shoe and give your foot more support, says Kate Ross. You can feel it by squeezing closed the two sides of the shoe at the heel. If the bottom half of the heel is a bit stiff, then there is probably a counter in there.

Keeping Clothes Longer

Caring for your clothing by wearing it and storing it properly will extend its life, making it an even better deal than when you bought it. All of our Yankee experts agree that if you buy good-quality clothes and give them the proper care, they should last a lifetime (or at least until your kids call the style police on you). Our experts believe in the basics: Hang up your clothes instead of leaving them in a ball on the floor. Don't walk around with your

---

BUY EXTRA SOCKS

Hardly anyone has time to darn socks anymore. But you don't want to pitch a perfectly good sock just because its mate is worn to a thread in the toe or heel. Here's what to do. Buy several pairs of socks in exactly the same color and style. When one hits the skids (or gets lost), you'll always have an extra mate.

A not-so-mad hatter

YOU MIGHT THINK that hatmaking is a lost art, or one practiced by only very old craftsmen. Kate Ross doesn't fit the stereotype at all. She's young, and under her skilled hands, the felt, velvet, silk, and cotton fabrics that she transforms into hats are very much alive. Kate grew up in Connecticut and earned her bachelor's degree in art history from Yale. But it was millinery—the making of one-of-a-kind hats—that captured her interest and gave her an outlet for her design talents. Kate studied hatmaking under master milliner Wayne Wichern at the New York Fashion Academy in Seattle. Kate now works out of her studio at the back of Head Over Heels, the hat and shoe shop that she co-owns with her aunt, Jan Russell, in Exeter, New Hampshire.

Kate explains that she makes her hats by shaping squares of felt on wooden forms called blocks, using steam and heat to make the felt pliable. The felt is left to sit for at least 24 hours so that it can dry and shrink to fit tightly around the block. Kate then takes the hat off the block, cuts away the excess felt from the brim edge, and hems the hat, which is now ready to be trimmed. Kate adds any kind of decoration that suits her or her customer's imagination—felt leaves in contrasting colors, silk ribbon, velvet flowers. When each hat is finished, it's as unique as the person who made (or ordered) it.

hands jammed in the pockets of your jacket (the pockets will wear out sooner). And stuff the toes of your shoes with tissue paper so that they'll hold their shape if you don't wear them every day. But their expertise doesn't end there. These folks also know a thing or two about the intricacies of folding knitwear, storing hats, and protecting buttons. Here are some of those imaginative tips for keeping your clothes in good shape. (For tips on dealing with clothes moths, see page 51.)

SMART STORAGE SOLUTIONS

Unless you're a college student, you probably don't store your clothing in a heap on the floor. Blue jeans and T-shirts can stand up to that kind of treatment, but most other clothing can't. With that in mind, we present these clever storage tips that will give your clothing a longer life.

Pad your hangers. Those wire hangers are death to the shoulders of jackets and tops, especially if the fabric is knit. But padded hangers can cost almost as much as the clothes themselves. You can make your own padded hangers by wrapping quilt batting, strips of foam, or heavy yarn around the wire hangers you get from the dry cleaner or at clothing stores. You'll save your clothing—and your money.

Part with your plastic garment bag. It's tempting to hang that special outfit in the plastic garment bag that the store gave you. "But plastic doesn't allow those natural fibers to breathe, and it doesn't let moisture out— and that can ruin the garment," explains Colleen L. Jones. Instead, store your garments in a closet with closed doors. Enough air will circulate to keep them fresh and clean without allowing dust to settle on them.

annals of ingenuity

WHAT SIZE FOOT BAG DO YOU WEAR?

for millennia, people walked around barefoot. Then came the Bronze Age, when someone fashioned a pair of "foot bags" in what is now northern Europe. Those foot bags eventually became moccasins, which are still in vogue today.

Let your clothes out of the bag. There are good reasons to remove dry-cleaned garments from their plastic bags. According to Colleen L. Jones, removing the bags allows the cleaning chemicals to dissipate instead of settling into your garments—which is no good for your health or your clothing. Also, if the bag is printed, the ink on the bag can transfer right onto the clothing.

Fold your knits. Although you often see sweaters and other knit tops on hangers in the store, it's much better to store them folded flat, advises seamstress Nancy Kimball. Knit garments tend to "grow," losing their shape when they're stored on hangers for long periods of time. Folding knit garments allows them to hold their original shapes—and you won't get those silly bumps in the shoulders from a hanger.

Store sweaters in pillowcases. What's the best way to store that special cashmere or silk sweater? Fold it and slip it into a clean pillowcase (muslin is best, but cotton is okay), then lay it flat on a shelf or in a drawer, recommends Colleen L. Jones. You can fit several folded sweaters in one case. The pillowcase will offer extra protection from dust and critters, and it also will allow the fabric to breathe.

MAKING ACCESSORIES LAST

If you're like us, you don't want just your outfits to last longer— you want everything to last longer, including your favorite shoes and purses. Here's how the experts keep those ties, belts, shoes, purses, scarves, and hats looking great longer.

Renew your ties. Here's how to keep your neckties and scarves looking new. When you take one off, simply rub it back and forth gently across your thigh. The motion will lift the nap and remove any wrinkles or creases. Your tie or scarf will be ready to go the next time you want it, and you won't have to risk burning it with even the coolest iron.

Let your belt hang. A good leather belt should be around for years. One way to keep your belt in good shape is to let it hang instead of winding it and storing it in a drawer, because winding stretches and creases the leather. You don't need to purchase a fancy belt rack. Just screw a couple of clothes hooks into the closet wall or inside the door and hang two or three belts on each hook. If you watch your waistline, your belts should last a lifetime.

Keep your hats shipshape. Here are two ways to make sure your Stetson or your prized Easter bonnet is looking its best every time you reach for it.

1. Stuff 'em. Instead of stacking your hats on top of each other on a closet shelf, store the good ones with enough tissue stuffed inside the crown so that they don't rest on their brims, recommends milliner Kate Ross. Otherwise, the brims will flatten, even in a hatbox. Storing them this way will help them retain their fashionable shapes.

2. Stack them sensibly. "To save space, you can stack hats inside a hatbox," Kate says. "But be sure to stack the larger hats over the smaller hats, like those nesting dolls that fit one inside the other, so they don't crush each other out of shape."

WHATSIT?

Q: This instrument is made of dark metal and has a blade that slides out of the handle and is sharp on one side only. The handle has a scalloped design that could be used for measuring. What is it?

A: This is the Protean Lancette and is a buttonhole cutter. Here's how it worked. You'd hold the tool with both hands and adjust the slide for the button size you wanted to cut. Then, holding it as you would a pen and with the cutting edge away from you, you would insert the point where you wanted to start the buttonhole until the gauge stopped you.

Tuck and roll. You already know about stuffing tissue in your shoes to help keep their shape. But did you know that you can extend their life, save space, and stay organized all in one fell swoop? "Roll up your clean socks and tuck them into your shoes before you put your shoes away," suggests Kate Ross. Then, when you're in a hurry in the morning, you can just pull out a pair of shoes and socks that match.

Take the tube. Tall boots can get creases across the calves or ankles if they are allowed to flop over in your closet. To keep them standing tall, insert a cardboard tube left over from a roll of wrapping paper into each boot. Or the next time you buy the end of a bolt of fabric, ask for the tube on which the fabric is rolled, suggests seamstress Nancy Kimball. Cut the tube to size and insert a portion into each boot.

CLEANING AND MAINTAINING YOUR CLOTHES

Most folks know that a little prevention goes a long way in most facets of life, and clothing is no exception. But sometimes stains do set, and we don't want to pay high professional cleaning bills to get them out. Our pros have some ingenious suggestions for keeping your clothes looking their best—from using hair conditioner to restore the softness of a silk blouse to covering metal buttons with aluminum foil before laundering. Read on for more tried-and-true ideas.

Zip it up. Can you really save loads of money just by zipping a zipper? You bet, says Colleen L. Jones. "Not only will this reduce the stress on the bottom of the zipper during washing," she says, "but the sharp edges of metal zippers won't snag and stress other garments being washed next to them." Zip up one zipper, and you could save a whole load of clothing from rips and tears.

Foil, don't spoil. You just bought a nifty jacket with polished silver or gold buttons, and you want those buttons to keep their

put the brakes on dry cleaning

"MY DAD, DONALD CONNOR, is a retired police officer and auto mechanic, so I'm used to him puttering around in his garage," says Colleen L. Jones. "But one day when I went out to the garage while he was working, I smelled something familiar: dry cleaning fluid. I asked him if he had any clothes hanging around the garage that had recently been dry-cleaned, and he said no. He was just busy cleaning the brakes of his car.

"I sniffed the brake cleaner, then looked at the label on the spray can. The active ingredient was perchloroethylene, the same active ingredient in dry cleaning fluid. Being frugal, I picked up my own can of brake cleaner in the auto supply section of a discount store, and now I use it to dry-clean my clothes. I just spray a little on a stain and let it air-dry. If the stain is particularly stubborn, I spray the cleaner on the spot, then blot it with a washcloth. I've saved plenty on dry cleaning bills since then."

shine. One way to do that is to grab some aluminum foil, says Colleen L. Jones. Cut a circle of foil about twice the size of the button and wrap it over the button, pressing the edges down like a piecrust. "Your button is now safely wrapped for washing and drying," Colleen says.

Fluff away dust. "If you have items of clothing that dust has settled on during storage, just toss them in the dryer on the Air Fluff cycle. It will get rid of the dust and keep the colors fresh without washing or dry cleaning.

Fight grease with grease. Have a grease stain on that favorite cotton shirt or pair of slacks? No problem. Grab a can of WD-40® from the garage or basement and spray a little directly on the stain—there's no need to rub. Wait 30 minutes and launder as usual. Be sure to test the WD-40® on a hidden area of the garment first, however, to make sure it won't do more damage.

Don't sweat it. If it's been a hot day and you find perspiration stains on your clothes, don't despair. Head to your medicine cabinet for the aspirin—not ibuprofen, not acetaminophen. Dissolve several aspirin—about 6 for a mildly dirty garment and up to 10 for a really filthy one—in 1 cup lukewarm water, then pour the solution directly onto the stain. Let it soak for 30 minutes, then launder as usual. Your clothes will come out fresh and clean, and you won't have to buy any expensive cleaning products.

annals of ingenuity

GIVE IT THE BOOT

for well over a hundred years, women have enjoyed wearing walking boots—high-heeled, low-heeled, laced, or fastened with buttons. Around 1860, the typical Yankee woman wore a walking boot that had a practical half-inch heel and a flannel lining for warmth. The average price for this wardrobe staple? Five bucks.

Get the ink out. "The best thing for removing ink stains on most clothing is Fantastik® spray cleaner," says technical designer and fitting specialist Colleen L. Jones. "Even though it's for cleaning kitchens and bathrooms, it does the trick on ink," she says. So before you toss out an ink-stained garment or spend extra money for dry cleaning, look through the cleaning supplies under your kitchen sink. You might already have the remedy right there.

Condition your silks. "Most silk garments are washable, even if the label says dry-clean only," notes Colleen. "Follow the dry-cleaning instructions while the garment is new, then, when it begins to lose its luster, start to clean and condition it at home." To wash your favorite silk blouse, fill the sink with enough water to fully immerse the garment, then add about a tablespoon of hair conditioner. Soak the blouse in the mixture for a few minutes, then rinse and hang to dry. Use warm water for whites and cold water for colors. "Silk is a protein fiber like hair," Colleen explains, "so after some wear, the follicles start to open up and rub against each other. Conditioner closes them up." The conditioner will keep the silk fabric feeling soft and smooth, and you won't have to spend a fortune at the dry cleaner.

Leave jeans a little damp. Want to keep those dark-colored jeans looking new? "Turn them inside out before washing and take them out of the dryer before they are completely dry," advises Nancy Kimball. "Overdrying causes fading, and doing this will help your jeans retain their color."

Practice Murphy's Law. You can make your leather accessories last longer by cleaning and conditioning them. But you don't have to buy expensive cleaning products. Grab that bottle of Murphy® Oil Soap (the kind that's made for cleaning wood floors) from the closet, apply a little to a damp sponge, and then rub the sponge over your purse, working the oil into the leather until it seems to disappear. There's no need to rinse. The oil soap will clean and condition the leather, making it soft and glossy. *Note:* Before you try this tip, make sure you like the smell of the soap.

Mind your own beeswax. If you want to keep your good leather shoes and accessories looking like new, use beeswax, says milliner Kate Ross. You can get beeswax at shoe stores or discount stores. "Warm the beeswax before you use it, so it is soft and pliable, or heat the shoes or purse slightly with a blow dryer," Kate says. Then apply the wax and work it in with a soft cloth. Kate warns that you shouldn't use this method on nubuck or suede, since beeswax will make them look like oiled leather.

Fast and Easy Repairs and Alterations

Sometimes clothes meet with an untimely injury—a lost button, a frayed cuff, a torn hem. Fear not, say our experts. There are plenty of ingenious ways to make quick repairs, some without even taking a stitch. And all of our experts agree on one method for customizing clothing: changing buttons. "Changing the buttons on a jacket changes the total look," says technical designer Colleen L. Jones. Here are some other great ways to fix and customize your clothes fast.

Update a frayed sweater with embroidery thread and this simple blanket stitch.

Make a blanket statement. If your sweater's cuffs are a bit frayed, don't dismay—you can pull them together again with a few decorative, stylish embroidery stitches, says Kate Ross. Using embroidery thread in the same or a contrasting color, do a blanket stitch from left to right all the way around the cuff. Your sweater will not only be repaired, but it also will be updated—and you won't have spent a cent.

Cut off your panty hose toes. Another pair of panty hose ruined by a hole in the toe? Don't toss them, says Colleen L. Jones. She should know, because she's a technical designer and fitting specialist who owns the Fancy Threads School of Custom Sewing in Newton, New Hampshire. She advises cutting off the end of each toe and machine-stitching a new seam across it, creating a new toe. (Do this on both feet so that they will be of equal length.) "It does shorten them a bit," Colleen notes, but in most cases they will still fit fine—and you won't have to rush out to buy another pair.

from great-grandmother to great-granddaughter

MY GREAT-GRANDMOTHER made dresses professionally on exclusive Newbury Street in Boston," says Rosella Campion, herself a garment industry veteran. "When styles changed, her customers brought their special garments to her, and she would take them apart to make new ones for them.

"Sometimes they would return from travels in Europe with bits of lace or embroidery that my great-grandmother would use to make a dress seem new by embellishing it. When cuffs on a jacket got worn, she replaced them with velvet cuffs and a matching collar. She would reuse as much as possible. When I outgrew a dress, she would enlarge it by inserting a band of velvet in the bodice of the dress.

"To this day, I follow my great-grandmother's example whenever I can. I have a black suit that I wear for both business and evening engagements. I just change the buttons for either occasion."

Button up with safety pins. If a button with a shank (a metal loop on the back) pops off a jacket, "slide a safety pin through the shank and pin it back on," recommends Kate Ross. "In fact, you can even customize clothing this way. Change a set of shank buttons by attaching them with safety pins instead of thread."

Double up on buttons. Expensive coats and jackets often have "backer buttons"—buttons sewn on the inside of the garment directly behind the outer button to give the outer button more strength and durability. Even if your duds don't have these, you can add them—and extra life—to your coats, says Colleen L. Jones. Choose a set of plain, flat buttons and sew them behind the outer buttons (on the inside of the coat or jacket), passing your needle through the holes of the outer buttons so that the two are sewn together. You'll reduce the stress on the outer buttons, and

a sweater to dye for

"I WAS WEARING my brand-new cotton sweater, which I loved, when I accidentally spilled bleach on it," remembers Kate Ross. "In tears, I tried to figure out how I could save my sweater. Then I got an idea. First, I rinsed out all the excess bleach with cold water. Next, since the sweater was a heathered blue, I bought two different colors of blue liquid dye that roughly matched the sweater's original color. I added about a teaspoon of one color to a glass of water, then I dipped a Q-tip in the mixture and dabbed it gently onto the bleach spot. I repeated the process with the other color, creating my own heathered effect. If I dripped a bit too much dye onto the sweater, I blotted it with a wet towel. My sweater has since had years of wear—and it's still my favorite blue sweater."

they'll be less likely to pop off—so you won't be searching for lost buttons or buying a whole new set.

Beat the button blues. Because blue jeans buttons are attached to the fabric with grommets, a missing button on the waistband spells disaster, right? Wrong. "You can repair the hole by tucking a piece of denim between the two layers of the waistband where the button came off, then stitching back and forth over the hole to secure the fabric," says Colleen L. Jones. (You may need to pull out any stray threads left by the missing button first.) Then buy a replacement jeans button with a loop on the back at any fabric store and sew it on by hand. The whole chore will take only a few minutes, and you'll have saved an expensive pair of jeans.

Hem those too-long jeans. Are your jeans too long? You can shorten them yourself without ending up with a funny-looking hem. Colleen L. Jones explains how. "Cut the jeans one and one-quarter inches longer than you want them to be. Fold them up one-half inch, then another five-eighths inch. Lay each leg flat and hammer the seam with a regular household hammer. Really whack it. This will break down the fibers so that the seam lies flat, making it easier to stitch." From here, you can either sew the hem by hand or stitch it on a machine. According to Colleen, "Most machines will stitch through it like butter." Once you're finished, you'll have a pair of jeans that fit perfectly without having to hire a tailor.

Just add pads. You found a jacket or dress that's almost perfect, but the sleeves are too long by just a tad. No problem, says Colleen L. Jones. For a quick fix without a single stitch, add shoulder pads. Many pads now come with Velcro closures so that you can remove them easily for laundering or move them from garment to garment. With the pads, your garment will fit perfectly, and you won't have to pay for tailoring.

New Uses for Old Clothes

If there's one characteristic common among Yankees, it's that we like to keep things around for a long time, extending their useful lives way beyond the warranty period. Our experts have found ingenious ways to do just that.

Cut off the cuffs. Have a cotton turtleneck or sweatshirt that's ready for the rag bin? Before you cut it up, snip off the cuffs and give them a second life: Slip them over rolls of wrapping paper to keep the paper from unrolling, suggests technical designer Colleen L. Jones. You'll not only squeeze the last bit of use out of your shirt, but you'll also put an end to a popular household pet peeve.

New Life for Old Ties

With today's dress-down trend in the workplace, many of us (or our significant others) have more neckties that we can use. But being the thrifty Yankees that we are, we don't want to toss them in the circular file. Here are a few stylish ways to put those old ties back to work. You can use your ties:

- As a belt for slacks or a skirt
- As a sash for a dress
- As a headband or ponytail holder
- As curtain tiebacks (Choose two ties that complement each other either in style or color and simply tie back one curtain panel with each tie. Then attach each tieback to the wall with a thumbtack or pushpin.)

Deck the walls. Old clothing can make a unique wall display in your home. Don't believe it? Think about your grandmother's vintage dresses that are languishing in the attic. Or maybe you have several of your grandfather's hats. Or perhaps your child's christening gown was especially beautiful, and you don't want to stash it in a drawer. Pull out some of these items and hang them up—on the wall. You can use pegs, coat hooks, hangers, or even curtain rods (just slide the arms of a garment through a rod). The garments will add color, texture, and a warm feeling to any room in which you display them.

Tie back your drapes with jewelry. Have a tangle of old costume jewelry stuck in a drawer somewhere? Don't throw those baubles away. Instead, use those beaded necklaces and chain belts to tie back the curtains in any room of your home. Select a "pair" of items that complement each other and loop one around each curtain. Secure each new tieback on a cup hook screwed into the wall behind the curtain.

Caring for Your Fine Jewelry

Whether you have a drawer full of jewelry or just a single wedding band, you want to keep your precious pieces gleaming and in good repair. Mario Ponte, a graduate gemologist and owner of Exeter Jewelers in Exeter, New Hampshire, recommends having the settings for gemstones checked by a professional jeweler once a year to be sure nothing has broken or come loose. He also suggests having good pieces reappraised every two or three years so that your insurance keeps up with the value of your jewelry. In the meantime, there are plenty of ways you can care for these treasures yourself. Here are some tips for keeping your fine jewelry looking just fine.

Don't use toothpaste. "Don't use toothpaste to clean your jewelry," cautions Mario Ponte. It's a myth that toothpaste is a

that's • ingenious!

i skirted the issue

"DURING THE 1970s, my closet contained bell-bottom hip huggers, beaded dresses, fringed moccasins, and a beloved brown leather miniskirt," says Jan Russell, co-owner of Head Over Heels, a hat and shoe shop in Exeter, New Hampshire. "Of course, styles change constantly, as does one's figure, and I was left wondering what to do with the skirt and my other fashion relics. Then came the gasoline crunch, when we all had to find entertainment close to home. Our hometown bowling alley provided a means of inexpensive entertainment. I enjoyed bowling, but I didn't have a bowling bag. So I pulled out my old leather miniskirt, stitched a straight seam across the hemline, inserted a leather pull cord to gather the waist, and voila: I had a custom-made leather bowling bag."

good cleaning agent for fine jewelry. Toothpaste may be great for your pearly whites, but it can scratch your jewelry.

Restore the brilliance. "Diamonds aren't indestructible," warns Mario Ponte. "They need to be cleaned and cared for regularly." To restore the sparkle to your diamond, stir up a solution of equal parts cold water and household ammonia in a cup. Dip your diamond piece into the cup and soak it for 30 minutes. Lift the piece out of the cup and gently tap around the mounting with an old, soft-bristled toothbrush to loosen any remaining dirt. Drain the piece on a paper towel.

Add more glitter to your gold. If your gold ring has become dingy, combine 1 cup warm water, 1 teaspoon dishwashing liquid, and 3 or 4 drops ammonia. Dip your ring into the solution and brush it with an old, soft-bristled toothbrush. Then rinse under lukewarm water and set it on a paper towel to dry. Buff it with a lint-free cloth, and your gold ring will look like new.

Make your silver shine. Here's how to restore the shine to all of your fine silver jewelry (and your silver flatware, for that matter). Line the bottom of a glass baking dish with aluminum foil, then fill the dish halfway with hot water. For every quart of water, add 1 tablespoon salt and 1 tablespoon water softener. Immerse silver only (not gemstones, which could be damaged) in the dish for several minutes. You'll see the tarnish begin to disappear. When the tarnish is gone, rinse your silver clean under running water and dry with a soft cloth. This is an excellent method to use when you have several pieces to clean, because you can do them all at once.

Give pearls the velvet touch. "Store pearls in a cloth or velvet pouch or bag," says Mario Ponte. "Never use plastic to store pearls, because it can cause them to discolor."

furnishing your
castle

THESE DAYS, SHOPPING FOR A single piece of furniture can be a shocking experience. The smallest coffee table or ottoman can set you back hundreds of dollars. An ordinary easy chair can cost thousands—if you buy retail. Luckily, you have lots of options. A few tips from our ingenious experts will help you sniff out the best discounts, explain why you should never go to an auction without a flashlight, and teach you to use a magnet to find out whether that lamp you're eyeing is solid brass.

Who are these experts? They include professional decorators

Phoebe Davidson of Natick, Massachusetts, and Karen Krowne of Wayland, Massachusetts, who offer some clever ways to choose the right accessories and select appropriate furniture for your home and your taste. Professional antique restorer Wayne Towle of Needham, Massachusetts, shares his advice for haunting antiques shops and auctions (including a way to get an early peek at auction pieces). John Lawrence is a furniture restorer from Wayland, Massachusetts. Among his expert tips are how to spot a handcrafted piece when you're shopping for the real thing and how to get the best deal at almost any auction.

So what are we waiting for? There's shopping to be done!

Choosing Furniture

Experts know that just because something looks good in the store doesn't mean it'll look good in your house. Before you fall in love with a couch, a fabric, or even a paint chip, follow these rules to save time and money.

Check your choice in natural light. Professional decorator Phoebe Davidson, of Natick, Massachusetts, never buys anything without taking it outdoors first. Things look different in fluorescent or yellow light than they do in daylight, which is extremely important if you're going to put something near a window. "I make sure that I can buy it on approval, too," Phoebe notes. If it doesn't look right, you want to be sure you can bring it back.

THE PROS KNOW

it's a look

THE KEY to adding a period look to your room, says interior decorator Karen Krowne, is to accessorize. Some design centers give you the impression that you have to buy period furniture. Don't, she says. You can give an oriental, French country, or arts and crafts feel to a room with an end table and a lamp. Add a print and some fabric, and you have an understated look for a fraction of the cost of a single piece of furniture. "And in five years, if you decide that you aren't Victorian or English country anymore, you don't have to buy a new couch," Karen says.

Try before you buy. Everybody has, at one time or other, chosen a paint color they adore, only to find that it doesn't look right covering a whole wall. That doesn't have to be a problem if your local hardware store will rent you a quart of paint (believe it or not, some will). This allows you to take home a small amount of paint in any of the store's pre-mixed colors and try it out for a dollar or two. It's a great opportunity to put a big swath of paint on the wall and live with it day and night for a couple of weeks. That way, you can make a much more informed decision than trying to go by a manufactured paint chip.

Plan your space. The trouble with buying furniture today is that it's big. Those enormous, overstuffed chairs look great in store showrooms, but they may not look good in your house. "They're comfortable," says Phoebe Davidson, "but who needs a couch that's forty-four inches tall?" You don't, unless you'll be putting it in a room that has a cathedral ceiling, like the showroom does. Phoebe says that she'd never shop for furniture without a tape measure and an idea of the space that needs to be filled.

Measure the furniture you want to buy, then plan your room. It's the oldest trick in the book, says Phoebe, because it works. "Come home and make a template of your room out of newspaper, including depth and width," she advises. Keep in mind that the average person needs 2 feet of space between pieces of furni-

---

annals of ingenuity

ADDING WORMHOLES

d uring the 1920s, architect Addison Mizner and his brother, writer Wilson Mizner, owned a furniture store in which they would "antique" dining room tables, chairs, and knickknacks to make them look older than they really were. When showing friends around the factory, Wilson would sometimes hand them air rifles so that they might take their own shots at the soon-to-be antique furniture. "Don't shoot them straight on," he'd warn. "A worm always charges at a piece of furniture from an angle."

that's • ingenious!

make your own swatches

YOU KNOW ENOUGH to take wallpaper samples or paint chips with you as you shop for curtains, throw pillows, and linens. How else will you be able to match the colors on the walls? But how are you going to match that Turkish rug or the mat from your favorite print? Use those free paint charts from the hardware store. Grab a few that seem close in color to the object you want to match. Take them home and compare them to the object. Cut out the exact matches and paste them onto a piece of poster board or an index card that you can fold over and carry in your purse or pocket. When you're trying to find a matching throw pillow or lamp shade, you'll have a handy reference.

ture (more if that person uses a wheelchair or a walker). If you plan your room carefully, your new furniture won't make you feel as if you're living in a dollhouse. One more thing: Ask the salesperson to show you how to measure your home's doorways, stairways, and turns to make sure you don't buy a piece that literally won't fit through the front door.

Make sure you have options. You love that antique bed, and you can get it for a good price, too. What you may not realize is that finding a mattress for your "find" might be a bit tricky. That's because some older pieces of furniture are smaller than their present-day counterparts. Some older chairs, for instance, are too small for an adult to sit in comfortably. Also, as furniture frames got bigger, so did some standard companion pieces, such as mattresses. Many older beds can't accommodate the new mattresses, which means that you'll be paying for a custom mattress—and that's hardly a bargain.

Steals and Deals on Furniture and Accessories

To get the very best deal on furniture, inherit it from your favorite aunt, says furniture restorer John Lawrence. These days, great craftsmanship is priceless. That's why antiques dealers spend all their time prowling around garage and estate sales. If you're in the market for new furniture and accessories, it pays to be creative.

Just re-cover it. Lifelong decorator Phoebe Davidson hears it all the time: "I want to redo the living room, but my husband loves this awful old chair." Her advice is simple. "Keep the old furniture you have, even if you think it's ugly, because you can fix it up and make it better than what's out there today," she says. A chair with a good frame can be completely redone, right down to the springs, and it will last forever. "So much of today's new furniture is all about looks," Phoebe notes. "Things are glued and stapled together rather than having double-doweled joints and corner blocks. And new furniture costs thousands. Furniture that's decades old was built to last."

Never pay retail. The number one rule when buying new furniture is never to pay retail. Retail stores inflate prices up to 400 percent. (That's not a typo.) Find out the retail price of the piece of furniture you want, then promise yourself to do better. Call the manufacturer and ask where its factory outlets are. Outlets sell the same furniture for much less than retail stores, and every state has discount furniture warehouses that sell name brands at deep discounts. Finally, look for wholesale dealers that sell designer furniture by mail order. Do an Internet search on the name of a particular manufacturer to find wholesalers that carry that brand. (*Note:* Use your credit card for all mail-order purchases to protect yourself from the few fraudulent dealers out there.)

Ask for designer leftovers. Decorators and interior designers sometimes make mistakes, and that can be to your benefit. They sometimes buy furniture, lamps, curtains, and other accessories that don't quite fit the space they're supposed to or don't fit their clients' needs. Many of those mistakes can be sent back to the factory, but some can't, and that's the stuff designers are looking to unload. Because designers typically buy furniture at a 50 to 70 percent trade discount, they might be willing to sell it to you for cost, just to get rid of it. If you're looking for a certain piece, call around to your local decorators (many are listed in the Yellow Pages) to see what they have on hand. If you find something that interests you, ask the decorator for the manufacturer's name, model number, and dimensions, then find out the retail price before you begin to negotiate.

WHATSIT?

Q: One of our readers found this contraption in an antiques shop. Can you guess what it is?

A: It's a shoemaker's lamp. The cobbler would set it near his bench, and the light from a candle placed in the center would be reflected into the glass balls and provide a bright light by which he could work.

It's curtains for you—and for less. When you shop for custom curtains, you'll find that some retail stores charge hundreds of dollars to make them. That's actually more than you'd spend to commission a decorator or designer to make and install them. Instead, you can buy your own fabric at a discount outlet, then find a seamstress or tailor in the Yellow Pages to sew them for you. That's what the decorators do!

Pillow talk. Adding pillows to a room is a quick, easy, and inexpensive way to change the whole look. Making the pillows yourself can save you even more money. Here are three ingenious strategies to help you get started.

1. Ask for scraps. The fabric store isn't the only place that sells fabric scraps at unbelievable discounts. Upholsterers have them, too. Why? Not because *they've* made mistakes in measuring, but because some designer goofed when estimating the amount of fabric a client would need to redo a chair or sofa. When that happens, the upholsterer is stuck with a couple of yards of fabric that won't cover even the smallest ottoman. But that fabric may cover your throw pillows nicely, and since the designer's client has already paid for the fabric, the upholsterer will probably give the scraps to you for next to nothing. All you have to do is ask to see any leftover fabric that might be for sale.

2. Make them yourself. You can sew most pillow covers by hand, says Karen Krowne, even if you don't know the first thing about putting in zippers. The truth is that most custom-made pillows don't have zippers. They don't need them. Just trace the pillow onto the wrong side of the fabric, adding an extra inch or two on all sides for the seam allowance. Sew three sides with your sewing machine or by hand, put the stuffing in, and then stitch the fourth side. When you want to change the cover, just repeat the process with new fabric.

3. Use fabric napkins. You might not even need to use scissors to make a decorative pillow cover. Many upscale retail stores sell beautiful, oversize fabric napkins. Buy them in pairs, choosing one napkin with a plaid or print design for the front and another in complementary plain color for the back. Make sure the napkins are large enough to fit your pillow form at home, or buy a form to fit at a fabric or craft store. You can even get seam tape that you iron on rather than bothering with needle and thread.

Check the scrap heap for a table runner. You're browsing at the fabric store and find a couple of yards of scrap linen on sale. Congratulations. You might have found a new table runner, says Karen Krowne. She suggests keeping the measure-

MOVE IT!

Decorators these days are getting lots of money for rearranging people's knickknacks. Taking an object out of its original context can be a striking way to update a look and express yourself. But you don't need a decorator, just your imagination. Have an old ceramic teapot? It could become a wonderful vase for flowers on your living room coffee table or guest bedroom dresser. How about a collection of old milk bottles or watering cans? Line those up on a knick-knack shelf in the dining room. Why go out and buy objects when you can use the ones you have to express your design style?

ments of your dining room table with you—say in your purse or personal organizer. That way, anytime you stop at a fabric store, you can check out the scrap table for potential runners. "Table runners are so easy to make," she says. "It's easy to add a little tassel or fringe. I use an iron-on hem tape and add a decorative border. It's a snap."

Antique Attractions and Flea Market Finds

Furniture restorer Wayne Towle knew that he was in over his head the day he watched an interior designer bid $90,000 for a chair without batting an eye. "With one phone call, he had it sold for twice that," says Wayne. "I was in awe." Auctions are full of professional buyers and sellers who bid on their own wares to drive up the price. But you can still find good deals if you know what you want and when to bid.

Stay for the end. One of the pitfalls of buying furniture at auction is that you're often bidding against professional antiques dealers and interior designers who don't mind spending $10,000 for a vase or a chair when they know they can sell it for $20,000. But if you spot something at an auction that you love and it's one of the last items on the block, you may be in luck. Casual shoppers and even professionals are usually gone by the last hour of any auction. If you're willing to wait it out, the auctioneer will likely be willing to take a loss on the last few pieces just to avoid hauling them home.

Bigger is cheaper. When you need a particularly large piece of furniture, such as a hutch or an armoire, you might have

THE PROS KNOW

a real-life kitchen

"THE PROBLEM with creating or decorating a kitchen is that you look at all those brochures of gourmet kitchens, and the three things you never see in them are food, kids, and papers," says decorator Karen Krowne. "Any sensible person knows that those are the three messes you'll be cleaning up every day, so who do they think they're kidding?

"The most difficult of these is paper, because gourmet kitchen designers don't realize that managing a household means taking care of bills, junk mail, grocery lists, report cards, and homework. They also don't seem to know that all of these pieces of paper end up on kitchen countertops.

"I took care of the paper problem in my kitchen by getting little wooden cubicles like they have in the post office. I had them made, but you can find them in some antiques shops or office supply stores. I put the cubicles up on the wall, and that's where the mail and newspapers go. The bills get sorted there and paid as needed.

"I also attached file folders—the kind meant to go outside the doors in doctors' examining rooms—to the ends of my kitchen island. Those are also available at office supply stores. The kids put their homework, soccer schedules, invitations, and report cards to be signed in there.

"So far, we haven't lost a single sheet of paper, and my countertops are still reserved for the one thing they were designed for—cooking."

don't polish that lamp!

ANTIQUE LIGHTING expert Bruce Sweeney of Wayland, Massachusetts, has seen it many times: A customer comes in with a once-valuable lamp that has been destroyed by too much polishing. "One lady came in with a pretty copper lamp. She was really excited because she'd discovered the copper under the dull finish. She was having trouble getting the rest of the old finish off and wanted me to polish it for her," he says, shaking his head. "I had to be the one to explain to her that this dull finish was the original patina. It had tremendous historical value, and once she removed it, she also removed three-quarters of the lamp's value. She'd turned a $40,000 lamp into a $10,000 lamp with one cleaning."

Bruce's advice to all antiques owners is the same. Before you refinish a dresser, hutch, or lamp, take it to an experienced restoration expert for an opinion about its worth. Most offer free estimates, which means free advice about how to proceed. If the finish on your lamp or dresser is worthless, they'll tell you, and you'll be free to go home and strip it yourself. If the finish is rare or an example of a particular artisan's work, they'll tell you that too, and give you advice about how to preserve it.

"Don't destroy the antiques you have," Bruce says. "I hate giving bad news."

good luck at an antiques show or auction, says Wayne Towle. "Only a few buyers are going to be interested in large pieces," he notes. "Let's face it, there are only a few homes that those pieces will fit in. There are only a few *trucks* that these pieces will fit in. That's why they'll cost less per pound than a small end table that'll fit in your trunk." Strike your bargain at the end of the day, when the owner really doesn't want to haul the piece home. "That's when you can make a great deal," Wayne says. Be aware, though, that the dealer probably won't offer delivery on the item, and you'll be expected to get it home yourself.

Buy tomorrow's antiques today. John Lawrence was a teenager when he started haunting house auctions, flea markets, and estate sales looking for furniture. Back then, no one was interested in art deco furniture. "It was still too new," he remembers. A couple of decades later, those same pieces are pricey classics. John learned a lesson: If you find a piece of well-made furniture, it doesn't need to be an antique to be valuable. "Mid-century furniture is a great value right now because it is very well made but hasn't caught the eye of collectors and antiques dealers—yet."

SPOTTING HIDDEN TREASURES

In this day of professional antique "pickers," who scour garage sales looking for undervalued goods, it's next to impossible to find an undiscovered Tiffany lamp or a seventeenth-century vanity gathering dust in someone's attic. Still, our experts know how to find great pieces that will last long enough to become antiques.

Check for telltale signs of authenticity. Occasionally, you'll find an antique piece that was handcrafted—or that somebody claims was handcrafted. Usually, it takes an expert to tell the difference. But John Lawrence says that there are a couple of signs to look for. "Handcrafted pieces contain small imperfections that signal a particular craftsman's work," he notes. Those imperfections might include a scoring mark down the inside of the dovetails, which shows that the craftsman had to mark a line to guide his hand cuts. If you turn a drawer over and run your hand along the bottom, you might notice slight waves in the wood, which might indicate that the piece was hand-planed. If, however, the bottom is made of smooth plywood, the piece was certainly machine made.

A scoring mark along dovetails can indicate that a piece is an antique.

Make sure it's solid. John Lawrence also advises using the wiggle test on any piece of furniture before buying it. "Look for

CARRY ON—AND IN AND OUT

If you want to get into an antiques show early, when the real deals happen, become a porter. Make friends with a local dealer, then offer to work carrying items into the show. That way, you can see what everyone else has before the general public arrives. "That's when many of the deals happen," says Wayne Towle. Dealers trade with dealers and give each other good prices.

structural integrity," he says. "Put your knee on the seat of the chair and wiggle the back. If it's loose, you'll need to take it apart and reglue it when you get home. That's not as easy to do as it sounds." You may be investing in professional repairs before you're done. John's advice is to stick to solid pieces.

Skip the stuffing. According to upholsterer Peter Alexson, who works in Framingham, Massachusetts, a good way to identify a quality chair is to find one with the least amount of padding. That probably sounds counterintuitive. People generally think that overstuffed chairs are the most comfortable. "Actually, padding usually covers a bad frame," he says. A solid frame built for decades of use doesn't need overstuffed arms. What's more, that stuffing will quickly be pulled out of shape by repeated use. "Men especially tend to slide down in their seats as they watch TV or read," Peter notes. "That constant downward motion is going to pull the fabric off an overstuffed chair and redistribute the stuffing." Then you'll need to re-cover it. Here's a better strategy: Find a good-quality chair instead, and you'll re-cover it only once in your lifetime. Not only that, but it will be more comfortable, too.

Peter also recommends avoiding furniture with hanging pillows on the backrest. "Sure, they look nice, but they'll be the first thing ruined with any use," he says.

Heavy is good. When it comes to moving furniture, lighter is better. But when it comes to buying quality furniture, the opposite is true. The best furniture, says Peter Alexson, is the heaviest. "In the old days, they didn't know how to cheat," he says. Frames were made of hardwood, and seats were built on steel coils and layers of dense padding. "You bring in an old love seat, and it takes three guys to set it up on end to retie the springs. These days, I can carry a new, full-size couch myself, because it has a hollow frame made of particleboard, filled in with plywood and foam."

THE PROS KNOW

beating the auctioneer

IT'S NOT EASY getting a bargain at an auction or estate sale, says furniture expert John Lawrence. "You're competing against collectors who will pay any price, and that's a losing proposition," he explains. "Or you're competing against people like me, who know exactly what a piece is worth commercially." Still, there are ways to get a great price on something that's just right for you—if you follow a few simple rules.

1. Bring the right tools. Pack a tape measure and paper on which you've written the dimensions of the furniture you're looking for so that you don't go home with something that's too big or too small. You'll also need a flashlight to help you inspect the underside and back of every piece, looking for hidden flaws.

2. Inspect the merchandise. Find the pieces that fit your criteria and check each one thoroughly. Pick it up to see if it's made of solid wood rather than cheap particleboard. Take out the drawers and inspect the carcass of a bureau to make sure it's not made of cheap wood and covered with veneer. Wiggle chair backs and rungs to make sure the structure is sound. Look for hand-cut dowels and evidence of craftsmanship, if that's important to you.

3. Have a bottom line. Know what you're willing to spend and stick to that price. That will save you the heartache of finding a similar piece at your local antiques store for less the very next week.

4. Wait it out. The worst time to buy anything at auction is in the first hour. The best time is in the last hour, when the auctioneer is tired and the crowd has gone home.

AVOIDING FAKES AND COSTLY MISTAKES

When is a bargain not a bargain? When it costs $50 but needs several hundred dollars' worth of restoration or when it is supposed to be a valuable antique but is actually a fake. Luckily, a few simple guidelines will help you spot the hidden price of so-called great deals.

Check the veneer. Furniture restorer Wayne Towle never buys a piece of veneered furniture without checking the veneer itself, a thin (usually between $\frac{1}{36}$ and $\frac{1}{50}$ inch thick) sheet of wood that has been glued to some surfaces, then stained and finished. "If it's delaminating, or lifting away from the wood, that's no good," he says. That means it will have to be stripped and refinished before long, and that's usually a messy, expensive job. Check the veneer by tapping it with your fingernail or the tip of a pencil. If the sound changes and becomes slightly hollow in spots, particularly near the edges of drawers or near the bottom, the veneer will need refurbishing soon. You can also wipe the piece clean and run your fingers over the wood. Look and feel for raised bubbles that indicate a veneer that's almost done for.

If the veneer on a piece of furniture is chipped (top) or peeling (bottom), just walk away.

Examine the hardware. If you're thinking of buying an antique piece, make sure the hardware is original. John Lawrence says that many dressers have had their hardware changed over the course of their lives. The replacement hardware is generally antique-looking reproduction quality. Although replacement hardware doesn't affect how the drawers open and close, it does reduce the value of the piece as an antique. "Open the drawers and see how the hardware is attached," John advises. If there are extra holes that aren't holding any screws, the original hardware is long gone.

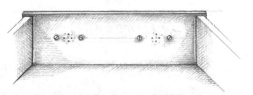

The hardware has been replaced on this drawer.

Think twice about rewiring. You fall in love with a beautiful old chandelier. It was made to hold candles, but the shop owner tells you that you can easily wire it for bulbs. "That sounds so simple, and yet it is a modification of enormous expense," says antique lighting expert Bruce Sweeney.

People often come into his shop with old chandeliers that they've tried to fit with stereo speaker wire. "Speaker wire isn't only ugly; it also will burn your house down," says Bruce, who uses specially made ultrathin electrical wire to make his modifications. He warns customers that if they have a fixture that was made before electricity, they might have to spend 10 times its worth turning it into a safe electrical fixture.

Another mistake people sometimes make is buying old wall sconces that they think they can rewire and use with today's outlets. "Many old sconces won't fit new electrical cords," Bruce says. If you're buying an antique wall sconce that you want to rewire, make sure it has a large base. Most of the older ones have small bases that won't

THE **P**ROS **K**NOW

check the brass facts

"AND THE HARDWARE is solid brass," the antiques dealer tells you of the armoire you're considering. Is that a fact? Well, when John Lawrence wants to see if the hardware on a piece of furniture is all brass, he uses the magnet test.

Brass is one of only a few metals to which a magnet won't stick. John puts a magnet against the hardware, and if it sticks, he knows it's brass-plated. If it doesn't stick, it's probably the real thing. There's one exception to the rule. Sometimes fixtures on cheap furniture are made of white metal or pot metal and are then brass-plated. A magnet won't stick to those either. In those cases, use your fingernail to scratch away the tarnish in an inconspicuous area. If the metal underneath the tarnish is whitish, it's not brass. If it's gold, it probably is.

---

annals of ingenuity

THE BLACK & DECKER MILK BOTTLE TOPPER?

b ack in 1910, S. Duncan Black and Alonzo Decker were a couple of guys trying to make a living inventing industrial machinery. Their early inventions include a machine that put caps on milk bottles and another that dipped candy. They probably would have gone on making little inventions for specific uses, but in 1914 they came up with something revolutionary: the electric drill. Rather than having one use in a single industry, it had hundreds of uses in every factory. During the economic boom that followed World War I, their drills became ubiquitous, and by 1924 the company was making a million dollars a year.

The name Black & Decker would have been known only to industrialists if not for the men's second brainstorm. In the wake of the next world war, they introduced a portable electric drill for home use. Many returning soldiers had a lot of time on their hands, along with a desire to get married and settle into homes. They became the first wave of do-it-yourselfers, and they made Black & Decker® a household name.

cover the outlet specified by new state building codes. "You'll be paying an electrician to come in and refit the outlet. Suddenly, that twenty-five-dollar find isn't such a deal."

FIXING UP YOUR FINDS

You don't need to be a pro to put the finishing touches on that chair or end table you just brought home. Here, our experts offer some simple ways to care for and enhance home furnishings.

Steer clear of synthetics. When you're choosing fabrics for upholstery, Peter Alexson recommends sticking to natural fibers. "Many new fabrics have a high polyester count, which is fine until you spill something on them," says the professional upholsterer. "Then you can use a blowtorch on that stain, and it won't move." Natural fibers, by contrast, are easy to clean.

Distress it yourself. "One look that's popular these days is the distressed look, says furniture restorer Kevin Bianchi. "The good news is that it's easy to achieve that look at home with an unfinished piece of furniture or one that's finished if you don't want to take the trouble of refinishing it." He says that the easiest way to make a piece of furniture look better and to hide its flaws is to paint it. The result resembles naturally aged and distressed wood.

Start by choosing two or three contrasting paint colors. Paint one color on the piece, then use a stick of paraffin or a candle to wax the areas that you want to look distressed. The areas around the drawer handles and the corners are good places to start. Then paint the entire piece with a contrasting color. You can even repeat your application of wax and add a third color if you like. Finally, use sandpaper to work through the colors in a few spots to create the impression of decades of wear.

Get yourself in a pickle. People often ask Kevin Bianchi to put a pickling finish on their pine or oak furniture. That's a light, milky white stain that has become very fashionable lately. "It's based on an old technique in which paints were thinned with sour milk," he says. Although there are stains on the market that will simulate this finish, it's actually easy to achieve this look at home with a little latex paint and some water.

"Thin some white latex paint with water," Kevin says. "Or paint the piece with white latex paint, then sponge the paint off with water before it dries." Some of the paint will seep into the pores of the wood. The rest will come off and show the wood grain. This technique works best on oak and pine because of their porous quality. "Don't do this on birch or maple, or even cherry, because the grain is too small and the paint will have nowhere to go," Kevin says.

Once you achieve the look you want, be sure to seal it using a nonyellowing acrylic finish. That is the crucial detail, Kevin notes.

refinish it like the pros

LIKE ANYTHING ELSE, refinishing a piece of furniture can be an expensive mess if you don't use the right tools. "Just dumping a chemical stripper on everything won't work," says furniture restorer Kevin Bianchi. If it's not a lacquer finish, you'll end up just moving the shellac or varnish around in circles rather than stripping it off. But how do you know if you're dealing with shellac, varnish, or lacquer? Here's how the experts figure it out.

1. Start with rubbing alcohol. Dab some on your furniture with an old rag. If the finish softens, it's shellac, and you can remove it with straight isopropyl alcohol, available from your drugstore.

2. Try turpentine—after you've wiped off the alcohol, that is. If the turpentine softens your finish, you're dealing with varnish, which turpentine will strip easily.

3. Lacquer thinner is next. If neither rubbing alcohol nor turpentine does the trick, try lacquer thinner. If that softens the finish, you're definitely dealing with a lacquer finish.

4. Get out the big guns. If you've eliminated everything else, now you know the finish is polyurethane, which requires a heavy-duty chemical stripper from the hardware store, along with watertight work gloves, safety goggles, and plenty of ventilation.

Too often people create the perfect white stain look, only to see it yellow over the years. One or two coats of the right acrylic will preserve the look that you want.

Lacquer your brass. Furniture restorer John Lawrence doesn't like polishing tarnished brass any more than the rest of us do. But he doesn't have to, because when he brightens up the hardware on his flea market finds, he gives them a coat of clear lacquer, available at any hardware store, to keep the tarnish from building up. "This will keep the brass looking good for five years or more," he says. Even drawer handles that get used every day will retain their shine for years.

chapter 6

easy home
f i x-i t s

IS THERE ANYTHING MORE SATISFYING than being your own
handyman? These days, it can be nearly impossible to find a repairman or a contractor willing to come to your house to fix even
a large appliance such as a refrigerator or to patch a hole in the
wall. You've probably been thinking that there must be an easier
way. Well, you're right. With a little ingenious information and a
bit of creativity, you can learn which appliances you can revive
simply by cleaning them and which ones would be a waste of
money to try to fix.

Ingenuity: Bred in the Bone

'm a home improvement nut," says Bill Keller. "It's in my bones, something I inherited from my grandfather, Bob Gapinski. Grandpa had an eighth grade education, but he was sort of like Leonardo da Vinci. He was a machine worker by day and a tinkerer by night.

"Grandpa was always building lamps out of hand-hammered copper and old glass beer quarts. His Christmas presents were the best because they were tools. They were heavy and always wrapped in newspaper. One year, he gave me an electric motor that didn't work. He knew that I would take it apart, figure it out, and fix it. I did.

"He died about ten years ago, and since then my uncle has been giving me some of Grandpa's tools. I have his only set of screwdrivers and his framing square—the one he used to build the house my mother grew up in. It may sound corny, but these tools mean something. They are strong and true, like he was. And they are a reminder that building pieces of your house, making it just so, is worth doing."

Accomplished do-it-yourselfers already know that they can save hundreds of dollars by doing simple jobs themselves. They also know that it's important to learn how the systems in their homes work. That way, when they do need professional help, they can more accurately describe the problem at hand. Knowledge will also make you feel less helpless when things go wrong.

That knowledge comes from our experts. Home improvement enthusiast Bill Keller of Lemont, Illinois, has tackled dozens of household fix-it jobs and renovations, such as installing lights in a drop ceiling. T. J. Wilson of Monticello, Illinois, completely renovated two houses—without ever hiring a contractor. He offers advice on everything from patching walls to preventing floods inside your home. Our favorite is his truly inventive method of cleaning a grimy oven exhaust fan. Contractor Rob Dixon, also of Monticello, Illinois, shares his wisdom about keeping bathrooms dry and repairing leaky toilets. Read on for loads of ingenious tips about maintaining your home and keeping your money in your pocket, where it belongs.

Kitchens

Cabinets that won't shut and scratched countertops are the kinds of pesky problems that make your kitchen seem shabby when it doesn't have to. You can fix that countertop and even update the look of your kitchen if you want to—and it can cost less than a trip to the grocery store.

When T. J. Wilson and his wife bought their first house, every room needed major improvements. "My wife and I bought a microwave oven, and it reduced our counter space by half," T. J. says. To solve that problem, they bulldozed one kitchen wall. They built a larger kitchen, rearranged the plumbing, and installed their own cabinets. Luckily, T. J. says, most kitchen repairs don't require heavy machinery. Here are some easy ways to make your own kitchen repairs.

DOORS

What with all the cabinets and appliances, there may be more doors in the kitchen than in any other room in your house. If yours are acting ornery, take heart. We have a couple of ingenious ways to make sure the doors in your kitchen close—and stay closed.

Play your cards right. Cabinet doors start to look like something out of Ma and Pa Kettle's kitchen when they won't close properly. If a door tends to swing open, or if you have to pick it up to close it, you probably don't need an overhaul (or a sledge-

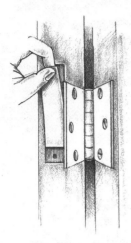

Slip a homemade shim under the hinge to realign a cabinet door.

hammer). Maybe all you need is a homemade shim to realign the door. "You can use a playing card or the cardboard from the bottom of a legal pad if you need something thicker," says T. J. Wilson. Cut the shim to fit under the hinge that's out of alignment and screw the hinge back on. Once you've straightened out the door, it should close perfectly and look as good as new.

Help your refrigerator door swing free. Ideally, a refrigerator door should close with just a little encouragement—say, a bump of the rump. If it doesn't, you're wasting energy on those occasions when the door doesn't close snugly. The answer is not only simple, but it's free, too. Almost every refrigerator is equipped with adjustable feet. If yours is, adjust them so that the corner directly under the door handle is the shortest. That way, gravity will work to close the door for you.

COUNTERTOPS

No part of your kitchen takes more abuse than the countertops. They get nicked and cut and scratched and burned. But there's no need to panic or call in the remodelers.

Wash and wax. Countertops suffer the occasional light burn from hot pots and utensils. You can revive yours by scrubbing the burned area with the same abrasive that you use to clean your pots. Problem solved, right? Well, not quite. You see, scrubbing with a powdered abrasive will likely remove the shine from Formica. So what's the answer? Ordinary car wax. Rub a little into the scratches, and the Formica will shine like new. (Be sure to try this in an inconspicuous area first to make sure you approve of the results.) And keep in mind that you'll want to use this extreme measure only with burns. You shouldn't use a harsh abrasive on ordinary stains, because it'll scratch the surface. Use a little baking soda instead, and your countertop will look great for years.

Soothe the scratch. Oops, somebody forgot to use the cutting board when chopping vegetables, and now you have some nasty cuts in that laminate countertop. Don't panic; just visit your local hardware store or any home center that sells countertops and ask for laminate repair paste. (It's sometimes called plastic seam filler.) It comes in lots of different colors, so you may need to buy a couple of shades and mix them to match your countertop.

Wipe the area with rubbing alcohol before you start. That'll remove all the grease and dirt. Then spread the paste into the scratches with a putty knife or your fingers. Wipe away the excess and let it dry. Your countertop will look like new.

Sand soapstone. Soapstone countertops are popular because they're durable and almost never stain. If you find that you've somehow scratched yours, don't panic, because you can use sandpaper to repair the damage. The depth of the scratch will determine the grit of the sandpaper. If the scratch is deep, start with a low number grit. Eighty grit is pretty rough and will sand the soapstone quickly. As the scratch gets sanded out, start using progressively higher-grit paper, stopping at around 400-grit paper. When the scratch is completely gone, go over the area with a little mineral oil.

Bathrooms

Bathroom repairs are a cinch if you keep one thing in mind, says Rob Dixon. Rob has repaired his share of leaky pipes, peeling paint, and rotting floors in more than two decades of work as a contractor. "The number one problem in bathrooms is controlling moisture," Rob says. It's the cause of mold, and it'll rot the wood subflooring beneath your tile and linoleum. If you want your bathroom—and your home—to stay maintenance-free for as long as possible, control the moisture in your bathroom. With a few simple repairs and some of Rob's tips, you can keep your bathroom in good working order without having to call a plumber.

WHATSIT?

Q: Here's a puzzler for all you carpenters out there. Can you identify this ingenious tool?

A: This is a tapered shell auger with a flat nose. These were made in sets from 2 to 8 inches in diameter and were used to ream out pilot holes in log water pipes. Only one side was sharpened. The other side had a hole for tying on a liner, which was a rod that increased the diameter of the bit just enough to bore a hole smaller than the next-larger-size bit. The nose of the tool is a flat disk that acted as a guide to keep the auger in the center of the pilot hole.

Be a fan of bathroom vents. If you already have a bathroom vent, you're halfway there. Vents push humid air out of the bathroom and keep the room dry. The trouble is that some of these vents don't go all the way to the outside of the house. Instead, they vent to the attic. "That's the worst thing you can have," says Rob Dixon. Sending moisture into the attic will begin to rot the wood up there. Worse, it'll ruin any insulation you have. Wet insulation conducts heat rather than trapping it.

Find out where your bathroom vent vents by visiting the attic. Make sure the piping goes all the way to the roof. Or stand outside your house to find the bathroom vents on the roof or an exterior wall. If you don't see them, you'll need to extend the vents yourself or have someone else do it to keep your repair costs from going through the roof.

Reach for the wax ring. The second most common source of damaging moisture in the loo is leaks in the floor. You'll know

---

annals of ingenuity

THROWING A WRENCH IN THE WORKS

If you know the name Jack Johnson, it might be because he was the first African-American heavyweight champion of the world. What you might not know about Johnson is that he patented one of the most common household tools in history.

Early nineteenth-century America was a chillingly intolerant place, and in 1912 Johnson was sent to Leavenworth Federal Prison for traveling with his girlfriend, who was white. While in prison, Johnson designed and crafted a tool for loosening and tightening fastening devices. And on April 18, 1922, he received a patent for the wrench.

---

you have one when the floor around your shower or toilet gets a little soft and squishy. That's a sign of rotting wood, and it needs to be fixed as soon as possible. Granted, that involves tearing up the flooring and replacing the plywood subflooring underneath, but there are good reasons to do it. One is that that moisture will eventually rot the floor joists and make the floor unsafe. (Imagine your upstairs toilet sitting on your dining room table.) Another reason is that the water leaking out of the bowl is dirty, and it will spread bacteria and odor into the floor. The usual source of this kind of leak is an aging wax ring, which attaches the toilet to the waste pipe underneath. It costs about a dollar at the hardware store. Sounds like a bargain, doesn't it?

Stop leaks before they start. If you notice a black residue in the toilet tank, it's a sign that your toilet may soon develop a leak, says contractor Rob Dixon. The residue is probably composed of bits of the rubber stopper valve that keeps your toilet from running. "Most cities use chlorine to bleach their water supplies," Rob says. Chlorine tends to eat away at the rubber stopper in a fairly short amount of time. Eventually, your toilet will begin to run all the time and waste water.

PREP IT YOURSELF

I like working around the house, so of course my wife and I bought a house that we would have to fix up," says Larry Bean of Natick, Massachusetts. "The first thing I wanted to do was tear down a wall between two small living room areas to make one larger room. I suspected that the wall was load-bearing, which means that it's the wall that helps to hold up the upstairs. I knew I was going to have to hire a professional to remove the wall and shore it up correctly and according to state building codes. What I didn't want to do was pay full price for that, because the estimates were fairly high. I found a contractor who would charge me just for the time and materials he used. I told him that I was going to do some of the work myself. He was thrilled to hear this. Many busy contractors actually prefer simpler jobs.

"To prep the area, I removed all of the furniture from both rooms. Then I used a saw and crowbar to tear down the drywall on each side of the wall, exposing the beams underneath. I cleaned up the area so there wouldn't be any debris in the guy's way. By the time the contractor arrived, all he had to do was shore up the wall and remove the studs. I told him not to bother to haul the studs away because I might have a use for them later (and I knew I didn't want to pay his fee for cleanup). The best part was that my little bit of work took half the price off the bill."

To solve the problem, replace the existing stopper with one made of siliconized rubber. It'll cost you only about $3 and last three to four times as long as the regular rubber stopper. And changing the stopper now will save you much more money in water leaks down the road.

Walls and Ceilings

Where would we be without walls? They hold our houses up and provide a spot to hang our favorite pictures. Isn't it time we gave something back? Here are a few surefire ways to patch your walls when they need some tender loving care.

Stick up for drywall patches. The trouble with patching large holes in drywall is that if the hole doesn't cross a stud, it's hard to set the patch into the hole without pushing it in too far. Amateur handyman T. J. Wilson has a clever solution: paint sticks, which you can get free from your local hardware store.

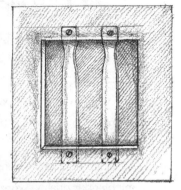

Glue the sticks to the back of the hole using quick-setting glue, or attach them with drywall screws. Then put in the drywall plug and add tape and joint compound as you would on any other patch. The sticks will add security to the patch until it dries. If the hole is small, you can use clean, dry Popsicle sticks instead of paint sticks. They'll work just as well.

Paint sticks are free and are an ingenious tool that can help you patch holes in drywall.

Patch things up with wallpaper. If you're looking for a way to patch a long crack in a wall without having to perform

A FRENCH (DOOR) RENAISSANCE

Home handyman Bill Keller found that the trouble with having an office in the basement was sharing space with the kids' playroom. He thought about installing a wall with a regular door, but instead he decided to use French doors rescued from another part of the house. They are wide enough to give the impression of openness. "And when the kids are noisy, I can just close the doors, and it's like they're not even there," he says. The children can be seen but not heard, and he can keep an eye on them while still getting some work done.

Meet the Expert

Mr. fix-it

I STARTED FIXING APPLIANCES when I was seven years old," says contractor Rob Dixon. "My mother had a beauty shop, and sometimes her customers would complain that their radios didn't work right. I offered to fix a few of them, and these ladies were more than happy to let me try. What did they have to lose? I even gave them my own homemade bills—I charged a dollar an hour for labor. They thought that was pretty cute.

"I learned a lot by taking things apart and putting them back together. I still do. If my blender doesn't work right, I dismantle it. Even if I can't fix it—and plenty of times I can't fix the plastic appliances they sell these days, because they aren't made to be fixed—I still learn something. The only thing that has changed is that I don't spend a lot of time tinkering with other people's appliances. I can't afford to charge a dollar an hour."

major surgery, here's the answer. Head to the hardware store and purchase some very inexpensive white vinyl wallpaper. First, scrape off any loose paint or plaster so you have a solid surface to work on. Next, use wallpaper paste to attach the wallpaper to the wall, covering the crack. Skim coat the paper if you need to (or just feather the edges so the seam isn't so obvious), sand it, and then prime and paint.

If you can't beat 'em, spatter 'em. If the walls in one of the rooms of your home have been patched so many times that you consider them a lost cause, don't call in the contractor just yet. Instead try this ingenious idea: Give the whole room a spatter paint job. It'll look terrific, and it will mask the patches and dings on the wall.

Appliance Fix-Its

The most ingenious way to save money is not to spend it on new appliances when the old ones work just fine. If your stove's exhaust is gunky or your refrigerator is too noisy, there's likely to be an easy, ingenious solution that doesn't involve spending a cent. Here are some of them.

REFRIGERATORS

The refrigerator is the heart of every kitchen. It keeps your vegetables fresh and your ice cream frozen. Keep yours running smoothly by following our ingenious expert advice.

TRASH IT OR SAVE IT?

Contractor Rob Dixon has been fixing appliances all his life. When he was little, he liked taking apart everything from blenders to toasters to diagnose the problem and fix it. Unfortunately, he says, these days many small appliances are made to be thrown away when they break. Here's how to tell the difference between a throwaway and a keeper.

Most appliances that aren't worth fixing cost under $30 and are made of cheap materials, such as plastic and stamped metal parts. They can't be taken apart, never mind fixed. "Who's going to inventory a $2 part for a $12 toaster?" Rob asks. Toasters, coffeemakers, irons and steamers, clocks, fans, and food processors fit firmly into this category.

Larger appliances such as dishwashers, computers, and televisions are more likely to be repairable and returned to good use. Sadly, though, Rob says that even these appliances are being made with enough special interdependent parts that they are difficult and expensive to repair. "We're becoming a society of disposable things," he says.

MAKE it LAST

Check your washer hoses

THE HOSES on your washing machine are the one thing that absolutely will rupture eventually, says T. J. Wilson. They are constantly under pressure. Eliminate the possibility of a cracked hose, and you'll get rid of almost all of the possibility of a flood in your home.

Set a schedule for yourself to check the hoses for cracks or other damage periodically. Once a year should be enough. Look for fine misting or drips just after you've run a load of wash. Put a tag on the hoses with the date that you purchased the machine. After 10 years, change the hoses on the machine whether or not they look as if they need it. The hoses are much less expensive than the deductible on your home owner's insurance.

A spontaneous flood is especially dangerous while you're away. For a little extra insurance (not to mention peace of mind), remember to shut off the water leading to your washing machine before you go on vacation.

Take a load off your refrigerator. As refrigerators age, they tend to have to work harder to accomplish the same tasks. If your refrigerator seems to be running marathons, it may need a good cleaning, says T. J. Wilson. "Remember that a refrigerator is just a heat pump," he notes. "It moves heat from one place to another." In this case, the coils on the back disperse the heat, but they also get covered with dust and gunk. Unplug the fridge and vacuum the coils once a year, and they'll run more efficiently.

If the coils are clean and the fridge is still running all the time, you may have a bad fan. The fan is supposed to cool the coils. If it's not working, the heat isn't being removed as it should. You can find the fan on your refrigerator by following the noise while it's running. If the fridge is running but the fan's not turning, unplug the fridge and clean the fan with a soft brush, or perhaps replace it. A fan certainly costs less than a repairman, and a repairman to fix the fan costs less than a new refrigerator.

Pipe down in there! The thing most people complain about is a noisy refrigerator. Over the years, refrigerators seem to accumulate noises. One possible reason is that the tubes leading to the compressor are touching the coils. You'll be able to tell because the black paint will be worn away where that's happening. You might be able to gently bend the coils to stop the noise.

It's also possible that the fan may have moved over the years and the blades are hitting something. Again, you should be able to move the fan back slightly and stop the noise.

LAMPS AND LIGHTS

A lamp's only job is to light up your life. All you have to do is keep the bulb(s) fresh. Here are a couple of ways to make that job a little easier.

Get the light out. Your brand-new lamp is great, except that when you try to change the light bulb, the lamp won't let go. It's frustrating, because you know that you're risking a broken bulb and a stripped socket each time you change the bulb. You could spend money at the hardware store on an epoxy that's specially designed to coat light sockets and unstick them, but contractor Rob Dixon uses plain old candle wax instead.

Put the new bulb into the lamp and tighten it just enough for it to light up. Leave the light on for 15 to 20 minutes—enough time for the bulb to heat up. Then turn it off, unplug it, take out the bulb, and rub paraffin or candle wax in the socket. Now the bulb will be easy to remove when the time comes.

TAKE A MAINTENANCE HOLIDAY

The most difficult thing to do each year is find time to do those little annual chores that can save so much time and money in the long run," says T. J. Wilson. "I learned that the hard way one Easter when our refrigerator stopped because I hadn't been diligent about vacuuming the coils. Now that's one of my annual Easter chores.

"I tie all of my maintenance to holidays, because those are usually days when I'm at home and have a little extra time on my hands, and because they're easy to remember. For example, on Labor Day I change the antifreeze in my car. On the morning that we get an extra hour from daylight saving time, I put batteries in our smoke detectors and check the fire extinguishers. By tying these chores to holidays, I never put them off, and I don't have to do them all in one day."

Have a blackout. Fluorescent lights are terrific because they provide uniform lighting. The most wasteful mistake that most people make is not replacing them often enough. If the light is turning black at the ends or if it blinks or provides only partial light, it's time to replace the bulb. Hanging on to the old bulb until it is completely useless is a false economy. What you're really doing is stressing the ballast that regulates the amount of electricity entering the tube. By the time the fixture starts humming or giving off an odd smell, it's too late. The entire fixture will have to be replaced.

MISCELLANEOUS APPLIANCE CARE

As you might expect, our everyday experts came up with some pretty ingenious appliance care advice that just didn't fall into any one category. So we've collected them here. The following tips will help you keep your dryer, garbage disposal, and your kitchen exhaust fan in tip-top shape.

Go on lint alert. You already know that you need to check the dryer vent outside your home and keep it clear of debris. But you may not know that lint gathers in other parts of your dryer, too, and that those areas need to be cleaned every year to keep the dryer at its energy-efficient best. Here's a simple two-step method for doing just that.

1. Remove the hose from the vent and vacuum it. Lint likes to gather in that hose, and it makes your dryer work harder.

2. Remove the back of the dryer. That's where you'll find whole nests of lint that also need to be vacuumed.

Your dryer will thank you for this annual cleaning by lasting years longer than it otherwise would.

Feed and water garbage disposals. All your garbage disposal needs is a constant flow of vegetable scraps, right? Wrong. Here are two ways to keep your disposal happy and healthy for years to come.

1. Put your garbage disposal on a low-fiber diet. If you want your garbage disposal to last longer, avoid materials such as corn-husks, artichokes, and banana peels. The long fibers of those foods can get twisted in the teeth and slow down the disposal or stop it altogether.

2. Add cold water. Always run cold water down the disposal while it's operating to keep any grease moving past the teeth. Cold water also will keep the motor cool.

Power-wash your exhaust fan. Once you've been through a few months of spaghetti dinners, fried chicken, and other delicious messes, you may find that the exhaust fan over your stove is getting noisy and dirty. You could spend an unpleasant afternoon scrubbing it, or you could just put it in the dishwasher. That's what T. J. Wilson does. He says that you may have to turn the fan over and run it through a second time, but it sure beats scrubbing it by hand.

If you've never done this before, you may have too much built-up grease for the dishwasher to handle. In that case, T. J. says, you might have to resort to sterner measures. "I sometimes take mine to my friend's body shop and have him run it through an automotive parts cleaner. But I don't tell my wife about this, because she disapproves of the harsh cleansers they use."

Painting

Putting a new coat of paint on an old set of walls can sure brighten up the room. Too bad it's such a messy job. Luckily, we've found some ingenious ways to cope with the mess.

Contain old paint. The trouble with leftover paint is that after a few uses, the lid tends to get painted shut, and the paint inside dries out quickly. A better way to store leftover paint is to use an old laundry detergent bottle. Not only will it keep the paint from drying out, but the wide-mouth spout is practically drip-proof. Just remember to write the color of the paint and the room where you used it on the outside of the container. Or drip a few drops onto the lid as a reminder.

Send your rollers to the deep freeze. The first thing you learn about painting a room is how expensive rollers are. You'll probably spend $5 for a couple of rollers for the walls and ceiling, but you can use them only once. Cleaning them will waste gallons and gallons of water, and when you're done, they'll still be too stiff to use. That adds up to even more waste, especially when you're painting an entire house and want many of the rooms to be the same color. Here's how to store those rollers so that you can use them again.

Drop each one in a resealable plastic bag and put it in the refrigerator. The cold will keep the paint moist enough so that

---

KNOW WHEN TO SAY WHEN

"The very best advice I can give on home improvement is to be careful not to get in over your head," says home improvement enthusiast Bill Keller. "I love fixing up my house, but I also believe that you should do only those things that you enjoy.

"When I installed French doors in my basement, I wanted to paint them. After it took me most of an afternoon to paint one side of one door, I realized that this wasn't fun for me. Rather than ruin my back and my patience, I hired a painter to come in and paint the other three sides. It took the painter no time to finish the job and cost very little money. If you can isolate the jobs that you want a professional to do and do everything else yourself, you can save money and have fun."

---

when it's time to work on the next room, all you'll have to do is get out the bag, put the roller on the handle, and start working.

You can keep a roller in the fridge for up to a month without having it dry out. Sometimes the roller will leave a paint residue on the bag that does dry and flake off. But you can wipe the flakes off the roller in no time and start painting.

Easy Household Enhancements

"I travel a lot on business, so I've seen a lot of hotel rooms," says Bill Keller. "I'd always wondered why those fancy hotel rooms were nicer than my bedroom at home. Shouldn't my own bedroom be the best? I took it as a kind of challenge.

"Once, I was having coffee in the Ritz-Carlton in Pasadena, California. I began to look around. What made this the Ritz? It had crown molding, and the molding melded into the cornice over the drapes. Interesting. It had fabulous pillows, beautiful bathroom fixtures, and perfect water pressure in the bathroom. Hmmm.

"I had no trouble adding the crown molding and making a cornice to match at home. That was easy. The pillows and bath fixtures took some work, but I learned that many fine hotels will sell their pillows if you ask. They'll also tell you where they buy their bathroom fixtures and showerheads if you'd like to order some of your own.

"And my wife found some beautiful wallpaper—the kind that has an entire pastoral scene on it that spans several panels of paper. Very fancy. In the end, it has taken some work and some investigation, but it's starting to feel more and more like the Ritz—only better, of course."

Feeling inspired? Here are some more quick and easy ways to enhance your surroundings.

Add see-through doors. Bill Keller completely renovated his home in Lemont, Illinois. When it came to the bar in his basement, he wanted a way to make the cabinets and shelves look fancy, but he didn't want to buy custom cabinets. His solution was to take the panel out of the cabinet fronts and replace it with glass. "Most cabinet doors have a frame and a panel. I kept the frame but replaced the panel with glass," Bill says. "If you were to order custom glass-front cabinets from a carpenter, that's just what he would do, too."

He added glass shelves inside the cabinets and then went to the hardware store to find quartz lights to install above the top shelf. "They're ridiculously cheap," he says. Now his glassware is on display in his bar area and looks as nice as if it were sitting in a custom-made display hutch. For a different look, you can also add a mirror behind the shelves.

Bill says that one of his uncles used this same idea on a couple of his kitchen cabinets to lighten up the dark oak woodwork in the kitchen. "You probably wouldn't want to do this on all the cabinets, but with one or two, it really opens up the kitchen," he says.

THE VACUUM CLEANER WITH LEGS

My wife and I wanted a central vacuum cleaner, but we didn't want to pay the price," says professional handyman Jim Gapinski of Des Plaines, Illinois. Luckily, Jim's been running his own contracting business for 20 years, so he was able to create an alternative.

"I put the piping throughout the house myself. It was just normal plastic pipes, like polyvinyl chloride (PVC) piping, but I used a thinner gauge," Jim says. "Getting it up through the walls was the toughest part. But I put an outlet in every room, just as the professional installers would do, with a cap over it.

"Then I went to buy the central motor. I found that it cost five hundred dollars. Hey, I'll admit it, I'm cheap. I certainly didn't want to pay that much for a motor. So I decided to use an old shop vac that I had in my basement workroom. I set an electrical box and placed the inlet to the central vac system near enough to the floor so that I could just roll the vacuum over to the piping, plug it into the wall, plug the hose into the PVC pipes and start it up. It works great. And when we're not vacuuming the house, I can unplug it and roll it over in my shop and use it there.

"We've had the system for four years now, and my wife's never been happier, because she doesn't have to carry the vacuum cleaner around anymore."

Try new handles. One of the easiest, least-expensive ways to update the look of your kitchen is to change the cabinet handles and drawer pulls. Head out to any home improvement center, and you'll probably find a whole wall dedicated to drawer and

New handles give drawers and cabinets a new look.

door handles. Some are plain, some are fancy, some even come in cute shapes, but all of them will cost a whole lot less than an entire kitchen face-lift.

MY DAD'S DREAM HOUSE

"One of the things I always admired about my dad was his ability to make anything," says Jim Gapinski, a professional handyman who lives in the house his father built in Des Plaines, Illinois.

"I remember when he built an open fire pit out in the backyard, then told us he was going to build a log cabin around it. This was back in the early 1960s. He told me that he'd wanted a log cabin since he was a kid.

"The first question was where to get the logs. He called the electric company, because he'd seen that they were replacing telephone poles in the neighborhood. Sure enough, they had some old poles that they'd let him have.

"The poles still had all the creosote on them from where they'd been put in the ground, and they had holes all over them. He cut off the creosote ends, then used a spoke shave to shave them down and remove the holes. He got these steel rods that were about a foot long and three-eighths inch thick to bind them together. Talk about work. We think we work hard now, but not like him.

"He finished that log cabin just like he said he would, and it's still beautiful. It sits in the backyard still. Someone once called it a playhouse, but that's not what it is. It's a real house. It's the house my dad saw in his head and then made."

Build a stairwell haven. When Bill Keller was finishing his basement, he discovered a space problem. "The builders had put everything in the worst possible place: a water heater in one corner, a sump pump in the other, and the stairs came down right in the middle of the room," he says. He wondered how he could use the space under the stairs. His solution was to install the television there. "I built a fifty-inch, big-screen TV right into the wall under the stairs, flush-mounted so that it looks like one of those expensive skinny TVs," Bill says. He wired an outlet under the stairs and cut out the drywall in the shape of the TV. Then he simply wheeled the TV and its cart back into the wall.

chapter 7

attic, basement, garage, and
workshop

THE TRADITIONAL STORAGE SPACES in a home are kind of like credit cards. Using them indiscriminately is great fun for a while, but sooner or later, they fill up. Then you're stuck paying the piper for something that you used up long ago. Okay, no one from Visa will call with dire threats if you stuff your attic with old clothes or leave ancient paint cans all over the garage. But you have nothing to lose and everything to gain by using the space more efficiently and keeping it organized and clean. And there's a domino effect: When you make more space in your storage areas, your whole house benefits, because you can move the stuff that really belongs in storage out of, say, the master bedroom.

If that sounds too much like "Eat your spinach; it's good for you," keep reading. There are painless ways to make your storage rooms more attractive and effective. And if you don't believe us, surely you'll take the word of our everyday experts. They've developed some ingenious tips from decades of pondering floor plans, packing collectibles, and pushing mowers, so they know which storage ideas work and which aren't worth the trouble.

For instance, collectibles expert Michele Karl of Seymour, Tennessee, helps you figure out the best way to store your valuables. Wade Slate, a professional handyman in Knoxville, Tennessee, chips in with some ways to make better use of your garage storage space. And automotive products professional Julie Amato, also of Knoxville, Tennessee, gives you the inside scoop about which car products you can save and which you should pitch. There's loads more, too, so join us as we transform the garage, attic, basement, and workshop from dumping grounds to valuable storage areas.

Up in the Attic

Attics can be spooky places—and not just because that's where monsters sometimes lurk. That's also where junk hides, haunting your dreams and concealing potential dangers, such as fire. Now's the time to face your attic demons—real and imagined. We promise you'll be pleased with the results.

GETTING ORGANIZED

We could probably get you to admit that your attic could be more organized. Here are some easy (we promise) ways to organize your attic, making it a more navigable, usable space.

some don't like it hot

UNLESS YOU'RE ONE of the lucky few with an air-conditioned attic, the space is bound to get hot, says retired electrician Jim Slate of Winnsboro, South Carolina. He should know. He's crawled in hundreds of attics to wire electricity. "It's not so bad if you have a huge, old-fashioned attic, but when you have a dark roof and there's only three or four feet between the roof and the attic floor, the air really heats up," Jim says.

Beyond the obvious discomfort, overheated attics present a safety concern. "Never store dry paper or thin dry cloth up there, because it could spontaneously combust and burn down the house," Jim cautions. Anything that comes in an aerosol can also should not be stored in an attic that gets hot. Here are eight other items that can't stand the heat—either because they'll be damaged or could be dangerous—and should be removed from the attic.

1. Candles
2. Crayons
3. Film
4. Glycerin soaps
5. Record albums
6. Spray paint
7. Tape
8. Unused envelopes

Organize by holiday. If you store seasonal items in the attic, quit storing them by type—centerpieces, decorative porch flags, and gift wrap, for example. Instead, start grouping items by holiday or season. That way, you're much less likely to leave a few items behind in the attic, and you won't have to open so many boxes and stir up so much dust to retrieve what you want.

For example, store all the Christmas lights, wrapping paper, cards, ornaments, wreaths, and so forth in one area of the attic. And if you aren't a decorating fiend, you may be able to fit all your Christmas stuff in one clean rubber trash can with a lid. The ones with flat tops are best so that you can stack other stuff on top. Another benefit: You may get a jump on decorating, writing out cards, or whatever holiday task you typically put off, because everything will come out at once.

USE THOSE RAFTERS

Rafters aren't just for holding up roofs anymore. In the attic or garage, you can store bulky, light- to medium-weight items on the exposed rafters, on top of plywood if necessary. Here are 13 possibilities.

Boxed or folded tents

Deflated rubber dinghies

Doors (which you can also use in
   place of the plywood)

Empty computer or stereo boxes

Lightweight lawn chairs

Luggage

Plastic wading pools

Rugs (rolled or stacked flat)

Stepladder

Storm windows

Surfboards

Twin bed mattress

Window screens

Think about the future. Attics are a great place to peruse mementos and ponder the passing of time. But you can do yourself a favor by doing that before you take heavy objects up there. Take into account what your physical condition might be when you want the objects to make the trip back down. If you're saving cartons of hardcover books for your retirement years, for example, store them in smaller boxes, or pare down the collection instead of storing it all. If you're saving furniture for your heirs, consider that the younger generation, too, will develop slipped disks and other such ailments over the years.

If you have your heart set on storing the stuff, you can hire someone to bring it downstairs. But if you're just putting off making a decision about whether to keep or toss heavy items, force yourself to decide now and save your older self some trouble.

Keep your valuables boxed. Some people are so organized that all their attic treasures are neatly arranged on shelves. If you haven't attained that goal with your precious collectibles, it's just as well, says Michele Karl, a collectibles expert and author of *Baby-Boomer Dolls: Plastic Playthings of the 1950s and 1960s* and *Composition and Wood Dolls and Toys: A Collector's Reference Guide.* "If you leave valuable items on shelves in the attic, they'll be exposed to the elements and get dusty," Michele says. "Instead, pack them in boxes, label the sides, and stack them."

that's • ingenious!

make your attic alluring

ARE YOU THE KIND of person who makes her way into the attic only twice annually, once to retrieve the Christmas lights and again to put them away? If so, your attic may be suffering from neglect. You'll get maximum use from that space if you regularly cull the items up there. One way to encourage occasional purging is to store items in your attic that you know you'll need on a regular basis. Here are four suggestions.

1. Motor oil. If you're a conscientious car owner, you change your oil every 3,000 to 5,000 miles. And if you store your motor oil in the attic, you'll have to go up there just as often. And don't worry—motor oil can endure quite high temperatures.

2. Your favorite old armchair. You know, the one that's too ratty for public view. Instead of tossing it out, move it to the attic, where you can enjoy its perfect fit occasionally.

3. Golf balls or fishing equipment. Rather than store these items in the garage, where they're easy to get at, put them in the attic. You may even feel guilty enough about cutting out to go golfing or fishing that you tidy up the attic a bit before you go.

4. Gifts. The ones you're not quite ready to give. This works only if you can remember that the gift is up there when it's time to present it. One way to remind yourself is to make a note on your calendar.

Down in the Basement

Your basement can be a refuge, a cool spot, and a place to stash things you don't want anyone to see (and maybe a few items you've never considered). Here are some ways to bring out the best in your bottommost room.

Light your way for safety. Consider the lights for a minute. Or, rather, what happens when the lights go out. If your fuse box or circuit breakers are in the basement, you need a safe way to reach them in the dark. Instead of putting a candle and matches next to the fuse box, put them along the top of the doorjamb leading from the upstairs to the basement. That way, you won't have to stumble down the stairs in the dark. Even better would be keeping a flashlight on a small shelf near the doorjamb. But always have the candle and matches, too, in case the batteries in your flashlight die.

Paint to avoid pitfalls. Even if you have regulation steps, the basement stairs can be treacherous, especially if they're dark, the ceiling is low, or people are careless when they head downstairs to grab a jug of apple cider or go check the fuse box or circuit breakers. To improve your staircase's safety record, consider painting the treads of each step with white, luminous paint. That way, people will be better able to see where they're stepping and where the staircase ends. Just make sure no one tries the new, improved steps while the paint is wet.

Chill out. If you have a chilly basement, share the wealth with the rest of the household. Pull the cool air upstairs by leaving the basement door open and placing a fan in the doorway. At the same time, the dry, warm air will circulate into the basement, which will help keep moist air from condensing there.

MAKE it LAST
Make your own root cellar

DOES IT SEEM as if your potatoes sprout overnight and your apples get mushy just as fast? It could be that the spot where you store them in the kitchen is too warm. I have a friend who keeps his own newly dug potatoes and bushels of apples from a local orchard fresh and crisp from October to May. He walks right by the kitchen with the produce and heads for his concrete floor basement, where the temperature is usually 40° to 50°F.

He puts the apples in a galvanized metal trash can and keeps the potatoes in a couple of those large popcorn tins people give each other at the office at Christmas. Both containers go right on the floor. For proper ventilation, he moistens sphagnum moss or some clean burlap and adds it to the top 5 inches of the tins, covering the apples or potatoes completely. If the moist layer dries out, he dampens it again with a spray bottle. And when he wants to bake an apple pie or fry some potatoes, he just reaches under the moss and gets what he needs.

I tried this myself with carrots in a fruitcake tin, and it worked well. They didn't sprout for 6 months, and I didn't have to keep that so-called economical 5-pound bag in the refrigerator, where it would have taken up the entire vegetable bin.

If your garage is fairly cool but not freezing in the winter, it will work just as well for cold storage.

Give the floor a faux finish. Tired of looking at that ugly concrete floor, with all its cracks and water marks? Paint it. There are lots of options, including a faux marble look that can make the cracks look natural, or some brightly colored stencils that mimic a patterned carpet. You can even stain the concrete in a contrasting diamond pattern to make it look like parquet.

But don't rush into the project. Concrete must be absolutely

SIX WAYS TO DRY UP DOWN THERE

Getting moisture out of the basement is like pushing water uphill. But it's well worth your time and trouble, because moisture in the basement can cause odor and insect infestations, not to mention mildew—one of those gifts that just keeps on giving. So try any (or all) of these moisture-reducing techniques.

1. Open all the doors and windows for a few days.

2. Take furniture outside in the sun to bake dry (and kill bacteria).

3. Place an electric fan on the floor for added circulation.

4. Try a dehumidifier.

5. Place a few charcoal briquettes in a shallow pan in strategic areas, such as near the washer and dryer. You can still use them for barbecues later.

6. If you're desperate, try rigging the basement for heat or using an electric space heater.

dry before you even think about painting it. Not sure whether yours is dry? Do a safety check with a rubber mat. Place it on the concrete and wait a couple of hours. If there's "sweat" on or under the mat when you lift it, go back to your drying methods and try again later. To test a concrete wall to see if it's dry enough for paint, use a rubber bath mat with suction cups.

Before you pour the cement in a basement with block or concrete walls, line the room with 2-by-4s, then wedge clapboards behind them.

Add concrete to eliminate moisture. If there's water leaking into your basement, you might be able to solve the problem by adding a few more inches of concrete to the floor. But leave a few inches around the perimeter of the new layer to create a gutter—a place for the water to flow while your feet stay dry.

Just be sure that the gutters all drain in the same direction and flow to a sump, where you can pump the water out whenever necessary.

Before you pour the new concrete, line the perimeter of the room with 2-by-4s. If the walls are block or concrete, place a clapboard between each 2-by-4 and the wall so that it's easier to remove the boards later. Let the concrete set for at least 24 hours, longer if your basement is particularly damp.

Garage and Workshop

Even if you never park a car in your garage, there are ample benefits associated with cleaning it and keeping it organized. You gain storage space, find stuff you forgot you owned, and get your workshop organized. If you're not sure what should stay and what should go or how to organize what's left, follow these experts' lead.

Walk through the drive-thru door. Professional handyman Wade Slate is an avid woodworker and operates a lawn care business from his detached two-car garage in Knoxville, Tennessee. Because he's contending with three times the average amount of lawn care equipment and tools, he really knows how to maximize storage space. At the same time, he has arranged his garage so that he can easily access the tools of his trade when he needs them, starting with the entrance.

"I'm too cheap to install an electric garage door opener," Wade says. "In my experience, they're often unsafe or break. But it's a pain to open and close that heavy door manually." So, to accommodate frequent trips in and out—without inviting burglars, squirrels, or neighborhood dogs—Wade recommends creating a door within a door.

Wade made that extra door by removing one of the lower panels of the garage door with a jigsaw. "But you could use a regular saw if you drilled holes at the corners to get yourself started,"

A GREAT DATE IN GARAGE DOOR HISTORY

for the first few years that cars were widely available, garage doors were a problem. That's because technically, there weren't any. If people stored their cars, it was in a barn or shed. The doors—swinging barn doors—were heavy, sagged, and required lots of space to open completely. Besides that, those old-fashioned doors were just too passé for the new motor age.

That bothered C. G. Johnson, an Indiana inventor. He knew that those heavy swinging doors just wouldn't do, so in 1921, he invented a new kind. His idea was an upward-moving door with horizontally hinged, connected panels. Johnson's door took up almost no space and, when properly balanced, was easy for almost anyone to open. He mounted a small prototype of his invention on the back of his car (a Model T, of course) and traveled around to market his door. Thus was born the modern garage door and Johnson's company, Overhead Door Corporation, which still makes garage doors today.

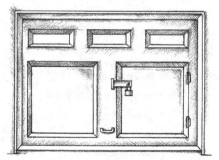

With just a few pieces of hardware and a jigsaw, you can create a walk-through door in your garage door.

he says. "And make very sure you don't cut through the door support at the bottom." Wade then framed out the opening with 2-by-2s and planed the edges of the panel to make them smooth. Last, he reattached the panel as a door with hinges and a heavy-duty latch with a padlock.

"I can come in and out with small stuff, and so can the kids," Wade notes. "I don't have to worry that they're going to smash their heads on that big door anymore either."

Store posters on the garage door. The garage door may be too cumbersome to open and shut all the time, but its size does have its advantages, says Wade Slate. He uses the wide-open space on the inside to store posters. "I have all kinds of sports and movie posters, and the little girls in the family have dog posters and whatnot," he says. "They have too much sentimental value to give away, but we don't have enough room to hang them all."

So Wade purchased two oversize, acid-free poster frames at a discount department store for around $15 each. He displayed one poster in each frame and stacked five or six others behind it, separated by sturdy, acid-free drawing paper. He mounted the two frames on the inside of the garage door, drilling through the corners with screws so that they wouldn't fall down when the doors open and shut. The posters add a bit of visual diversion to the garage, and they'll be easily accessible should Peter Frampton ever make a comeback.

Use tape to mark the spot. Even if you regularly store trash cans, mowers, pressure washers, or bikes in the same space in your garage or workshop, the second they're moved, other objects materialize to take their place. When you get tired of rearranging because the kitty litter is now where the birdseed should go, start saving places. Here's how.

Use electrical tape to make an outline of the bottom of the object on the garage floor, right where you always "park" it. Then next time you move the lawn mower out to cut the grass, you can ease it back into its empty parking space. A variation on this idea will keep your workshop tools organized. Hang each tool in its own spot on some Peg-Board, and then outline the tool with black marker or even a pencil.

Deliver your tools from the elements. Mailboxes are made to withstand rain or sleet or dark of night, right? That's why they're great for increasing your garage storage space. Mount one on the side of the garage or on a post outdoors and use it to store tools or even the paperwork and warranties from all of the products you keep in the garage. Mailboxes are often cheaper brand-new than similar-size plastic containers (and definitely more waterproof than any other containers with drawers). And they make great mobile units. Stock one with a set of gardening tools, gloves, seeds, and so forth. Then it's ready to go to the garden first thing come spring. It can spend the season outside, then come back in the garage in the winter.

Store your sandpaper. You need to have sandpaper in your workshop, but how should you store it? It gets scattered here and there, and it seems as though you can never find the grade of sandpaper you're looking for. To avoid this frustration, stack your leftover sandpaper and clip it to an old clipboard. Hang the board on a nail in your shop, and you'll always know where to find it. What's more, you'll be able to flip through the "pages" and find the grade of sandpaper you need for the job at hand.

Reach for baby wipes. If you're looking to organize small pieces of hardware, baby wipe containers may be the solution. The containers are durable and stackable. And even though they're not transparent, there is an ingenious way to always know

GARAGE DOOR SAFETY

It might look funny in a slapstick movie, but it's no joke when a defective automatic garage door comes down on a car or, worse, someone's head. To test whether your door's safety reverse mechanism is in good shape, lay a brand-new roll of paper towels on the floor where the closed door would ordinarily meet the concrete, then activate the door. When it touches the paper towels, it should immediately bounce back up. If it crushes the roll instead, get the safety reverse fixed immediately, before someone or something gets hurt.

MAKE it LAST

Wax on, dirt off

ONE OF THE BEST WAYS to protect your garage door is to give it a coat of car wax regularly. The wax will help the door repel dirt and moisture. Apply it the same way you do to your car.

---

what's stored inside: Use a hot glue gun to attach a sample of the contents to the front of the container for easy identification.

Drive out expired auto products. Garage shelves the world over bulge with old automotive products, says Julie Amato, store manager of the Knoxville, Tennessee, Auto Zone for the past decade. Right beside those products are grubby bottles that look like obvious choices for disposal but could continue to go in the car engine for another 10 years and still work well. Which are which? Here's the scoop.

1. Antifreeze can still please. "It doesn't expire and is made to withstand very low temperatures," Julie says.

2. Oil is okay, too. Motor oil can retain its properties at the highest temperatures, so it, too, is an indefinite keeper.

3. Gas goes bad. Gasoline absorbs moisture, which renders it useless, so don't hang onto leftover gas after the mowing season unless you buy a product that stabilizes gasoline. "It won't save you money, but it will save the inconvenience of disposing of gasoline legally, which usually means a trip to the hazardous waste disposal site," Julie says.

4. Sad facts about car wax. When you live in a cold climate, don't count on car wax to last more than one season. "It will freeze and go bad," Julie cautions.

5. Tire spray can stay. If the cleaner you use on your tires freezes, it will get cloudy. But don't worry, because that's okay; when it thaws, it will still work.

6. Brake for new fluid. Never try to get by with last year's brake fluid. "It goes bad, so buy a new bottle every year," Julie advises. "It's just not worth worrying about whether your current container is current with something as important as brakes."

Weed out garden chemicals. Buying in bulk is a great philosophy for almost everything except insecticides, pesticides, and fertilizers, says Bunni Hood, the manager of a family-owned greenhouse in Knoxville, Tennessee. She recommends organic gardening methods whenever possible, but if you do have chemicals languishing in your garage, be sure to purge any leftovers. "All chemicals can be dangerous to children and pets," she says. "So try to buy only what you need for the year."

Even if accidental poisoning isn't a risk in your household, keep in mind that chemicals do lose their properties quickly. Liquids usually break down within a year of purchase, Bunni says. "You definitely should dispose of any liquid that has solidified," she notes. As for granular fertilizers or agricultural lime, make sure they stay dry; they're useless if they're clumpy.

WHATSIT?

Q: One end of this very old tool is a sharply pointed, short knife. The other end has a very small metal wheel much like a glass cutter. What is it?

A: This is a glazier's tool. It was used to cut and set glass in window sash. The small wheel scored the glass, and the two jaws broke off small pieces. Next came a knife sharpener and a twisted-wire corkscrew (which this one is missing). The corkscrew was for pulling the cork from a linseed oil bottle. The oil was mixed with whiting to make putty, and the short blade on the end was a putty knife, with a pin to guide it along the sash. The bulge in the center was used as a tapper to break the glass after it had been scored.

chapter 8

your home's
exterior

MANY EMOTIONS COME with owning a home. There's the pride you get from earning your piece of the American dream, but there's also the realization that it will take a lot of work to keep that dream from turning into a nightmare.

In these pages you'll meet the ingenious experts who will help you keep the dream alive. Greg Jasinski, for example, is a professional painter from Lockport, Illinois. He reveals the best way to clean paint rollers. Professional handyman Jim Gapinski of Des Plaines, Illinois, offers ways to make your roof last longer. And

CHECK YOUR HOME'S ARMOR

Rain, snow, sleet, and hail may not stop the mail, but they can sure do a number on your home's exterior. As you look around the outside of your house, you'll notice that almost everything about it is designed to keep out the elements, especially water. According to Jim Gapinski of J. R. Repairs in Des Plaines, Illinois, "When it comes to maintenance, you need to keep your eye on any area where two different types of building materials come together." That could be where brick meets siding, roof meets chimney, siding meets windows, and so on. "Each of those places usually has some type of flashing or caulk to keep out everything from water to insects," Jim says. That flashing is usually the first thing to go, so it's where you'll want to concentrate your attention when you're checking out your home for potential repairs.

construction expert Dwight Martino of Worth, Illinois, will have you using caulk like a pro in no time. There's more, too, so let's get started!

Painting Your House

If you have ever owned a wood-sided home, then you've probably noticed that the luster of a fresh paint job begins to fade just about the time you get your brushes cleaned and neatly stored away. It doesn't matter whether you choose latex or oil-based paint. There's nothing Mother Nature can't penetrate in only a few years.

The good news for do-it-yourselfers is that painting isn't brain surgery (although the first tip here demonstrates that the most successful paint job starts in the brain, not the bucket). The downside for the occasional painter is that by the time you start getting the hang of it, the job is usually done.

Paint your house one side at a time. Wood-sided homes need to be painted every 5 to 7 years. But with all the prepping, priming, and painting, it's not surprising that many people who do paint their own homes hire a painter the next time. Here's how to stay ahead of the curve and give your house a fresh coat of paint every 4 years—in just a quarter of the time.

Simply commit to painting one side of your house every year. It's a method with numerous benefits. First, the job can usually be tackled in a single weekend. Second, because you're concentrating the job in a short time, bad weather is less likely to interfere. Third, with the extra attention you give a smaller part of the house, you can spot problems before they require expensive repairs. Finally, you can spread out the cost of materials over 4 years. Use this ingenious method, and you'll save time, money, and the nuisance of a wasted summer.

GIVE BOZOS THE BRUSH-OFF

When it's not properly cared for, a paintbrush will dry out of shape and end up with frizzy bristles. In the trade, such an afflicted brush is affectionately referred to as a Bozo brush, because its bristles resemble the clown's trademark hair. Bozo brushes are obviously useless for painting windows or trim, because they can't cut in a clean line. Here's an ingenious four-step way to keep your brushes in tip-top shape.

1. After you clean your brush, wrap the bristles in newspaper while they're still wet.

2. Lay the brush down and flatten the bristles by running your hand over the newspaper, away from the handle.

3. Fold the newspaper back onto itself just past the end of the bristles and secure it with tape.

4. Hang or store the brush flat until you need it again. You'll be ready to cut in the perfect line every time.

A LOW-TECH CLEANING SOLUTION

Go to any paint store, and you're sure to find at least a half dozen pricey gadgets designed to clean paint rollers. So which one works best? "None," says professional painter Greg Jasinski of Greg's Painting in Lockport, Illinois. Roller combs loosen the roller's fibers, and most other gadgets are just messy. "I just stand the roller on one end in the slop sink, run lukewarm water down into the center of the roller and let the water overflow," Greg says. After 10 minutes or so, the roller is spotless.

Try prep work without the pressure. Staining a deck or a sided house? Here's how to skip a step and shave a few days off the job. Don't use a power washer to clean the surface. Greg Jasinski, a professional painter from Lockport, Illinois, with 16 years of experience, doesn't even own a high-pressure washer. "You don't need one," he says. "Just use a garden hose. Whatever doesn't come off doesn't have to."

Despite this seemingly lax approach, Greg insists that prep work is the most important part of any good paint job. "But pressure washers just open the pores in the wood and force water in," he says. If you do use a pressure washer, give the wood a few days to dry before you paint.

Wet your brushes. Painting is simple. You just dip your brush into the paint and then slap it on the house, right? Not quite. Before he paints, Jim Gapinski, a professional handyman for more than 25 years, takes one simple step to make his paintbrushes last longer. "I soak them in water before I get any paint on them," he says. Wetting the brush first "keeps the paint from soaking into the heel of the brush." That keeps the paint on the end of the brush, where Jim wants it, and makes cleanup easier, too.

Brace your bushes. Greg Jasinski always carries a sheet of plywood in his truck when he's working on outdoor painting jobs. "I wedge the plywood between the house and a bush, then use a short painter's pole to hold the whole thing away from the house." This ingenious contraption gives him plenty of room to work and keeps the bushes from ruining his paint job. He also covers bushes with a heavy-duty drop cloth to avoid getting scratched.

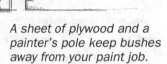

A sheet of plywood and a painter's pole keep bushes away from your paint job.

Make a homemade ladder level. Try this the next time you need to paint a wall next to some exterior (or interior) stairs. To make up the rise of a single step, Greg Jasinski places a piece of ¾-inch-thick wood on top of a full paint can. One leg of the ladder sits on the stair and the other on the paint can. But, he cautions, "use a full can of paint." You need the weight to keep the can steady. Of course, this method isn't completely secure, so you'll need to have someone hold the ladder as well.

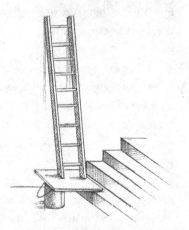

This ingenious ladder level makes painting walls along a stairway easier.

Give your paintbrushes the gift of life. Found an old, stiff paintbrush in your garage? Don't throw it out. Breathe new life into it by soaking it in fabric softener. Greg Jasinski learned this trick from one of the old-timers with whom he works.

"Lay the brush in fabric softener for two to four hours, then rinse it off," Greg says. "The softener will condition the brush and remove the pigment. And your hands will come out baby soft, too." But, Greg adds, "never stand brushes up on their bristles in any cleaning solution." Rather, lay them down to prevent the bristles from bending.

T H E P R O S K N O W

paint in the shade

UNLESS YOU'RE working on your tan, says Greg Jasinski, "work out of the sun." That means staying in the shade. "Direct sunlight causes brushes to gum up quickly and leaves you less time to work with the paint," Greg says.

Your best bet is to start on the south side of the house in the early morning or late afternoon. Paint the west side of the house while the sun is still rising and the east side while the sun sets. You can do the north side anytime. If you must paint in the sun, "add a paint conditioner to help make the paint easier to work with," Greg says. A paint conditioner thins the paint and prevents it from getting gummy or drying too fast in warm weather. You'll find conditioners at paint stores and large home centers.

Lay the paint on thick. Cinder blocks are the toughest surface to paint. No roller nap is thick enough to do the job right. So if the blocks aren't playing fair, cheat, says Greg Jasinski. "Cheat the paint on the joints," he advises, by using a brush first, then hit it with the roller. Keep a brush at hand to touch up those hard-to-reach nooks and crannies.

Strain your paint. When you paint outdoors, your brush often picks up small rocks, paint chips, and wood slivers, which get mixed into your bucket of paint. Try this ingenious solution to remove those annoying bits. Use an old nylon stocking to strain the paint or stain into a new bucket. The nylon can even be washed and used over and over again.

Chill your brushes and rollers. Don't feel like cleaning a brush or roller between coats? Just put them in the refrigerator overnight. This clever technique works because paint won't dry below about 50°F.

Wrap brushes in aluminum foil or plastic wrap; place wet rollers in plastic grocery bags and tie the bags tight around the handles. This is also a great idea if you're finished with a job but just don't feel like cleaning up right now. One caution: Don't try this with oil-based paint, which will make your refrigerator smell.

Roof Repair and Maintenance

Jim Gapinski has replaced plenty of roofs as a professional handyman. "The worst part is removing the old roof," he says. "There are special tools, but anything that works is fair game." He says that if you're going to tackle the job yourself, the best advice is to "have plenty of nephews. Hand each one a shovel, pitch fork, or pry bar and tell 'em to go to it."

"Once the old roof is off, putting on the shingles is easy," Jim says. And if it's done correctly, some roofs can last a lifetime. Jim recently replaced a 50-year-old wood shingle roof on a chicken coop that his father built. "I saved a few of the shingles. You can actually see where they were worn thin by water," he says.

If the time has come to replace your roof, you're in luck: It's a perfect opportunity to do some things differently that can make your roof last a lot longer.

Use a cricket. Jim Gapinski says that the best way to extend the life of your roof is "never to use a lap joint." A lap

that's • ingenious!

turn it pee green

COPPER FLASHING HAS always been a popular choice for its rich, old-world appearance. If you like the look of old (green) copper flashing but don't have the patience or the nature to do the job, use urine (yes, urine) to speed up the aging process. Depending on how hands-on you want to get, you can apply it with a brush or a spray bottle. Urine is highly acidic and creates a chemical reaction that speeds up the process of "aging" copper.

Lap joints (left) allow leaves and other debris to rot on your roof, a problem you can easily solve by installing a cricket (right).

joint, in which one set of shingles gets tucked under another, is what most roofers use to join two parts of a roof. It's the most common configuration because it's the cheapest. But the problem with lap joints, says Jim, is that "stuff like leaves don't wash out of those areas, so it just sits and rots."

Instead, Jim installs something called a cricket. It's a type of flashing that "looks like a little metal valley." It's available in galvanized or copper and is essentially a gutter that runs on all the inside corners of your roof. "It's only a few inches wide, and you don't even really notice it," Jim says, "but it makes all the difference."

Put water damage on ice. If you're reshingling your roof, Jim Gapinski recommends having your roofer install an ice and water shield to prevent ice damage. "It's a type of rubber sheeting that goes under the first few rows of shingles and seals the area around the nails to prevent water from getting in," Jim explains. "Water damage occurs because ice backs up under the shingles, then water gets in those nail holes." The upgrade shouldn't add too much to the cost of your roofing job, but, Jim says, the added expense is "a lot less than the cost of fixing water damage."

Wash your roof. If a dark, moldy substance leaves black streaks on your asphalt shingles, take a tip from construction worker Dwight Martino. "You can get rid of that stuff with Lysol," he says.

144

"That stuff" is mold, and it usually appears in shady areas or on the north side of the house. Like anything else, if the shingles never dry, they'll develop mold. "Undiluted Lysol in a pump sprayer will kill the stuff instantly," Dwight says. "Then it's easy to just hose it off."

Damn those ice dams. If you live in a region with cold, snowy winters, you know about ice dams. "They're a real problem," says Jim Gapinski. "They cause water damage, and that's the worst thing for your house."

Every winter, Jim is called in to intercept ice dams, a perennial nuisance for home owners who live in colder climates. They form when water freezes in gutters and backs up underneath shingles, causing millions of dollars' worth of damage to homes every year. Jim removes the ice by applying ice-melting chemicals to the roof and gutters. Calcium chloride is a chemical substitute for rock salt and is sold under different brand names as an ice melter. "Never use common rock salt on your roof," Jim says. "It will leave a residue and discolor the shingles."

After carefully removing icicles and excess snow from the bottom of the roof, Jim spreads a generous amount of calcium chloride directly on the ice. Within minutes, "you can hear it snap, crackle, and pop, then the water begins to flow," he says.

THE PROS KNOW

weather your shingles

IF YOUR ROOF has wooden shingles, there will probably come a time when you will have to replace a few of them. But then you'll have a section of shingles that looks completely different from the rest of your roof. Well, here's an ingenious way to get new shingles to match the old ones.

Dwight Martino of D. Martino Construction Company in Worth, Illinois, recommends spraying the new shingles with "a fifty-fifty solution of vinegar and water. The acid from the vinegar will turn the shingles gray almost instantly without harming them." Use a spray bottle for small areas or a pump sprayer for larger areas. "The shingles will get a little lighter after they dry, but you can hit them with another coat until they match," Dwight says.

Now Thatch's a Great Roof

thatch is the oldest roofing material known to man, and in many countries, it's still one of the most common. You may associate thatch with the British Isles, but the material also is used in Africa, Asia, and the South Seas. But thatch isn't only charming. Depending on the material used, it's watertight, inexpensive, and durable. With proper care, a thatch roof can last 70 years. How does that compare with your roof?

Gutter Care and Repair

Brian Cannaday of Clean 'N' Clear Maintenance Services in Hinsdale, Illinois, found out just how bad things can get if you don't clean your home's gutters on a regular basis. "Once I found a dead cat all covered with leaves in a customer's gutter," he says. "I almost passed out." Brian struggled with whether to tell the home owners about his discovery. "I didn't know what to say. 'Are you missing a cat?'"

Fortunately, most gutter jobs don't lead to such extreme discoveries. However, Brian says that you can prevent leaves (and the occasional deceased mammal) from clogging your downspouts by attaching a small piece of screening over each downspout with silicone sealant. Here are some more ingeniously easy ways to care for your gutters and downspouts.

Guard your gutters. Unless you enjoy getting up on a ladder to clean your gutters frequently, gutter guards are a great idea, especially if you live in a heavily wooded area. The guards, which are essentially vinyl or plastic screens, usually snap onto existing gutters. They allow water to roll in but keep out leaves and twigs, which are notorious for clogging downspouts. You'll find gutter guards at almost any home improvement center.

Bigger is better. "Almost anything will wash down a downspout that's big enough," says Jim Gapinski. That's why he's a fan of oversize downspouts. "A standard downspout is just a little hole in the bottom of the gutter," Jim says. If you often get clogs, he recommends upgrading to oversize downspouts, which are more than double the size of regular ones. "They're as wide as the bottom of the gutter and about four inches long," Jim explains. You can find oversize downspouts at most large home improvement centers.

Be a snake in the gutter. Curt Bohlmann has an easy way to clear clogged downspouts. He snakes a garden hose up the downspout to remove the clog. "The last place I want to be during a rainstorm is up on an aluminum ladder," Curt says. "And this way, you don't even have to turn on the hose. You just run it up there and poke through the clog, and all the debris will flush right out."

Rebuild your old gutters. Are your old galvanized gutters rusting through in spots? Relining the bottoms of your gutters with aluminum is a marvelously ingenious and frugal way to fix the leaks without the expense and trouble of replacing your

---

MAKE-YOUR-OWN GUTTER SHOVEL

Cleaning gutters is one of those necessary evils, like going to the dentist or paying your taxes. But there is a way to do it without getting your hands dirty: Make a gutter shovel from an empty plastic bottle.

You'll need a bottle about 3 inches wide, with flat sides and a handle. One-gallon laundry detergent bottles work well. Cut off the bottom, then use the bottle to scoop the leaves out of your gutter.

gutters. You'll find the aluminum, which is usually sold for flashing, at home improvement centers.

Cut the aluminum into 3- to 4-inch-wide strips to fit into the bottom of your gutters. Attach the aluminum to the clean gutter with "liquid brush grade" fibered roof coating. The material, which is a kind of adhesive, is available at home centers. Apply a coat to the bottom of the gutter, then press the aluminum into the wet adhesive. Keep the aluminum from lifting by placing a full can of soda every foot or so along it. After the adhesive dries, apply another coat on top of the aluminum. Here's the frugal part: You can get 100 feet of aluminum from an 8-inch by 50-foot roll for less than $15.

Windows and Doors

Early humans had the right idea: Find yourself a cozy little cave and move right in. Now that's what we call maintenance-free living. No sagging doors. No sticking windows. No screens to fix. And best of all, no dirty windows to wash.

But we've evolved, and with that evolution has come modern conveniences. Although windows are handy for seeing through walls and doors are helpful for keeping out dinosaurs, they're not as maintenance-free as a cave. Luckily, evolution also has brought us some ingenious ways to take better care of our windows and doors.

Give your doors a face-lift. Over time, the weight of a heavy exterior door can cause the upper hinge to loosen, leaving a home owner with a bad case of sagging door syndrome. Symptoms include difficulty closing the door and drafts. To nurse the door back to health, remove the center screw from the top hinge and replace it with a 3- to 3½-inch drywall screw. The longer screw will run all the way into the stud and pull the hinge tight against the jam.

Bondo: Not just for poor drivers anymore. Bondo brand automotive body filler is a great repair material for a variety of areas around your home's exterior. It's great for fixing dents in metal doors and makes a terrific wood filler, too. Jim Gapinski likes it for fixing rotten windowsills. He recommends removing the rotten wood with a chisel, then applying a wood hardener like the one made by Minwax. The hardener reinforces the decayed wood fibers and seals the wood against further moisture. After the hardener dries, mix the Bondo according to the package directions and fill in the gaps. Smooth it with a disposable putty knife, and then sand, and paint.

that's • ingenious!

get back on track

MANY TYPES OF double-hung and sliding windows made in the 1950s and 1960s had aluminum tracks. When windows become difficult to open and close, Brian Cannaday of Clean 'N' Clear Maintenance Services uses a little petroleum jelly to give the windows a lube job. "Just coat the tracks with Vaseline and work the window back and forth," Brian says. He contends that it's just as good as the white lithium grease the pros use.

Don't scratch the glass. When there's paint or a decal on a window, you probably reach for a razor blade to remove it. But did you know that you can scratch the glass when you use a razor? Before professional window cleaner Brian Cannaday removes tape residue or paint spatter with a razor blade, he takes one precaution that protects the glass from scratches. He wets the windows with a little dishwashing liquid mixed with hot water to make it slippery. "This forms a protective coating on the window," Brian says. When he's finished, he never sees fine scratches when the sun shines through the glass.

Wax your windows. Large picture windows are the toughest things to keep clean, according to Brian Cannaday. But here's a secret he's been keeping to himself. "I wax my picture window with automotive wax," he says. "I haven't done this for my clients—they'd probably think I was nuts—but I do it on my own house."

Apply a coat of carnauba wax to a clean, dry window. "That's the kind of wax that you have to wipe off once it dries," Brian explains. He insists that the wax's "hard shell finish" makes the dirt and water "sheet up and roll off."

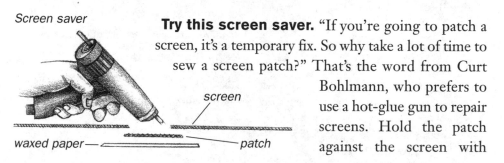

Screen saver

screen

waxed paper——

patch

Try this screen saver. "If you're going to patch a screen, it's a temporary fix. So why take a lot of time to sew a screen patch?" That's the word from Curt Bohlmann, who prefers to use a hot-glue gun to repair screens. Hold the patch against the screen with

---

THE ULTIMATE WINDOW CLEANER

Imagine streak-free windows—without a squeegee. When it's time to wash her windows, Karen Gapinski sends her husband, Jim, out to work with her secret formula. In a bucket, he combines 1 gallon hot water, ¼ cup liquid dishwasher detergent, and 1 tablespoon Jet-Dry brand dishwasher rinse agent. Jim washes the windows with a brush, then just hoses them off. The water sheets up and rolls off the windows without streaking—and without Jim's having to use a squeegee.

Why does this mixture work so well? Rinse agents are designed to lower the surface tension of water, causing it to sheet off dishes during the final rinse in your dishwasher. It does the same thing on your windows, eliminating streaks.

SEAL THE DEAL—AND THE GARAGE DOOR

The rubber seal at the bottom of a garage door can dry out, crack, and fall off, leaving a gap between the door and the floor. That gap is a problem because it allows heat to escape and lets leaves, insects, and rodents in. Here's a simply ingenious way to repair that old rubber seal with a bicycle inner tube.

Start by removing the worn-out seal, then cut an inner tube in half after removing the valve stem. An inner tube from a 27-inch wheel will yield two strips of rubber about 7 feet long when they're joined. Use several lengths to equal the width of your garage door. Flatten the inner tube and screw it to the bottom of the garage door about every 12 inches, but don't tighten the screws all the way. After you have all the rubber in place, go back and tighten each screw. The inner tubes will serve as a seal and compensate for variations between the garage door and the floor.

some waxed paper, then use your hot-glue gun to apply the glue between the screen and the patch. The waxed paper will keep the glue from oozing out the other side, but it won't stick. Just glue around the edge of your patch to keep out the bugs.

Corking Caulk Tips

Drafts are common around doors and windows, so it's important to replace caulk whenever it starts to dry, crack, or separate. The thing is, there's no easy way to remove the old caulk. (Hey, that's why they call it work!) And as a general rule, the older the caulk, the harder it will be to remove.

"First-generation caulks were oil-based," says Dwight Martino, who operates his family's 50-year-old construction business in Worth, Illinois. "When the oil dries out, you'll need nothing short of a jackhammer to get it out. When I come upon that type

MAKE it LAST
Put a lid on it

CAULK TUBES aren't known for their shelf life. Once you cut off the tip of the tube, you'd better start caulking. And if you don't empty the tube, you might as well throw it away, because once the caulk dries in the nozzle, it's unusable. Most frugal do-it-yourselfers have tried in vain to save a half-empty tube of caulk, only to find it useless the next time they need it. But there is a perfectly ingenious way to solve that problem. Make a workable caulk tube cap out of a wire nut. Wire nuts are plastic caps used for twisting and protecting electrical wires. You can find them in the electrical aisle of most hardware stores. Simply thread a large 10- to 12-gauge wire nut on the plastic tip, and your caulk will be as good as new the next time you need it.

of caulk, I apply a little kerosene with a small brush and let it sit for a while." The kerosene penetrates the caulk and "breathes some life into it," Dwight says. "Then you can use a putty knife or a small chisel to work it out."

For newer latex-based caulks, Dwight suggests softening them with a hair dryer. "Most people can't control a heat gun," he says. "Two seconds too long, and you'll blister the paint." But a hair dryer safely softens the caulk enough to remove it with a scraper. Here are some more ingenious tips that'll make replacing caulk a little less taxing.

Heat it up. Do-it-yourselfer Curt Bohlmann of Des Plaines, Illinois, has some advice about applying caulk: Make sure it's warm. But never warm a caulk tube in the oven or microwave.

(That could be very bad.) Curt says that simpler is better. "Just leave the caulk tube in direct sunlight for half an hour before you use it," he advises. In colder weather, place the tube near a radiator or heat register.

Extend your reach.
Having a hard time getting caulk into those hard-to-reach areas? Curt Bohlmann likes to use a drinking straw as a caulk tube extension. "The straws with a flexible section—aka bendy straws—are great," he says. "That accordion neck will get in just about anywhere." Just shove the straw onto the end of the caulk tube and secure it with duct tape. Use one hand to direct the straw and the other to squeeze out the caulk.

that's • ingenious!

perfect your bead technique

MOST DO-IT-YOURSELFERS who dabble with caulk use the wet-the-finger method to smooth it. But there are two problems with this technique: First, you have to wipe your finger frequently to get rid of the excess caulk. Second, who wants to put a finger back in his mouth after running it along a bead of caulk? Not only that, but sooner or later, you're going to run out of fingers. Instead, use a plastic spoon to create the perfect caulk bead. Run a plastic spoon over the caulk, with the spoon facing forward as you skim. The spoon's rounded tip will create the perfect shape and scoop up the excess caulk at the same time.

Miscellaneous Exterior Tips

Just so you don't miss out on all those useful tips that don't quite fall into any category, we offer this collection of ingenious suggestions about your home's exterior.

Add a little mood lighting. Dimmers aren't just for indoor use. Try them outdoors, too. They create a lovely mood on patios and porches. Dim the lights for a special occasion or crank 'em up for security. Dimmers even work on quartz floodlights.

Take the plunge. The occasional stray basketball can do a number on aluminum siding, but you can pull out larger dents with a toilet plunger. First, make sure the siding is clean and dry. Position the plunger in the middle of the dent, push in, and then gently pull the plunger out. The dent should pop right out. But keep in mind that this trick works best on large dents with no sharp creases.

Save the hose. One of the first casualties of an early frost is usually the garden hose, which splits when the water inside freezes and expands. So be sure to put your hoses away before the temperature dips near freezing. Keep in mind, though, that even a hose stored in an unheated garage or shed can get ruined if there's water inside it, make sure the hoses are well-drained, too.

THE PROS KNOW

brush your bricks with beer

BRICKS THAT have been exposed to excessive moisture often develop a powdery white substance called saltpeter. The problem is especially common at the base of brick homes. Home improvement expert Dwight Martino recommends using the "old stale beer technique" to remove it. "Saltpeter is caused by a reaction between lime and portland cement," Dwight says. "Somehow the beer neutralizes that reaction." Use a stiff nylon brush to scrub the stale beer onto the bricks, then hose it off. After the bricks dry, use water sealant to prevent the moisture from seeping back in.

MAKE it LAST
Cap your chimney

YOU CAN MAKE YOUR FIREPLACE CHIMNEY last a lot longer by installing a chimney cap. Many chimneys are constructed with water-soluble grout. In addition to keeping sparks in and animals out, the cap prevents water from deteriorating the grout.

Here's a simple way to do that. Just lay the hose out on a slight downhill grade—say on your yard—and let gravity do the work for you. If you think your yard is flat, think again. Most yards are pitched slightly away from the house to promote good drainage.

Mark your territory. After the first big dump of snow, proud owners of snowblowers are usually the first ones out, ready to show the world that they have a leg up on old man winter. Unfortunately, snowblowers are also very efficient sod removers if you don't know exactly where your driveway is. Here's how to keep track. Before the first snowfall, mark the corners of your driveway and sidewalk with stakes or reflectors. That will make it easier to tell where your driveway stops and your lawn begins.

WHATSIT?

Q: One of our readers found this object in the dirt when his 150-year-old home was jacked up to replace rotting sills and floorboards. What is it?

A: It's a container for carpenter's chalk. It was used for snapping chalk lines on a timber or floor. The chalk line was passed through the large hole and came out through the smaller one. The case was full of chalk, and as the carpenter drew out the length he wanted, he would clamp the line tight and either have a hook on the end or his helper hold the other end tight. Then by lifting the line then releasing it, he would snap a chalk line on a timber to guide tools.

chapter 9

home safety
hints

Y YOUR HOME CAN'T TRULY BE YOUR CASTLE unless you feel safe inside it and secure about your belongings when you're away. Although there's no way to guarantee that you'll never have an accident or suffer a break-in, there are dozens of ingenious measures you can take to reduce the chances that you'll have to deal with these problems.

To help, we've rounded up a slew of safety experts who really know their stuff. Police lieutenant Nick Mabardy of Natick, Massachusetts, tells you how to protect your home from intruders.

You'll also meet our fire safety experts, including fire inspector Donald Ingram of Needham, Massachusetts; building commissioner Michael Melchiorri of Natick, Massachusetts; and building inspector Daniel Walsh of Needham, Massachusetts. They'll show you how to devise a fire safety plan, explain why your home needs three fire extinguishers, and tell you why you should carry a smoke detector when you travel.

We'll discuss other safety issues, too, including being prepared for floods and earthquakes. In the section about tornadoes, Terry Marshall, the director of emergency management in Adams County, Nebraska, will show you how paying attention to the size of hail can clue you in on the size of the storm. And believe it or not, there are ways to secure your belongings to make cleanup easier if a storm does strike your area.

Finally, we offer several tips about keeping neighbors, seniors, and kids safe in your home.

Securing Your Home

Home safety isn't just a matter of staying healthy in your home. It's also about keeping your house secure against break-ins when you're not around. Nick Mabardy has been a police officer for 33 years, and he knows that thieves target houses that offer easy access first. Here are some ingenious ways to remove your home from that list.

Don't fence me in. When people put up tall privacy fences around their backyards or allow their shrubs to grow up over their windows, it's the same as sending an invitation to criminals. That greenery offers an excellent place for crooks to hide while they're breaking in. Keep your shrubs trimmed. Be especially careful to plant shrubs far away from any basement windows—that's where criminals most frequently gain access to homes. And make sure a

---

GET FREE ADVICE FROM THE PROS

Many police departments offer free home security surveys, and most of the time, all you have to do is ask. A police officer will come to your home and find the most likely ways that a burglar could enter. The officer will check the locks on your doors and windows and give you a detailed written report that outlines the places where your home is vulnerable. With that information, you can fix any problems and add more security to your home.

---

fence doesn't completely obscure your back door. If there's a chance a neighbor might spot someone while they're breaking in, criminals will be less likely to try it.

Shed some light on the situation. According to Nick Mabardy, lighting is the number one deterrent to break-ins. So if you have a light on a timer in your living room, you're protected, right? Not necessarily. That technique doesn't work if you have only one light that turns on and off at predictable times. The trick is to have two or three different lights on separate timers, so that the living room light comes on at six and turns off at nine, while the bedroom light comes on at eight and goes off at ten. "It gives the illusion that someone is home," Nick explains. "To tell that you're not, the person will have to study your house for some time, and he's likely to be noticed." You can also install lights with motion detectors for the backyard, so when someone comes into your yard, it looks as if they're being watched.

Clear the path to security. Heading off for your annual ski vacation? Before you leave, be sure to hire a neighborhood kid to come by the house to shovel the walk and driveway in case there's a snowstorm. An unshoveled driveway is a sign to even the most casual observer that the house is unoccupied. "People think that leaving the walk unshoveled is a good idea because thieves will be afraid to leave their footprints," says Nick Mabardy. "Criminals know that by the time you get home to study those footprints, they'll be long gone, and so will all of your valuables." The best defense is to have a house that looks lived-in. Besides, shoveling is the last thing you want to do when you get home from vacation!

Case your own house. If you've ever locked yourself out of your house, you've probably wandered around the yard looking for a way in. If you found an open window in the laundry room and squeezed yourself through it in broad daylight without attracting any attention, you know how easy it would be for a stranger to do the same. Taking the time to eliminate these easy entry points with window locks and deadbolts will make it harder for someone to break in. Now all you have to do is remember to take your keys.

Don't be a show-off. Criminals don't just look for houses that are easy to break into; they look for houses that contain something worth stealing. Keeping that new stereo equipment, computer system, or art collection near a window is a mistake for which you could pay dearly. Draw the shades in your home office to conceal office equipment, and store other valuables out of sight. By the same token, bragging to friends and acquaintances about your priceless collections or expensive jewelry could be an invitation to a thief.

Pull the old sticker switch. When you invest in a home security system, the manufacturer will give you a set of stickers to put on the doors and windows of your house to warn thieves that an alarm system is in place. The theory is that this will deter most thieves, who would much rather find an easier target. But what about the rest of the thieves? We've all heard that some experienced thieves have developed ways around certain security systems. Here's how you can pull a fast one. If you know someone who has a different security system, ask them if you can switch stickers with them. You'll still get the effect of warning inexperienced burglars that you have an alarm system, but they just won't know which one.

Fire Safety

You probably think that your house is as safe as it could be from fire, but you're probably wrong. Fire inspector Donald Ingram has been investigating house fires for more than 20 years. He's always surprised at the careless decisions that cause so much damage and loss of life. He suggests a few simple, ingenious steps that you could take right now to help prevent a fire in your house.

Go underground. Many people don't put smoke detectors in their basements. That's odd, say fire safety experts, because (a) the

---

SMOKE DETECTOR TO GO

I n addition to the smoke detectors in my home, I have an extra one that I take on vacation," says building commissioner Michael Melchiorri. "It's a small battery-powered unit that I bought at the hardware store for ten bucks, but it gives me peace of mind whenever I'm away from home.

"I've been a building inspector for a long time, and I know that just because a house or hotel has a fire alarm system doesn't mean that it works. I just unpack my smoke detector and set it on top of the TV. It's especially useful when I rent a cabin in Maine for a fishing trip each summer. I know there aren't going to be any smoke detectors up there, so I just bring my own."

---

annals of ingenuity

MILESTONES OF FIRE-FIGHTING HISTORY

feeling pretty safe from fire in your home? Here are just some of the people and inventions to thank.

1648 The first fire wardens are appointed in what is now New York.

1679 The first paid fire department is formed in Boston.

1736 Benjamin Franklin forms the nation's first volunteer fire company in Philadelphia.

1863 The fire extinguisher is patented by Alanson Crane.

1872 Philip W. Pratt of Abington, Massachusetts, patents the first automatic sprinkler system.

1878 America's first firehouse pole is installed in New York City.

1878 David B. Kenyon, captain of Engine Company No. 21 of the Chicago Fire Department, invents the firehouse sliding pole.

1878 The fire escape ladder is patented by Joseph Winters.

1911 The Fire Marshals Association of North America sponsors the first National Fire Prevention Day.

1969 The first battery-operated home smoke detector is patented.

---

basement is where the furnace is, (b) it may also contain a workroom with lots of wood and flammable substances, and (c) it might even be a playroom for children. All of these factors demand the security of a smoke detector that will warn you of danger and allow you to escape long before the flames travel up the stairs.

Reduce clutter, increase safety. Building inspector Daniel Walsh says that cleaning your basement may make your house safer. Too many people store excess papers, linens, off-season clothing, and other combustibles in one spot in the house. They may further exacerbate the situation by storing any or all of these things near the furnace. Make sure flammable items are as far away from the furnace as they can be, and find another spot to store old papers to make your home safer and more attractive.

Don't block your escape route. Sure, you have clutter. Who doesn't? But if you tend to stack books and boxes in the wrong place—such as on the back stairs, which you're supposed to use as an escape route in a fire or other emergency—you're asking for trouble. One sure way to improve safety in your house is to make sure doorways and stairways are clear at all times.

Keep a trio of fire extinguishers around. Building commissioner Michael Melchiorri advocates having three different kinds of fire extinguishers in the home.

1. One for the kitchen. In the kitchen, you'll want an extinguisher that's made to fight grease fires.

2. One for the broom closet. Choose an all-purpose fire extinguisher for the broom closet. Look for one that's labeled "general-purpose" or "ABC."

3. One for the workshop. Michael has one for his workshop that's made especially for wood fires.

By having the right kind of fire extinguishers around the house—and by keeping them handy so that you can reach them fast when you need them—you'll dramatically increase your chances of putting out a fire before it spreads. Make sure you know how to use each fire extinguisher before you have to. The last thing you need is to waste time trying to figure it out as the flames are rising. And always call the fire department, even if you think you've put out the fire. Often a fire will start up again later.

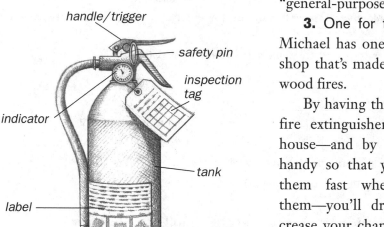

handle/trigger

safety pin

inspection tag

indicator

tank

label

Fire extinguisher

HAVE A FIRE SAFETY PLAN

Do you know what you would do right now if your smoke alarm went off? How about if it went off in the middle of the night? Building commissioner Michael Melchiorri's children know exactly what to do. Michael's father, Silvano, spent 33 years in the Natick, Massachusetts, Fire Department, and he has impressed upon his children and grandchildren the importance of planning for an emergency. Here are some ways to perfect your plan.

Practice makes perfect. Michael Melchiorri has made a written plan with his kids to make sure they know how to get out of the house from every room. "I've talked to them about staying low. It's what my father taught me," he says. He's right. In most cases, it's the smoke and not the fire that kills.

Throw 'em a rope. If your kids sleep on the second floor of your house, their most likely means of escape in a midnight fire might be through the window. Make their escape route as safe as possible by purchasing chain or rope ladders, which are available at large chain hardware stores for less than $50. Each one should be stored near a window, perhaps in a hope chest. You can hope that the kids never have to use them! But have them practice just in case—with you supervising, of course.

Build a safety ledge. If someone sleeps on the third floor of your house, you may not be able to find rope ladders long enough to reach the ground. In that case, it might be a good idea to have a contractor build a small balcony outside the bedroom window. It doesn't have to be very wide or large, just big enough for someone to stand on and breathe fresh air until the fire department arrives.

Conduct a broom check. When your children visit their grandparents, they can take their fire safety know-how with them.

INTRODUCE YOUR KIDS TO A FIREFIGHTER

Imagine for a minute that you're a small child—6 or 7 years old—and your house is on fire. Your bedroom is filling with smoke. It's hot, and you're terribly frightened, so you hide under the bed.

Soon an enormous stranger—is it a monster?—crashes through your door. He's carrying an ax and wearing a big, scary mask. And now he's after you!

Think about it: To a frightened child, a firefighter in full fire-fighting regalia may be a terrifying sight, and not necessarily a figure to whom she'd run for safety.

What's the answer? Make arrangements to take your child to a local firehouse and introduce her to a firefighter—and what he looks like when he's doing his job. That way, if and when the time comes, your child will run to—and not from—the firefighter.

Ask them to check the batteries in the smoke detectors at their grandparents' home by using a broom handle to reach the test button. Your kids can show off their fire safety awareness and help their family members stay safe. But watch out. When they come home, they're likely to test their own smoke detectors, too. Of course, that's probably a good thing.

Acts of God

Unfortunately, you can't control every aspect of your family's safety. You can protect yourself from most fires and accidents, but you can't protect yourself from bad weather. It's tempting just to forget that dangers such as hurricanes and floods exist. But hope is the worst kind of preparation. Instead, with just a little bit of advance planning, you can turn even the direst emergencies into mere inconveniences.

GENERAL PREPAREDNESS

If you know what kinds of weather-related emergencies are most likely to affect you, there are ways to prepare for them that go far beyond getting out the candles and extra blankets. Make sure you add these ideas to your list.

Use your phone-a-friend lifeline. Well before disaster strikes, it's a good idea to find an out-of-state friend or relative who will agree to be your family contact in an emergency. As rescue crews roam the city answering 911 calls, the local phone lines will probably be jammed. You and your family will have better luck calling long distance to let someone know how and where you are. Once you do find a long-distance contact, make sure everyone in the family knows that person's phone number.

Bring noisemakers. You've always heard that you'll need a flashlight and a battery-powered radio for times when you may need to take shelter in your home. And you've probably always assumed that those are for light and information. That's true, but disaster relief experts know that those items serve an additional function. If the worst should happen and you are knocked unconscious during an emergency, the rescue workers will keep looking for you if they hear a radio going or see a beam of light from a flashlight. Those are signs that someone is in trouble. So to make sure people know where to find you, keep both the radio and the flashlight on during a storm.

Get it on tape. If you want to protect yourself from the hassles that will surely follow any weather-related disaster, get out your video camera. "Making a videotape of your home and locking it away in a safe-deposit box will make your dealings with the insurance agency much easier," says Terry Marshall, director of emergency management in Adams County, Nebraska. If your

---

10 Essentials for Your Storm-Preparedness Kit

In case disaster strikes, you know you're supposed to have a flashlight and a radio handy. Here's what else you'll want to have squirreled away in a backpack or duffel bag within easy reach.

1. Extra batteries.

2. A 3-day supply of water. You'll need 1 gallon of water per person per day.

3. Written directions for how to shut off the gas, electricity, and water to your home in case authorities advise you to do so.

4. An extra set of car keys and a credit card or some traveler's checks.

5. A list of the medications each family member needs.

6. Sturdy shoes and work gloves.

7. Food.

8. The phone number of your insurance agent.

9. A rudimentary first-aid kit that includes bandages, gauze, peroxide, antibiotic cream, and tweezers.

10. An electronic game to keep the kids busy.

---

house suffers any damage in a weather disaster, the first thing you'll be asked to do is list all of your possessions. That will be much easier with a videotape to prompt you.

CARING FOR YOUR PET DURING AN EMERGENCY

Your pets give you love and loyalty, and they depend on you for their care. That's never more important than in a natural disaster. Your pets may warn you of an approaching storm, because they react to abrupt changes in barometric pressure. Likewise, they'll rely on you for protection during and after the storm. Here are two ways to give your animal family members the care they need.

Make Fluffy a disaster kit. Sure, have a kit to take care of your own needs during a severe storm, but have you thought of your pets? Think about your pets now, and you won't have to worry about them later. Here's what their disaster kit should include.

1. Leashes and harnesses to help you transport your pets

2. Current photos of your pets in case they get lost

3. The name and telephone number of your vet

4. Food and water, bowls, and perhaps a litter box and a favorite toy in case they go to foster care or a boarding facility

And of course, make sure their carriers are handy.

Make reservations. Finding a place to shelter your family pets in an emergency can be a trial. Red Cross shelters won't take pets, and many hotels won't accept them either. Instead, take a few minutes before a storm strikes to contact animal shelters, hotels, and even friends, asking which ones would be willing to take your pets in case you have to evacuate your home. Once you have a list of pet-friendly places and their phone numbers, keep this with your disaster information, so it will be at hand when you need it.

TORNADOES

Terry Marshall has seen dozens of tornadoes—and the high winds and destruction they bring—in his job as director of emergency management. He says that the best warning sign that a thunderstorm harbors a tornado is the size of the hail. "The larger the hail, the more severe the storm," he says. It's the most severe storms that bring tornadoes, and they usually strike right after the hail ends. That's when the real storm might just be getting started. Here are some of Terry's tips for getting through a twister.

Head for the basement. Once a tornado has been sighted in your area, you should head for the basement or the lowest level

DON'T GO ON TORNADO WATCH

"I live and work in Hastings, Nebraska. It's in the part of the country that weathermen like to call tornado alley," says Terry Marshall. "We get a lot of storms every year that have the capacity to produce high winds, hail, and tornadoes. The trouble is that most people hear the sirens of a tornado warning and think that's their cue to go out in the street to see if they can see the funnel cloud with their own eyes. Or worse, they get in their cars and go out looking for it to get it on videotape.

"In more than twenty-five years in emergency management, I've seen many dozens of tornadoes—and I wish I hadn't seen any. I've watched buildings, homes, and barns instantly destroyed, as if they'd been blown up with sticks of dynamite. I've seen the funnels cut a path through a neighborhood, then turn around and come back for more.

"I know a few things about tornadoes that most people don't. For example, they don't all have a funnel shape. And they aren't all dark and easy to see. The dark color comes from the dirt and debris that the storm has pulled up from somebody's land. Until it touches ground or destroys a home, it has no color at all.

"The worst part of my job is sifting through rubble, trying to find people who refused to take shelter when the authorities asked them to or who got in their cars and tried to outrun the storm. For my sake, take shelter when the weatherman says there's a tornado in your area. Leave the storm watching to him."

of your house. The strong winds may smash windows or pull off the roof, so you'll want to be as far away from the destruction as possible. If you live in a mobile home or are staying in a camper, you should evacuate immediately and head to the home of a friend who has a basement.

Hide in the closet. If you have no basement, take shelter in a windowless room such as a bathroom or closet. A bathroom is good because it has a minimum of loose debris and because the bathtub will likely offer some extra protection.

Stow yourself under the stairs. Terry Marshall says that another excellent place to hide is under a stairwell. It's small and sturdy, and that's what you're looking for in a shelter.

Don't open the windows. Back in the 1950s, the prevailing advice was to open the windows before a tornado approached. "The idea was to equalize the pressure inside and outside the house to minimize damage," says Terry Marshall. He warns that this advice is outdated for safety reasons. New windows take a while to unlock and open. You should spend that time finding shelter, not standing in front of a pane of glass that might shatter at any moment. "Property is replaceable," Terry says.

HURRICANES

High winds and flooding are the greatest dangers in a hurricane, and they're the elements that bring the greatest destruction. When you're looking for a place to hide, remember to find a room or area that's secure and on high ground. That means your basement is not a good choice. Try a windowless closet or the bathroom instead. Here are three more tips to get you through a hurricane—and the aftermath.

Check your policy. Many people who move into coastal areas don't realize that their home owner's insurance might not cover flooding caused by hurricanes. If that's the case with your policy, ask your insurance agent to give you information about the National Flood Insurance Program (NFIP). The NFIP makes federally backed flood insurance available to communities that agree to adopt certain policies to reduce future flood damage.

Clean up before the storm. Before a hurricane strikes, tidy up the yard. How's that? Well, the severe winds brought on by a storm can turn the most ordinary objects in your yard into missiles that can cause damage to your home and neighborhood. By removing stray toys and bringing lawn furniture and tools inside, you'll be making your neighborhood safer and your poststorm cleanup easier.

Stay away from windows. Because windows can shatter in a hurricane, you should retreat to a windowless room like a bathroom for safety. Pulling the blinds and closing the windows will give you extra protection against shattering glass and may make your cleanup easier.

EARTHQUAKES

Most of us are conditioned to think that earthquakes occur only in California. Not true! An earthquake can occur in almost any part of the country. No matter where you live, you'll want to know where to take shelter should the earth begin to shake.

Check every room. The best way to get through any seismic episode is to know where to take cover immediately. So to prepare for an earthquake, take a walk around your house now and identify safe areas in each room. Desks and heavy tables are good for hiding under. Or you may find an inside wall that seems safe from falling debris. Be sure to choose a spot away from windows, mirrors, and other glass objects that could shatter. And steer clear of bookcases, heavy pictures, and any furniture that might tumble over.

Brace the chandelier. During an earthquake, lots of things will be shaken up, but you don't want them turning into dangerous debris. If you live in an area where earthquakes are likely,

MAKE it LAST
Save your breakables

MOST COOKS have loads of glass in their kitchens—and I'm not even talking about plates and drinking glasses. I mean the bevy of spice bottles, vinegar bottles, olive oil bottles, and sauce jars that are stored in your pantry. If you live in an earthquake-prone area, you can save yourself a real mess—and all that food— by placing breakable bottles on the lowest shelves in the pantry. That way, they won't have far to fall. You can further secure the area by putting latches on the doors. Even the plastic latches sold as child safety devices will keep pantry doors closed, and that will help keep the bottles contained so that they won't fall out.

you should take time to secure overhead lighting fixtures, particularly those—such as chandeliers and pendulum lights—that don't mount flush to the ceiling. Tighten loose screws and replace any defective parts.

You should take similar precautions with cabinets where breakable dinnerware is stored. Keeping cabinet doors closed will help keep your dishes from turning into debris.

Go on fire watch. You know that when the ground starts to shake, your belongings will end up in a heap. You're probably most concerned about staying safe as the debris lands. Unfortunately, that's only one of the possible outcomes of an earthquake. Another related hazard is fire. Flammable liquids stored in your home—everything from pesticides to alcohol—can become accelerants to a fire if they're not stored properly. Store these things in low cabinets that lock securely, so that they don't leak and spread danger during a quake.

171

FLOODS

Heavy rains and snows can have serious consequences for people in low-lying areas. When the weatherman predicts flooding, you may have hours or even days to make safety preparations. But if the prediction is for flash flooding, you may have very little time to escape. Don't worry; just as Noah had the Man Upstairs to get him through the Flood, you have our expert advice.

Get gas. When the weatherman warns of possible flooding, head to the gas station. If floodwaters do approach your area, you'll probably be asked to evacuate. Having a full tank of gas when you hear the evacuation order is the best kind of readiness.

Be wary of water. If floodwaters seep into your basement, you may be tempted to wade around in them to rescue your valuables. That's a mistake for two reasons. First, the water is unsanitary and could make you sick. Second, it may have come in contact with an electrical short—and that makes it deadly. So in the case of flooding, the best defense is a good offense. If you have valuable papers and photographs, store them in a watertight container on the highest level of your house.

Tie it up. Not all floods come from rainwater. Some are caused by water heaters that get knocked loose during a violent storm. You can prevent your water heater from becoming a water main by strapping it to the wall studs around it.

Walk slowly and carry a big stick. During a flood, you should always avoid walking through the water. Floodwaters move swiftly, and even a few inches of water is enough to drown in once you've been knocked off your feet. If you have no choice but to walk through still floodwaters to reach safety, grab a long stick such as a broom handle to help guide you. Use the stick to feel your way through the waters so that you can tell exactly how deep it is. Make sure you know where the ground is before you take each step.

Look for critters. Once you return to a home that has suffered flood damage, you'll want to have that same broom handle, hockey stick, or other long pole. In addition to causing damage to your home, floodwaters will occasionally bring visitors inside. Small wild animals, especially snakes, may have been flooded out of their homes, too, and sought shelter in yours. Use the broom to overturn objects and check for unexpected houseguests. The good news is that your return should frighten them away.

Don't light up. Once you returned to your home, you may find that you don't have electricity. You'll be anxious to survey the damage that's been done, but don't let your anxiety lead you to make a deadly choice. Never light candles or cigarette lighters inside a home that has been vacated in a natural disaster. Many things could have happened in your absence, including a gas leak. Use your flashlight to inspect for damage, unless you know that the gas has been turned off and the house has been aired out.

Making Your Home Safe for Others

Once you've eliminated common safety hazards that might affect your family members, you have to start thinking about ways to make your home safe for casual visitors and neighbors. Swimming pools, hot tubs, and swings out back have become what lawyers call "attractive nuisances." Unfortunately, if a neighborhood child comes into your yard, even when you're not at home, you could be liable for any accidents that happen. Here's how to prevent them.

Fence in your pool. If you have a swimming pool, a hot tub or even a tennis court, you should invest in fencing for your

FIVE INGENIOUS WAYS TO REDUCE YOUR INSURANCE BILLS

Let's face it. Everybody hates insurance, because it always feels as though you're paying something for nothing. Here are five tips to help you pay a little bit less.

1. Get all your insurance from one company, and it will probably offer you a discount of 10 to 15 percent. If the company doesn't offer, be sure to ask.

2. Find out what sort of discount you can get on premiums for adding extra security measures to your home and car. For example, you'll probably be able to get a discount on auto theft insurance if you have a car alarm. There are lots of inexpensive household alarm systems that may give you a discount on your home owner's insurance. If you're a nonsmoker, you can probably get a discount for that, too.

3. Raise your deductibles on your car and home owner's insurance. Changing your deductible from $250 to $500 can take 10 percent off the annual cost of your insurance. Think of insurance as coverage for catastrophic events, not for smaller incidents and repairs.

4. Look through your policy for line items to deduct—for example, the line in your car insurance for replacement transportation. That means you're paying the insurance company for a service that you will probably never need. Even if you do need it, it will probably cost less than your deductible.

5. Never buy specialty insurance. That's the stuff they sell at the airport before you get on a plane. Airport insurance policies that will pay your mortgage if you become incapacitated and additional insurance policies on rental cars are unnecessary and often overpriced.

backyard. Some states require fences of a certain height and even padlocks for the gates to such areas to keep people out when there's no adequate supervision. This is an excellent idea no matter where you live. It lets neighborhood kids know that they need your permission and supervision before they use your pool or tennis court.

Use the big cover-up. Hot tubs can be wonderful, but they can also be dangerous. Even though the water is shallow, it's still deep enough for someone to drown in. If you get a hot tub for your back porch, invest in a hard cover. It costs a bit more than an ordinary plastic tarp, but it saves energy by sealing in the heat. And it can be padlocked to keep out kids and animals that might otherwise get in and get hurt (the hot water can be very dangerous). This also will keep your own kids from getting in the tub when you're not around.

Gear up. The amount of debris tossed around by a lawn mower should make you concerned for any person you hire to mow your yard. Even if you're hiring a neighborhood kid to do some yard work, insist that she dress properly. Don't allow sandals or bare feet. Insist on sturdy shoes and eye protection (sunglasses will do) before she starts to work. You should also provide something—a broom handle, an old hockey stick, or another instrument—for her to dig out clogged grass clippings from the mower so that she won't be tempted to use her hands.

ADAPTING YOUR HOME FOR SENIORS

If you have an older friend or relative who is coming to live with you, or even just to visit, you can make a few changes to help that person feel safe and comfortable. Here are some of our expert tips to help you out.

Get a handle on things. When you reach a certain age, your biggest fear is falling, and even a small step may seem treacherous. If visitors have to take a step up from your front porch to

D-style handles make climbing stairs to reach a door easier for older folks.

your house, you can give them extra support by installing a handle outside your door. It doesn't have to be expensive. You can buy a simple D-style handles, which would normally be used on a drawer, at the hardware store.

Attach the handle to the door frame, with the handle going up and down. Screw it right into the frame at a height of 3½ to 4 feet. That's just the right height for someone to grab onto and give himself a boost as he comes up the step. It's especially useful for visitors who use walkers, because even a single step up can be awkward for them.

Give 'em a hand. You've checked to make sure that the handrail on your staircase is secure. Now make sure it's long enough. Most people don't lean on a handrail until they are on the stairs, but older folks need a little extra help with even that first step. By installing a handrail that is accessible from the landing at the top and bottom of a staircase, you can prevent a number of accidents, and you can make your visitors much more confident and mobile in your home. An extra 6 to 8 inches on each end should do the trick. You also may want to install a handrail in your hallway to provide extra support along the way.

A GLOWING RECOMMENDATION

When Barbara Falla of Natick, Massachusetts, worked full-time as a nurse, she noticed that hospitals often applied glow-in-the-dark tape to steps so they were lit even when the lights were low. Now she uses the tape at home to make sure older visitors and young children can see where they're going. The tape is available at most craft stores and some hardware stores.

Bright lights, big safety. You may think that night-lights are just for kids, but older people need them, too. If you're afraid that someone will fall in the middle of the night, consider putting a night-light in the hallway between the bedroom and bathroom or near the top and bottom of the staircase. This is a particularly good idea in the winter, when people often start the day when the world is still dark.

Make the water heater cooler. Older relatives may have trouble tolerating high water temperatures. You can prevent scalding accidents by lowering the temperature on your water heater from 140°F to 120°F. You'll still have plenty of hot water for a shower at that temperature, you'll save money on your heating bill, and you'll protect a loved one.

Create space. It's easy for most people to negotiate their way around furniture, but if you're inviting guests who use walkers, you may want to rearrange your furniture to make sure they have enough space to get around the room and down hallways. Most people need 2 feet of space between pieces of furniture for a comfortable walkway, but people with walkers need the entire width of a standard doorway, which is about 2½ feet.

WHATSIT?

Q: The small cup on the right sits inside the little bucket on the left. The bucket sits in the top of this object, which is about 9½ inches high. In the bottom is a small lantern, and the base evidently holds oil. There is also a handle for carrying or holding. What is it?

A: This appears to be a sailor's stove and hand warmer, used when a man had to stand watch alone on deck. Using this ingenious contraption, he could heat water in the pail, make a cup of hot tea, and warm his hands while drinking it.

You'll also want to remove any loose throw rugs that may get snagged under the walker and cause an accident. By the same token, you'll want to keep any toys, stray magazines, television remote controls, and other obstacles tucked neatly away to prevent falls.

Just point and click. Some seniors move to Florida. Others take up golf. But Michael Melchiorri advises retirees to invest first in an automatic garage door opener. "Opening a garage door doesn't seem like a big deal, but as you get older, it can be a real health risk," Michael says. Bending down and pulling up on the door can cause back injuries and heart attacks. With an automatic opener, people can just push a button and avoid the sudden strain that could be fatal.

MAKING A CHILD-SAFE HOME

When children come to visit, they bring all their energy and curiosity with them. Unfortunately, that curiosity can put them in danger. You can help eliminate potential problems with a bit of planning. Department stores sell a variety of childproof products to lock cabinets and cover electrical outlets, all of which are a good idea. In addition to those, you can make your own ingenious safety devices.

Put a cork in it. If you have a toy box or hope chest at home, you might have an accident waiting to happen. Children tend to be careless with lids, and the next thing you know, a lid comes

crashing down on a child's little fingers. Prevent this by taking the corks from a couple of wine bottles and nailing them to the corners of the toy box. If the lid comes down, it will hit the corks, sparing the child's fingers or even his head. This ingenious device also will keep kids from shutting themselves in trunks or hope chests.

Cut corners. There are lots of baby catalogs advertising products that will pad the sharp corners of tables and other furniture. Barbara Falla's solution is simpler. She uses the insulation made for copper pipes to do the trick. It's inexpensive and easy to find at most hardware stores. Just glue it on or attach it with finishing nails to give your child's or grandchild's world a softer edge.

Have a traveling first-aid kit. As your family grows, so should your first-aid kit. For instance, new mothers should have ipecac syrup and activated charcoal powder on hand to give to a child who swallows one of several poisonous substances. What

GET A CERTIFIED BABYSITTER

"When my husband and I first moved to Natick, Massachusetts, years ago, I knew that I needed to hire a babysitter for our two young children," says nurse and social worker Barbara Falla. "Like many new mothers, I knew that I wanted my kids to be safe, but I wasn't sure exactly how to screen a sitter to find out if she had the right stuff. Luckily, I interviewed Linda, a girl who lived down the street.

"Linda came to the door with her Red Cross Babysitter's Certificate of Safety in hand, even though she was only 11 years old. At that time, I had no idea what this certificate meant. She explained that she'd taken a course in which she'd learned things like the Heimlich maneuver and CPR. I thought I would be interviewing her for the job, but instead she interviewed me. She wanted to know where the first-aid kit and fire extinguishers were. She wanted the phone number for the poison control center, the fire department, and our doctor.

"Of course, Linda got the job, and she was our babysitter for many years. She never needed to use any of that information, but I was awfully glad that she had it. I'd recommend sending any babysitter to the Red Cross, even if you have to sponsor the course yourself. It costs about $60 but saves a lot of worry."

CHILD PROOFING YOUR HOME— IN A HURRY

When Barbara Falla's grandson comes to visit, she takes a quick walk around the house looking for ways to make it a little safer for him. Here's how you can do the same thing when a last-minute visitor brings a young child to your home.

1. Move the potted plants out of reach. They could become a toxic snack or be pulled over, heavy pot and all, and cause an injury.

2. If the on/off knobs for your oven are near the door, just pull them off and put them in a drawer until your little visitor goes home. That way, he won't be able to turn on the burners and get hurt.

3. Remove all toiletries from under the bathroom and kitchen sinks unless you can lock the cabinet doors securely. Store the stuff on a high shelf out of reach.

4. Pick up throw rugs. They are the first things a child will trip over.

5. Put breakable knickknacks on a high shelf.

6. Check your upholstery and clothing for loose buttons. Any small object that can break off easily can become a choking hazard.

7. Tie up the cords from your blinds and curtains to keep them out of reach.

you might not remember, though, is that you may need these items when you go to visit relatives.

When you visit your parents or other relatives, and certainly if your child stays with them for an afternoon, make sure they have these items on hand and know when and how to use them. (You might present them with a Red Cross first-aid book if they're not sure, or get literature from the poison control center and have them keep it in their first-aid kit.) You can also take along the phone number of the poison control center and tape it to the phone. Accidental poisoning is one emergency in which every second counts.

PART 2

GETTING THE MOST FROM YOUR

home life

In some circles people are known for their jobs. But just as many folks are known for the things they do on their own time: They can whip up gourmet meals with leftovers or they're terrific fishermen. Maybe it's just that their fingernails are always neatly manicured.

If your aspirations include giving stellar parties or simply not being picked last for the company bowling team, you've come to the right place.

This section is devoted to the things that make living a richer experience. For instance, in these pages you'll learn to be a better softball player, find out how to stay healthy and safe, discover ways to throw more stress-free parties, and learn to be a craftier craftsperson. Does that sound like a tall order? Our ingenious experts are up to the challenge.

clever cooking
ideas

WHAT'S FOR DINNER? It's the eternal question that rings out every afternoon in kitchens all across the country. The secret about cooking is that it doesn't have to be a chore. Bring a little ingenuity into the kitchen, and you can whip up a delicious meal in a few minutes with just a few items pulled from your pantry.

For this chapter, we consulted an array of cooking experts, who represent many facets of cooking. Nancy Seaton of Hastings, Nebraska, is an enthusiastic home cook who offers up some hearty home-style recipes. Lynn Naliboff, a New York City–based food

GREAT AMERICAN COOKING

learned to cook in the army, during World War II," says Ed Jensen of Hastings, Nebraska. "In the photos of my unit, I'm the one in the middle, wearing the chef's hat. When I came home from the war, I opened a bakery and cafe in Hastings, and ran it for thirty years. I fed and got to know almost everyone in town. They loved my peanut brittle, my sour cream raisin pies, and my wedding cakes. The most famous dish I made in those years was a sort of German version of shepherd's pie. I don't know where the recipe came from; maybe I picked it up in the army.

"Anyway, you brown one pound of ground beef with some onions, drain off the fat, and put it in an eight- by eight-inch pan. Spread on a layer of sauerkraut and cover that with a layer of leftover mashed potatoes. If you have some leftover fresh or canned vegetables, you can chop those and put them between the layer of kraut and potatoes, but you don't have to. Heat the whole pan at 350°F for a half hour, and there's your dinner.

"People came into my café and asked for that dish—asked for seconds, too. The ladies across the street at the beauty parlor would even go off their diets for it every Tuesday. It's the simple foods that people like best."

editor, explains a quick and easy way to feed—and impress—last-minute guests.

We rounded up some professional chefs, too. Chef Karl Ronhave of Portland, Maine, shares some of his cooking tips, including a suggestion for stretching dishes. And personal chefs Sandy Phillips of Medfield, Massachusetts, and Karen Bates, of Kansas City, Kansas, offer ingenious ways to use up leftovers. Finally, chef Tim Rodgers, associate dean at the Culinary Institute of America in Hyde Park, New York, tells you which kitchen gadgets you shouldn't live without. You might be surprised by what shows up on his list—and what doesn't.

Simple Meal Solutions

It's six o'clock, and you just got home from work. Everyone in the house is hungry—including you—and opening a cookbook or going to the store sounds far too ambitious.

This is the scene that home cooks face far more often than they'd care to admit. But don't give up. Rather than reaching for the phone to order pizza or an expensive take-out meal, heed the advice of our ingenious experts. They'll have you whipping up meals with what you probably already have in your kitchen and turning leftovers into mouthwatering treats.

MARVELOUS MEALS WITH FOUR (OR FEWER) INGREDIENTS

Cooking delicious meals with just four ingredients sounds like the impossible dream. But the truth is, people actually love simple dishes. Ask Nancy Seaton, who's been volunteering in the snack bar of her local hospital for more than 20 years. "Give someone a grilled cheese sandwich, and the whole world looks better to her,"

GREAT MEAL, CORNER POCKET

Need a dinner idea that's easy to prepare and a snap to clean up? Food editor Lynn Naliboff offers this ingeniously simple idea. Cut out four 8-inch squares of aluminum foil and spray each with nonstick cooking spray. Place small wedges of potatoes and onions and strips of green peppers in the center of each square. Place one 4-ounce chicken breast, pounded, on top of the vegetables, then drizzle each with 1 tablespoon of your favorite marinade. Fold up the edges of the foil and seal, then cut a small slit in each packet with a knife. Bake at 400°F for about 40 minutes.

---

she says. Nancy knows a thing or two about home cooking. She grew up in a family with two working parents, and her mother, who worked as a surgical nurse until she was 75 years old, knew a few tricks about feeding her family quickly and nutritiously.

Make some macaroni and tomatoes. We used to beg Mom to make macaroni and tomatoes," Nancy recalls. The recipe was ingeniously simple. Her mother added a 28-ounce can of stewed tomatoes to 2 cups cooked macaroni. Then she'd bring the whole thing to a boil and add salt and pepper. "We loved it," Nancy says. Of course, you could add some cheese if you wanted, or perhaps a package of frozen spinach, thawed and drained. And that's still only four ingredients.

Help your hamburger. Nancy Seaton's mom also made an easy hamburger and rice dish. She loved it because it was fast and she could use uncooked Minute brand rice. Here's how you can do the same. In a skillet, sauté about ½ cup chopped onion with a pound of hamburger. Once the meat is browned, drain off the fat and add 1 cup uncooked Minute rice and a 28-ounce can of stewed tomatoes. Simmer for 30 minutes, adding salt and pepper and a little water if needed. If you like, add a 10-ounce package of frozen mixed vegetables to give the dish a stewlike consistency.

Liven up your chicken with salsa. After a while, ordinary chicken dishes can get boring. You can liven yours up with a little heat. Cut up enough boneless chicken to feed your family and sauté it in olive oil with some chopped onion or even some sliced mushrooms. Add a 16-ounce jar of salsa, then stir until it's heated through. Shred some Monterey Jack cheese on top and voilà! Dinner is served. All it needs is a side salad. If you're feeling adventurous, add a dash or two of ground cumin or coriander to the chicken as it cooks.

Make lazy man's lasagna. Lasagna is one of the simplest and most satisfying dishes around, but it's also time-consuming to make. If you just don't have the time (or the inclination) to layer those ingredients, just stir them all together. Here's how.

Cook 1 pound ziti. Heat up some homemade or store-bought sauce and stir that into the cooked ziti along with 8 ounces ricotta cheese. If you want to add a green vegetable to this dish, shred a small zucchini onto a clean dish towel and squeeze out all the juice. Add it to the ziti. The zucchini will give the sauce a meaty texture (with none of the fat) and add garden-fresh nutrients.

FEEDING UNEXPECTED GUESTS

The great thing about living in a small town, says cooking enthusiast Nancy Seaton, is that you have so many friends. The challenge is feeding those friends when they drop by without much warning. After years of practice, she's accumulated some clever fixes.

Prepare a minibarbecue. If you need an appetizer that will appeal to a crowd of men, Nancy recommends keeping packages of those little smoked sausages (Little Smokies is one brand) on hand. When company shows up, heat the sausages in the microwave on Medium for about 1 minute to get a little of the grease out. Then combine a 10-ounce jar of grape jelly and a 10-ounce jar of chili sauce (honest) and pour it onto the sausages. It makes an

WHATSIT?

Q: One of our readers "spent good money" on this item at an auction but has no idea what it is. It is made of lightweight wood and is 7½ inches long and 2¾ inches wide. Any ideas?

A: These corrugated paddles were called Scotch hands and were used more than 50 years ago to roll pieces of butter into balls. They were a factory-made product.

the great dump cake

NO ONE HAS ever accused me of being a great cook," says T. J. Wilson of Monticello, Illinois. "That's why I married one. In fact, the only good recipe I have is for something called Dump Cake. I got it from a friend in college. It's a fast and delicious dessert that even a college-age male can produce flawlessly during halftime and still see all the first-half highlights. These days, my wife and I keep the ingredients on hand for those evenings when unexpected guests arrive.

1 can (14 or 16 ounces) cherries or other canned fruit, with juice
1 can (15 ounces) crushed pineapple, with juice
1 box (18¼ ounces) yellow or white cake mix
¼ to ½ cup butter
¾ cup brown sugar
  ground cinnamon for sprinkling

Preheat the oven to 400°F. Pour all the fruit with their juice into an ungreased 9- by 13-inch cake pan. Spread the fruit evenly in the pan.

Sprinkle the dry cake mix evenly on top of the fruit, but don't mix. Cut the butter into small pieces and sprinkle them on top of the cake mix. Then sprinkle on the brown sugar and cinnamon to taste. Bake for about 45 minutes or until a toothpick inserted into the center of the cake comes out clean.

"The most difficult part of this recipe is resisting the urge to stir it," says T. J. "Don't. The juice on the bottom of the pan will boil and percolate up through the cake, making a kind of fruit crisp that tastes great with ice cream. It'll make you very popular during the second half of that football game. I guarantee it."

impromptu barbecue sauce that's quite tasty. "It's a Fred Flintstone type of hors d'oeuvre," Nancy says. "Men lap it up."

Bake a batch of cookies. Nancy's mother used to make these quick Special K cookies when she was short on time. Melt ½ cup peanut butter and 1 cup chocolate chips. Stir in 3 cups Special K breakfast cereal. Drop the cookies onto waxed paper by the teaspoonful. They set up in 30 minutes or so and are delicious.

Make some macho nachos. Next time you have nacho-loving guests over during football season (or anytime) but don't want to deal with the cheesy mess, try this easy version. Open a 15-ounce can of chili (the kind without beans) and a 4.5-ounce can of diced green chilies. Dice or shred 16 ounces of Cheddar or Monterey Jack cheese. Combine all the ingredients in a microwave-safe bowl. Heat in the microwave on High for about 3 minutes or until the cheese melts. Stir and serve with corn chips.

Whip up an easy appetizer. If you have a can of refrigerated crescent rolls, a package of frozen chopped broccoli, and some fresh garlic and Parmesan cheese, you have the makings of a wonderful appetizer to serve last-minute guests, says Lynn Naliboff. Unroll the crescent dough and separate it at the perforations. Thaw the broccoli and place it in a medium bowl. Mince 2 cloves garlic and add to the broccoli. Add ¼ to ½ cup (depending on how cheesy you want it) grated Parmesan cheese. Spoon about 1 tablespoon of the broccoli mixture onto the center of each crescent dough triangle. Roll the dough up and bake according to the package directions. Serve the rolls alone or with some warm pasta or pizza sauce on the side.

Guac around the clock. Uh oh, the gang has stopped by and you're strapped for some munchies. Or are you? Here's a fast-to-fix guacamole. Mash 1 avocado and combine with some prepared salsa. Drizzle a little fresh lime juice on top and place in the refrigerator for about 30 minutes. (Place the avocado pit in the guacamole to prevent it from turning brown.) Serve with tortilla chips or crackers.

Scream for this ice cream topping. Here's one you won't believe. Let's say some friends have stopped by for dessert. You have vanilla ice cream in the freezer and no way to dress it up. Well, look in the pantry. If you have a 14- or 16-ounce can of cherries or cherry pie filling and a 12-ounce can of cola, you're in luck. Pour them both (including the cherry juice) into a saucepan and simmer over medium heat to reduce the mixture by one-half. The sauce will thicken into a tasty topping for the ice cream.

that's • ingenious!

improv in the kitchen

"AT THE BEGINNING of my career, I sometimes had trouble keeping up in the kitchen," says chef Karl Ronhave. "I was always frantically prepping for the crush of business during the dinner rush hour. Sometimes lesser tasks fell through the cracks.

"I remember one night I was supposed to make a simple tomato and basil soup as an appetizer, but I was so busy that I completely forgot. At five-thirty, the doors opened and six tables filled up right away. Ten minutes later, I was standing in the kitchen looking at three orders for tomato and basil soup. Rather than disappoint those customers, I decided to improvise. I chopped some basil, sautéed it in a little oil, poured in some cream, and stirred in a little tomato paste that I found on the shelf. Never before—or since—have I had so many compliments on a soup."

PIECRUST IN A JIFFY

Company's coming and you have no time to make a piecrust. Don't worry. Just use two knives or a pastry blender to cut 1 stick butter into 1 cup plus 2 tablespoons all-purpose flour. The best part? There's no need to roll it out. Just pat the mixture into a pie plate and add whatever filling you have on hand. This ingenious crust won't work for a two-crust pie, but it'll come through like a champ for a pecan, pumpkin, or custard pie or a fruit crisp.

Make any cake a Black Forest cake. Want to spruce up an ordinary chocolate cake mix for company? In a large bowl, combine a 20-ounce can of cherry pie filling, 3 eggs, and a package chocolate cake mix. Mix well (the mixture will be a bit thicker than usual) and pour into a greased and floured 9- by 13-inch sheet pan. Bake according to the package directions. Remove from the oven and let cool. Serve with icing or whipped cream.

COOK ONCE, EAT TWICE: USING LEFTOVERS

Not everybody loves leftovers, but cooks sure do. It gives them the night off and gives the food budget a rest, too. Savvy cooks know how to use up what's left in the fridge and freezer. Sometimes that means reminding your family that it's there, and sometimes it means dressing up yesterday's meal to fit today's appetite.

Create a cooking rotation. When you bring home groceries, it's always tempting to stuff them into the bulging fridge, pushing all the older stuff to the back. But that's the last thing you should do, says personal chef Sandy Phillips. Instead, move older items to the front of the fridge so that they get used—or at least noticed—before they go bad. That way, you won't end up with

FEEL LIKE CHICKEN TONIGHT?

Chances are good that you'll be eating some sort of chicken dish this week, whether it's a roaster or cutlets. Chances are even better that you'll have some leftovers. Whatever the chicken, it's easy to turn tonight's chicken dinner into tomorrow's chicken surprise, says Lynn Naliboff. Here are some of her favorite ways to use leftover chicken.

- Cut up leftover cooked chicken cutlets and serve them cold over a green salad.
- Shred leftover roast chicken for a savory chicken salad sandwich.
- Toss leftover grilled chicken into your favorite pasta dish for a hearty dinner.
- Create a chicken Parmesan pizza. Top a ready-made pizza shell with store-bought pizza sauce, shredded mozzarella cheese, and strips of leftover breaded chicken cutlets.
- Turn a plain baked potato into a full meal by topping it with shredded Cheddar cheese and cubed cooked chicken.

one lonely yogurt container rotting in the back corner. Sandy designates a special shelf in her refrigerator for leftovers. Her family knows to go there first for snack foods before preparing something new.

Label it. Frugal cooks know that freezing meats and leftovers is a great way to save time and money. The trouble, says personal chef Karen Bates is with the system. "Things used to get buried in my freezer," she admits. Back then, she had four kids and had to use the kitchen efficiently just to get everyone fed each week. So one day when she stood in front of the open freezer door holding spaghetti sauce that might be older than one of her kids, she knew the system wasn't working. Now she uses labels.

You can write on freezer bags with a permanent marker, but

the best labeling solution is plain old masking tape, which holds well in cold temperatures and provides a good writing surface. Then when you're ready to wash the bag or container and use it again, you can simply peel off the old label, rather than having to cross out an old one.

Write the name of the item and the date on the tape so that you'll know to use it within 3 months. Foods held longer than that form ice crystals, which indicate that the food is on the verge of going bad.

Be a cubist. Some leftovers present simply baffling problems. For instance, when a recipe calls for only half a can of stewed tomatoes, what do you do with the other half? You've made too much pesto, but you know the other half won't last in the fridge. It's times like these when your ice cube tray can come to the rescue. Fill the tray compartments with leftover anything— from wine to chicken stock to tomato sauce to pesto—and freeze it. Once the cubes are frozen, pop them out and transfer them to a resealable plastic freezer bag. The beauty of using this technique is that you can remove exactly what you need without having to thaw the whole bag.

PIPE SOME POTATOES

Lynn Naliboff loves leftover mashed potatoes. "They're one of the most versatile leftover foods around," she says. "You can use them to thicken a sauce or stew or as a topping for a quick shepherd's pie. For a fast but elegant side dish, place leftover mashed potatoes in a pastry bag or a resealable plastic bag with one corner snipped off. Pipe the potatoes in puffs on an ungreased baking sheet and bake at 350°F until they begin to brown, 5 to 10 minutes, depending on the size of the puffs."

YOU MAKE THE CALL

There's an episode of the Mary Tyler Moore Show in which Mary throws a dinner party. She wants everything to go perfectly because a congresswoman is the guest of honor. Mary decides to serve the entrée from a platter, allowing guests to serve themselves. That's a problem, because she offers the platter to her boss, Mr. Grant, first. Of course, he takes almost all the food, leaving nothing for the other guests. Hilarity ensues. It usually does on television.

If this happened to you, it probably wouldn't be quite so funny. But there's a lesson to be learned from Mary's dilemma. Anytime you fear you might be a tad short on food, family-style service ain't the way to go. Instead, plate the food yourself in the kitchen. That way, you control the portion size.

STRETCHING FOOD TO FEED MORE PEOPLE

Sandy Phillips remembers the Easter when everyone said yes to her offer of a sumptuous holiday meal. Unfortunately, the RSVPs arrived late; in fact they showed up the day after she'd done her grocery shopping. "I had no idea what to do," Sandy confesses. Luckily, some fast thinking helped, and she's willing to share her expert solutions.

Put your portions in perspective. "The thing about Americans is that our portion sizes are out of whack," Sandy says. The good news is that if you've bought enough food for 8, you can probably feed 12 without anyone going home hungry. So the first step is to relax and dole out smaller, healthier portions to your guests.

Let them eat salad. And lots of it. When Sandy's guests showed up, she was able to dive into the refrigerator and come up with enough vegetables to make a salad. Serving a first course of bread and salad, or even a plate of cold vegetables, pickles, and radishes, is a terrific way to take the edge off your guests' hunger so they won't notice that there's not much food on the table when the feast begins. At the very least, a big salad will take up space on the table and make it look full of food.

Stuff 'em with starch. "My mother-in-law was helping me cook that Easter, and she was a lifesaver," Sandy recalls. Her mother-in-law forbade her to go to the store for more food. Her recommendation was to boil a few more potatoes and come up with one more side dish. At the end of the day, no one went home hungry, and Sandy didn't have to spend an extra $20 to $30 just to feel more secure about entertaining.

FOOD FIRST-AID

The roast is too salty. The soup is too thin. The hollandaise is falling apart. Can this meal be saved? Of course it can; read on.

that's • ingenious!

freeze your spuds

"COOKED POTATOES don't freeze well because they get so mushy," says Karen Bates. "It's a lesson home cooks learn the hard way. For me, freezing mashed potatoes became a personal challenge. After all, a delicious meat loaf and mashed potato make-ahead dinner isn't the same without the mashed potato part. I finally discovered the secret ingredient to perfect mashed potatoes that can be frozen and thawed. It is fat.

"When you mash potatoes, you add liquid to help break them down, then butter, sour cream, or some other type of fat to season them. I found that if you stir the fat in first and then add the liquid, it helps bind the potato so that when it freezes and thaws, it keeps almost all of its original texture."

Try a thickening agent. If your sauce or a soup is a little on the thin side, turn to the same thickening agents that chefs use. Add a little tomato paste or cornstarch (thin it with a little water first to get out the clumps). Beef up gravy with a little flour. Thicken soup with some instant mashed potatoes.

Beat it. Once in a while, Karl Ronhave will turn his back on a hollandaise, and the whole darn thing will separate. Despite what you may be thinking, that doesn't mean he has to start over. What a waste that would be. Instead, Karl adds a bit more butter to the sauce, places the bowl over low heat, and whisks the mixture. "All you're doing with hollandaise is beating air into the sauce until it thickens," Karl says. "Just by beating more air into it, the sauce will repair itself."

that's · ingenious!

turn up the heat

CHEF KARL RONHAVE has been working in restaurant kitchens for more than a decade, and he remembers more than a few evenings when he ran short of an ingredient or two. But you can stretch most dishes by adding spice or heat to them, he says. For example, when he needs to get more bang out of mashed potatoes, he adds a little cheese or maybe some horseradish. It makes the dish more filling and memorable, so that he can serve smaller portions.

Turn cake into trifle. Ed Jensen ran a bakery and café in Hastings, Nebraska, for 30 years, so he knows a thing or two about salvaging baking mistakes. When Ed had a cake that didn't rise evenly, he didn't throw it away. Instead, he made it into a different kind of dessert—a trifle. First, he cut the cake into cubes and put half of them in the bottom of a deep, clear bowl. Next, he added a layer of pureed raspberries or raspberry

MAKE it LAST

Eggs to the back

REFRIGERATORS OFTEN come with built-in egg containers, but they're in exactly the wrong spot. Never store eggs in the door of the refrigerator. That's the part that warms up a little every time you open the door.

To stay fresh (and bacteria-free), eggs need to stay cold, which means they belong inside the fridge—toward the back and on the top shelf, please. Store them right next to your other dairy products, which also need to stay cold to stay fresh.

jam, a layer of fresh fruit or cut-up bananas, the remaining cake cubes, some whipped cream, and maybe some nuts. Suddenly, that second-rate cake was transformed into a first-rate dessert.

Recycle your roast. Once you've overcooked meat, you're done for. That's the old wisdom anyway. But clever cooks have found a way to reuse meat that would seem tough or dry if served as the main course. Karl Ronhave says that overcooked meat can be reused as sausage. Simply grind the meat, mix it with spices, and stuff it into casings. Then heat and serve.

COLA IN, SALT OUT

What happens when your ham is too salty? Nancy Seaton shares the solution her mother swore by. Whenever she suspected that a ham was going to be too salty, she poured a can of cola over it before she put it in the oven. The sweetness in the cola leached out (or at least masked) the excess salt. Maybe that's why ham goes so well with sweet relish.

serve soup, save money

PERSONAL CHEF Sandy Phillips serves her family soup about once a week. Does she do this because it's economical, because it's easy, or because it uses up all those vegetables that look like they've seen better days? Yes.

You, too, can serve an instant soup from those forgotten veggies. Just heat up some chicken or beef broth or some bouillon cubes and water. Chop the vegetables (making sure to remove any brown spots) and add them to the liquid. Next, add your favorite starch—rice, vermicelli broken into small pieces, a cup of lentils or barley, or even a can of chickpeas swiped from the half-empty pantry. Bring to a boil, reduce the heat, and simmer. Sprinkle in whatever herbs seem appropriate and serve.

Karl also says that when a cut of fish gets a tad overcooked in a professional kitchen, it's likely to show up the next day in a fish chowder. There, the slightly firmer texture of the fish works well.

SALVAGING FOODS THAT ARE ABOUT TO GO BAD

You open the refrigerator door, and what do you see? A crisper drawer full of vegetables that are on the edge of extinction. Before you mourn their passing (and all the money that's about to be wasted), take a deep breath. There are ways to save them.

Roast old vegetables. The trouble with vegetables that have been sitting around a day too long is that they just don't look appetizing anymore. And you know that steaming them isn't going to make them look any peppier. That's why you should do what professional chefs do with their peaking vegetables: Roast them. Chop up those vegetables and toss them with a tablespoon of olive oil, some salt and pepper, even a little garlic or a favorite herb. Preheat the oven to 400°F. Spread the vegetables on a

IS IT FRESH?

Using products that are a bit past their prime can be a frugal way to stretch ingredients—unless you're talking about meat, dairy products, or eggs. Those ingredients should never be used unless they are fresh, because that's the only time they're safe. Here are two ways to test those foods' freshness.

Eggs can't swim. One way to determine whether an egg is fresh is to drop it into a bowl of water. Eggshells are porous and are continually losing moisture from the inside. As that happens, the egg white gets smaller and smaller, leaving a growing pocket of air inside the shell. If the egg is fresh and full of moisture, it will sink like a stone. If the egg is past its prime, the air pocket will cause it to stand up like a soldier or, worse, float in the water. If your eggs can swim, their freshness is fishy. Throw them out.

The nose knows. If you want to know whether a piece of meat or fish is fresh, your nose will tell you. Everyone knows what bad chicken smells like, and bad fish smells like, well, fish. Fresh fish should smell of the ocean, but not very fishy. Chef Karl Ronhave knows that fishy-smelling fish has been dead a little too long. If the fish is slimy, too, that's a sure sign that it's past its prime. Dangerous bacteria have begun to consume the fish.

Karl buys his meat and fish from a butcher or fishmonger rather than a supermarket. Those specialists often sell to restaurants and cafeterias in the area. That means that the fish and meat they have in stock doesn't stay around long enough to go bad. "If you must buy your fish at the supermarket," Karl advises, "take a good whiff of it before you buy it. Then you'll know how fresh it really is."

baking sheet and bake for 30 minutes or so. Roasting intensifies the flavor of vegetables, which is why they'll taste great. Unfortunately (or is that fortunately?), there won't be any leftovers.

Smooth your fruit. At the Culinary Institute of America, the person in charge of preparing the fruit plate for morning brunch at the school's restaurant is also in charge of making the smoothies. That way, every piece of fruit that isn't perfectly formed or that's just a bit overripe can go directly into the blender with a little ice and a little skim milk or juice to make a delicious drink.

If the berries in your fridge are peaking and you're not craving a smoothie at the moment, just put them in the freezer and wait a couple of days until the mood strikes. Then blend the fruit with juice and yogurt and enjoy.

Cooking Equipment You Shouldn't Live Without

Chef Tim Rodgers hates most kitchen gadgets. As associate dean of the Culinary Institute of America, he's seen his share. He's been teaching aspiring chefs at the institute for 14 years, and he always gives them the same list of essentials.

Choose your knives carefully. Go to a kitchen supply store, and they'll try to sell you 20 knives. But you need only 2, as long as they're good ones. "Go ahead and spend fifty dollars on a good eight- or ten-inch chef's knife, and it will outlive you and your children," Tim says. In addition to that chef's knife, pick up a paring knife for smaller jobs. With those two, the home cook can do almost anything.

Buy a cheap peeler. Forget the peeler with a padded handle and removable blade you'll find at

---

annals of ingenuity

O CANADA—PASS THE GRAVY

It's a case of Canadian ingenuity. In 1961, Edward Asselbergs, who worked for the Canadian Department of Agriculture in Ottawa, created the world's first instant potato flakes.

Now don't pooh-pooh instant mashed potatoes. It's true that they can't hold a candle to the real thing, but those flakes do come in handy when you need to thicken a soup or stew.

THE JOY OF PLASTIC

Plastic bags and plastic wrap are the unsung heros of the kitchen, says Tim Rodgers. They can cut time and aggravation and help you cook more safely. Here are three ways to put them to work in your kitchen.

1. It's a grater cover. When a recipe calls for grated lemon peel, just wrap the outside of the box grater with plastic wrap, then grate as usual. When you're done, just strip off the plastic wrap and scrape off the peel with a knife.

2. It's a stock cooler. After you make soup stock, you have to cool it before putting it in the freezer. But as soon as you turn off the heat, bacteria begin to grow. The danger zone for foods is 40° to 140°F. That's why safety-conscious cooks use resealable plastic bags to speed up the cooling process. Pour the stock or soup into a bag, then place the bag in a bowl of ice water. The liquid will cool faster so that you can freeze or refrigerate it safely.

3. It's a pastry bag. Cloth pastry bags are expensive and hold odors. Tim's students use resealable plastic bags instead. Just scoop frosting into a bag and seal it. Cut a corner off the bag and decorate at will. When you're finished, just throw away the bag.

---

gourmet cooking shops. The cheap ones were made to take the beating you're going to give them, and when they can't take it anymore, just throw them out and start over. That's what chefs do. "The expensive ones tend to take too much off the vegetable, but the cheap ones work the way they're supposed to," Tim says.

Opt for heavy pots. Forget those flimsy little Teflon pans. Chefs use big, heavy pots that heat up slowly and evenly. You'll find them at restaurant supply stores or auctions, and they'll last forever. The best thing is that they have metal handles, so you can brown food on top of the stove, then put the whole thing in the oven to finish it.

chapter 11

ingenious
entertaining

EVERYBODY LOVES A PARTY. Where else can you find good food and sparkling conversation with all your favorite people? Of course, hosting a party means making the plans, cleaning the house, cooking, and dealing with the thousand and one details leading up to the big event. You also have to face the general anxiety that comes with planning an event and opening your home to people you care about or would like to get to know better.

Not to worry. Our experts have a treasure trove of ways to help you plan a seamless event without spending your life savings. For instance, expert entertainer Norma Hansen of Hastings,

Nebraska, will teach you how to create a stunning menu that won't keep you up cooking all night. Caterer Susan Lane, who owns the Open Kitchen Gourmet Shop in Weston, Massachusetts, has some ideas for innovative centerpieces and keeping your kitchen from looking cluttered during even the most hectic parties.

You'll also learn how to throw a party for kids without worrying about tears and tantrums, how to keep kids entertained, and how to organize these parties so that cleanup is a snap. Let the party begin!

Getting Started

Most people think they'd like to entertain more. The thing that stops them is fear, especially about how to get started. When you start to feel harried about entertaining, just refer to the advice of our everyday experts to get over that first hurdle.

PROPER PLANNING PREVENTS POOR PARTIES

Norma Hansen has been entertaining friends for decades. Now that she's a widow living in a small apartment, she enjoys seeing her friends even more and throws dinner parties as often as she can. "The thing to remember is that inviting someone to your house for dinner is the ultimate compliment you can give them," Norma says. "You don't have to try too hard to impress them once they arrive." Norma has several ingenious rules about planning an easy party, even if you're doing it on your own in a small home.

Keep the menu simple. "Select a simple menu," Norma advises. "Of course, that's not to say that the food you serve can't be elegant." For example, Norma limits the number of elements in any meal to four—but each of those elements shines. There's a

PLAN A PERFECT PARTY

If the mere thought of planning, cooking, and cleaning for a party has you exhausted, separate the tasks, make a plan, and do as much as you can ahead of time. Here's a game plan that will help you do just that.

1. Two weeks before your event. Plan the menu and make your shopping lists. Start thinking about decorations or themes, if any.

2. One week before your event. Clean the house thoroughly. Move furniture to accommodate the bar or serving areas. Borrow extra chairs if necessary. Get all this done, and all you'll have to do is tidy up before your guests arrive. Shop for nonperishables.

3. Three days before your event. Preview the table setting; set up two or three places to see how it's going to look. This is also a good time to make sure you have enough silverware, plates, glasses, and serving platters. Shop for perishables.

4. The day before your event. Make your last trip to the store. Do you need ice? Now's the time to get it. Assemble the dishes you can in advance, including pasta salads and desserts.

5. The evening before the event. Set the table. Assemble any dishes that can sit overnight. Make a detailed written timeline for the day of the party, including when dishes need to go into and come out of the oven.

salad course, a meat course, a vegetable course, and a dessert. "You make the dinner elegant by buying the best ingredients you can afford, not by cooking complicated dishes," she says.

That rules goes for your bar, too. Hosts often fret about stocking an extensive bar for their guests. Buying alcohol and mixers for everyone's favorite drink is needlessly expensive and frustrating. "People come to your house to see you and each other, not to drink their favorite drinks," Norma says. She offers wine with dinner and two other types of cocktails. That policy contains both the expense and the storage space for an extensive bar.

Make your mark. One way to make a simple dinner seem more exotic is to add your own special touches, says Norma. For her, that means ending the meal with a delicious homemade dessert (one that can be made well in advance, of course). "It puts the crowning touch on the dinner," she says. In addition, she may put together a substantial salad with mesclun greens or with a few fresh raspberries tossed in. Adding a couple of personal touches will wow your guests much more than a complex soufflé or hollandaise sauce that will leave you stressed-out and grumpy when the dinner begins.

SETTING UP FOR EASY CLEANUP

Caterer Susan Lane has prepared parties in her own home and many others. The challenge, she says, is to keep the clutter cleared without taking time and energy away from your guests. Here are some ingenious ways to do just that.

Bus dishes like a pro. If you have a serving tray with handles, like the one you might use to serve breakfast in bed, leave it out in the party area. You can even invest in a couple of inexpensive wicker trays of this kind. "Then you—or whoever is helping you—can just stack the dishes and cups on the trays and bus the stuff into the kitchen," Susan says. After time, guests will get the hint and stack their used dishes on these trays for you. This will save trips back and forth and keep neglected cups and plates from overturning and making an even bigger mess.

Keep trash out of sight. Susan Lane always sets up her parties the same way. She hangs a trash bag on a nail in the garage. As the party progresses, she takes dishes out to the garage, where she scrapes the leftover food into the hanging bag. Then she stacks the dishes (also in the garage, where they won't clutter up the kitchen, making it look like a disaster area). "It keeps the kitchen looking neat, which will help you and your guests relax," Susan says. And when you're ready to clean up, the dishes are stacked neatly in one place and ready to wash.

Make quick work of drinks. When Susan Lane hosts a cocktail party, she adds a kitchen-size trash barrel to her garage cleanup area. As she buses dishes, she also brings out abandoned drinks and pours leftover liquid and ice into the barrel. "You don't even need a liner," she says. "You can just dump out the liquid in the backyard after the party ends and wash the barrel." Remember to remove and discard any fruit before you dump the drinks. The used glasses can stay out in the garage with the dishes until you're ready to wash them.

Plate the food in the kitchen. There's no rule that says you must have decorative serving dishes on the dining room table. Dinner party enthusiast Norma Hansen has never seen a need for them. "I don't have room on my table for serving dishes," she says. She also doesn't have room in her kitchen for people to serve themselves. "I always plate the food myself in the kitchen and ask one of the ladies to help me bring the plates to the table. I think people like being served, and I like having fewer dishes to wash at the end of the meal."

Centerpieces

After the food and the guest list, nothing causes more angst than the centerpiece. A simple vase with flowers seems so ordinary, yet an ice sculpture is, frankly, over-the-top. Luckily for entertainers everywhere, our experts have found an ingenious middle ground—one that won't have your guests craning their necks to talk around your so-called good taste.

this idea is a real lemon

AS A NEW YORK CITY-BASED food editor, Lynn Naliboff spends a good deal of time coming up with snazzy entertaining ideas. "I can't take credit for creating this mini-lemon vase," she says, "but it is one of my favorite centerpiece ideas." Filled with your favorite flowers—anemones, Gerbera daisies, and roses are good choices—this miniature vase adds a simple but elegant touch to the table.

"Find a lemon that's fat and round," Lynn says. "Then use a paring knife to make the bottom flat so that the lemon will stand upright. Make sure not to cut through the lemon, or your vase will leak!

"Next, use a grapefruit spoon to hollow out the lemon. Again, don't cut through the peel. Line the lemon with plastic wrap, fill with water, and arrange your flowers inside. If you find that the weight of the water and the flowers topples the vase, place a fishing sinker in the bottom."

Scatter rose petals. Professional caterer Susan Lane is often called on to top last season's decor. Still, she feels that simple is best. "It's nice to buy cheap roses, remove the petals, and scatter them over the table. It creates a really stunning effect," Susan says.

Go natural. Susan Lane also likes to use seasonal foliage to decorate a table. "I go out near the railroad tracks to find wildflowers or cut a couple of branches from the blooming forsythia out back," she says. "Filling champagne flutes with colorful fall leaves you've collected yourself is a great way to bring the natural beauty of the outdoors into your party."

Create a flotilla. In the fall, when apples are in season, they make a wonderful centerpiece, says Susan Lane. Fill a short-sided galvanized bucket with water and float some apples on top. Remove the apples that float stem side up and set them aside. Put the rest away for snacking. Carve out the cores of the apples you set aside and replace them with small votive candles. When you're ready to set out your centerpiece, fill the bucket with water, light the candles, and float the apples in the water. "These buckets look really sharp in an entranceway or on a buffet table," Susan says. Your guests will be talking about them for weeks.

Double the impact. Veteran entertainer Norma Hansen doesn't have a lot of extra money to spend on fancy centerpieces, but she doesn't need to. Instead, she creates her own simple but

---

MAKE it LAST
Keep your salads wilt-free

EXPERIENCED ENTERTAINERS know the value of preparing food ahead of time. It lessens party day work, and allows the host to spend time with her guests instead of in the kitchen. But there are exceptions to the rule. For instance, it's okay to wash, dry, and cut up the greens and other vegetables that will go into your green salad, but don't dress the salad until just before you plan to serve it. If you dress your salad the night before your guests arrive, you'll end up with a wilted mess. And that's not very appetizing. So go ahead and do as much in advance as you can. But leave that salad alone until you sit down to eat. Your guests will thank you.

How Much Is Enough?

How much food should you prepare for a cocktail party? Susan Lane has lots of experience feeding crowds of all sizes. Here are some of the formulas she uses to calculate her needs.

Hors d'oeuvres. "Each person will eat between four and eight hors d'oeuvres per hour at a cocktail party. If desserts will follow dinner, your guests will probably eat only four before dinner."

Drinks. "People will usually have three or four drinks in a two- to three-hour time frame."

Glasses. "The trick is to make sure you have enough glasses, because people will set the first one down and take a fresh one with the next drink. You'll need three or four glasses for each guest."

Ice. "You'll need one pound of ice per person. That might sound like a lot, but trust me on this one. You'll need ice to chill the bottles on the bar and ice for each glass."

---

ingenious table toppers. Her secret for transforming a small flower arrangement or a collection of different-size candles in crystal holders into fabulous centerpieces? She sets each one on a small mirror. By doing so, she instantly doubles the color of the flowers and the sparkle of the candlelight.

Parties for Kids

One of the joys of parenthood is sending your child to someone else's house for a party. Kids adore parties, and they're sure to come home happy, sated, and (best of all) exhausted. Of course, the downside is that you'll have to return the favor, which means inviting all those kids to your house. Here's how to survive, while making sure everybody goes home happy.

KEEPING LITTLE ONES ENTERTAINED

You have cake and presents, now what? For some parents, children's parties have become a sort of competitive event. Moms and dads try to outdo other parents for the most elaborate decor and the most exciting entertainment. The only ones not impressed are the kids. They don't need to be impressed; they need to have fun. Here's how to make sure they do.

Be prepared. Sure, your invitation said that the party would start at 1:00 P.M., but there's going to be at least one parent who thinks that you won't mind if he drops Junior off at 12:30 or 1:30. Kids will show up at different times, so it's good to have an activity ready that will involve each child as he or she arrives. You may want to set up party hats for smaller children to decorate or have a game ready outside for older kids. That way, the kids who arrive early can keep busy until all the guests are ready for the group activities.

---

annals of ingenuity

HISTORY OF HOT AIR

What would a party be without balloons? Well, if you showed up today at a birthday party with one of history's first toy balloons, which were inflated animal entrails, your approval rating would likely drop a notch or two. It seems that our ancestors, though ingenious, had pretty strong stomachs.

It wasn't until 1824 that the first rubber balloon was invented, but it wasn't as a toy. Professor Michael Faraday made the balloons for use in his experiments with hydrogen at the Royal Institution in London. "The caoutchouc [rubber] is exceedingly elastic," he wrote in the Quarterly Journal of Science that year. "Bags made of it . . . have been expanded by having air forced into them . . . and when expanded by hydrogen they were so light as to form balloons with considerable ascending power."

Children wouldn't benefit from Faraday's discovery until the following year, when rubber manufacturer Thomas Hancock began producing do-it-yourself balloon kits. No doubt another party staple—the whoopee cushion—was not far behind (so to speak).

Keep it short. Veteran parents know that the number one rule for a great kids' party is to keep it short. In fact, 2 hours is the absolute maximum length for a party. The kids will be worn-out and overstimulated by then. More than likely, so will you. And that means you'll all be crabby. The good news is that you'll probably need to schedule only two or three short activities—such as a game, a treasure hunt, and a sing-along—to get through it.

Check that clown's references. The ad in the Yellow Pages says that he's an award-winning magician, but what does that mean? What if his jokes are racy or his act is messy? The best way to tell whether the storyteller, singer, or clown you're thinking about hiring is the right one is to see his act. Most performers allow prospective clients to visit a party where they're entertaining to see whether their acts are right for you and the kids.

Present the presents one at a time. Let's face it, watching someone else open presents is boring even when you're an adult. Imagine how hard it is for kids, most of whom can't stand being out of the spotlight. That's why so many present-opening ceremonies descend into a chaos of tears and paper ripping as all the kids open all the presents at once. Get around this potential headache by having your child greet each guest as he arrives. While the other kids do their opening group activity, have your child accept his gift from the new guest, then allow the two of them to open the gift together. That way, each guest gets to take part in the paper tearing—the best part. Your child can learn to give gracious thanks to each guest, and you can quietly jot down who brought what for the thank-you notes to follow.

Keep little ones indoors. When you're hosting a party for munchkins, it's tempting to send them outside. Kids love to be outdoors, running and jumping and playing, and what could

---

MAKE it **LAST**

Throw down a tarp

JUST BECAUSE you're hosting a party for your child doesn't mean that your carpet has to suffer. Yes, a dozen little feet can grind a ton of crumbs and icing into the carpet before you can say "Make a wish," but you can avoid that with a painter's tarp from the hardware store. Spread it out under the table where the kids will eat, paint, or glue glitter, and let it catch the celebratory debris.

---

be better? Actually, that's great for kids who are age 6 or older. They're able to calm down after they've been running around outside and have some practice at sitting still. Three- to 5-year-olds can't really focus and will never calm down. Instead, keep those little ones indoors in a small room. Remove all distractions, including food and parents, and allow the kids to focus on one group leader and one activity at a time.

KEEPING THINGS TIDY

It's crazy to assume that a group of kids are going to spend 2 hours playing hard and eating fast at your house without leaving sticky destruction in their wake. But a mother can dream, can't she? Actually, there are a few techniques to help this dream come true.

Hire a sitter. Once kids are over the age of 5 and their parents are more likely to just drop them off at parties, discipline and control become major issues for the host. If you need a little help just turn to your trusted babysitter. A 2-hour shift won't cost much, but it will give you another pair of hands in the kitchen or at least someone who likes spending time with kids.

Let them eat cake—last. It's no secret that kids go to parties to get cake; they're no dummies. But once they start eating that cake, it gets in and on their clothes, in their hair, and under their shoes, where it will then spread to every uncleanable surface in your house. Minimize the mess caused by this feeding frenzy by dishing out the treat just before they head out the door. Then it's a mess for their parents to clean up.

AVOIDING MELTDOWNS

Kids under the age of 6 don't have much control over their emotions. Too much sugar, not enough sleep, and a little pressure to perform can add up to a scream-athon. And at a birthday party, crying is more contagious than the chickenpox. A couple of our patented techniques will give you a no-tears event.

Eliminate all choice. Adults love choices. After all, being able to make them is one of the perks of being a grown-up. Kids, especially kids under the age of 6, don't have much experience making choices. Ask a 4-year-old if she wants a hot dog or a cheese sandwich, and she'll say a hot dog—until somebody else wants a

---

EVERYBODY LOVES CHOCOLATE

Outdoor entertaining is one of the joys of summer—lounging around the backyard, sipping cool drinks, and chatting with friends. Here's a deliciously ingenious tip that will enhance your party—and your garden. Just before the big day, mulch your garden beds with a 1-inch layer of cocoa shells. The shells, which are a by-product of the chocolate-making process, give off a rich, chocolaty aroma that will delight everyone. Cocoa shell mulch is more expensive than other organic mulches, but it will add a wonderful touch to your gathering.

cheese sandwich. Give a group of kids some crayons to play with, and they'll all fight over the green one. Avoid this by avoiding choices and sharing. Give all the kids the same kind of food, goody bag, and set of crayons, beads, or paints for the activity.

Wrap the snacks. The first time Colleen Donahue-Bean threw a party for her daughter Devin, then 3, she was warned about snacks. "The guy we hired to sing songs told me that snacks were a bad idea early in the party," Colleen says. "But I thought, what harm could it do?" So she set out bowls of popcorn, peanuts, and fish-shaped crackers. Fifteen minutes into the party, she was out of crackers and the kids were screaming. "When the next party rolled around, I put a handful of crackers into individual sandwich bags and handed those out after the first activity but before the cake," she says. The kids ate happily and quietly. When each child finished her bag, she knew that snack time was over.

Ban piñatas. Piñatas seem like a good idea. The kids finally get to take a big stick and whack away at something while their parents actually encourage them. It's good, clean fun—until somebody hits the poor beast and the candy rains down on everyone. That's followed by a mad dash to collect it and the inevitable fighting and, of course, tears. Avoid these scrambles by eliminating big piles of candy from your party. You may want to ban candy altogether. Instead, fill individual goody bags with stickers, small toys, or trail mix. Nobody cries over trail mix.

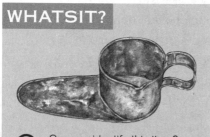

WHATSIT?

Q: Can you identify this item? Here's a hint: It would make you the life of any old-time party.

A: This is called an ale shoe or a slipper ale warmer. Filled with ale and placed next to the fireplace or on the stovetop, it warmed the ale to the right temperature for drinking.

chapter 12

beauty and personal
c a r e

WHO WOULDN'T LIKE to take a plunge into the fountain of youth?
Well, believe it or not, you can—and you can bypass the pricey cos-
metics counter at your local department store. You don't need $50
face cream or $60 manicures to renew and rejuvenate your natural
glow. Instead, reach for fruits, vegetables, herbs, and other low-
cost, healthy helpers to restore your complexion, soothe your skin,
erase fine lines, and make you look years younger. Best of all, the
natural ingredients suggested in this chapter are bargain-priced,
and the homemade recipes are simple—and safe—to make and use.

SHOP SMART FOR YOUR HEALTH

Tropical fruits are loaded with vitamins and minerals that keep your skin youthful and your hair full and shiny. Mangoes and macadamia nuts are two items to add to your beauty shopping list, say Dr. Angela Stengler and Dr. Mark Stengler.

Mangoes are rich in vitamin C and beta-carotene, two powerful antioxidants that block harmful free radicals, which damage healthy skin and hair. One mango a day provides 80 percent of your daily beta-carotene and 95 percent of your daily vitamin C requirements.

Macadamia nuts are rich in protein, vitamins A and E, thiamine, niacin, iron, and calcium. Loaded with monounsaturated fats (the cholesterol-lowering type), macadamia nuts expand blood vessels to provide nutrients to your skin and hair.

So how do we know so much about natural beauty and personal care? Well, we called on our team of crack beauty specialists. Angela Stengler, N.D., and Mark Stengler, N.D., are naturopathic physicians from La Jolla, California. Sally Cadwallader, from Costa Mesa, California, is a licensed cosmetologist who has been solving beauty dilemmas since 1963. And Stephanie Tourles is a licensed aesthetician who lives in West Hyannisport, Massachusetts. She's written two beauty books, *Naturally Healthy Skin* and *50 Simple Ways to Pamper Yourself.* Together, our beauty dream team has answers to most questions about looking and feeling your best.

Caring for Your Tresses

Hair that glows, shimmers, and shines is within your reach. The foods you eat, the medications you take, how well you handle stressful situations, and the climate in which you live all influence the health of your hair and scalp. For instance, did you know that dry, flaky skin may be a sign that you aren't eating enough foods with essential vitamins and minerals? And eating too many dairy products and sugary foods can cause dandruff. Want to learn more? Read on for loads of practical, down-to-earth tips and tonics that will restore your hair to its crowning glory.

Ground flyaway hair. Frustrated by flyaway hair that seems to go here, there, and everywhere—except where you want it? Tame those tresses with a hair tonic recommended by Susan Baker, an aesthetician and herbalist from Atlantis, Florida. In a small spray bottle, combine 4 teaspoons lime juice, 1 teaspoon lemon juice, and ½ cup room temperature water (ideally distilled or filtered water). Tighten the cap, give it a few shakes, and spray the mixture directly onto your dry hair before you step outside. This citrusy concoction will naturally stop the hair-raising static electricity that is generated on those winter days when the humidity is near zero indoors.

Get in the pink. Pink grapefruit not only treats your taste-buds and supplies your body with vitamin C, but it also works wonders on your hair. Pink grapefruit naturally strips your hair of any built-up residues, chemicals, medications, or shampoo. Pink grapefruit's astringent and antiseptic qualities stimulate the scalp and leave your hair shiny and squeaky-clean, says Susan Baker. After you wash your hair, rinse it with some unsweetened juice, then rinse again with water. Regular grapefruit will do the same things, but it doesn't smell as nice.

Reunite split ends. It's been 8 weeks since your last haircut, and those split ends are driving you mad. But you don't have time for a cut. Fear not; you can seal the deal with just three items from your pantry.

GET THE AVOCADO ADVANTAGE

Sally Cadwallader makes her living keeping other people's hair looking ship-shape. So what does a cosmetologist do to pamper her own locks? Sally reaches for a ripe avocado. "Avocado is a natural protein moisturizer for your hair—the perfect remedy if it's been harmed by too much sun, surf, or wind," she says. Her once-a-week deep-moisturizing conditioner restores shine, manageability, and full body.

1. In the kitchen, peel the avocado and remove the pit. In a medium-size glass bowl, mash the avocado into a thick paste. Head for the shower.

2. Shampoo your hair with lukewarm water, then rinse. Take small handfuls of the mashed avocado and work it into your hair and scalp.

3. Cover your hair with a plastic shower cap and enjoy a 10- to 15-minute shower. The moist heat will help the avocado penetrate your scalp.

4. Remove the shower cap and thoroughly rinse the avocado from your hair. Skip the commercial conditioner and let your hair air-dry.

"When the Santa Ana winds act up, I do this for my hair once a week, and it prevents it from becoming dry and flyaway," Sally says. "It makes my hair feel soft and full of body."

In a small bowl, beat 1 egg yolk. Then mix in 2 tablespoons olive oil and 1 teaspoon honey. Dampen your hair and massage in this mixture with your fingertips. Cover your hair with a plastic shower cap, then relax for 30 minutes. This gives the kitchen helpers time to treat your damaged hair. Rinse with warm water, shampoo as usual, and tell your hairdresser you can wait another week or two.

Rub away scalp stress. Pamper your scalp with a do-it-yourself massage every time you shampoo and condition your hair. It's not only a luxury. Regular scalp massages can help prevent dandruff and encourage the flow of blood and nutrients to your hair follicles, says Dr. Angela Stengler, N. D. She recommends the following four-step method.

1. Soak your hair with lukewarm water. Gently glide your fingers from your forehead hairline to the nape of your neck to untangle snarls.

2. Pour a small amount of shampoo into your cupped palm. Rub your hands together and run your open palms from the top of your head to the ends of your hair.

3. Place your fingertips at the nape of your neck and massage your scalp with small, circular motions. Slowly work your way up to your forehead, taking about 3 minutes. Rinse and massage in your conditioner, especially to your hair ends.

4. Rinse thoroughly with lukewarm water for 1 minute more than you think is necessary. Wrap your hair in a towel to absorb excess water.

Lavish your hair with lavender. Remember those old TV ads for the shampoo Gee, Your Hair Smells Terrific? Well, there's a natural way to treat your hair occasionally to a clean, floral scent. Pour a few drops of lavender essential oil, which you can purchase at a pharmacy or health food store, into a small spray bottle. Fill the bottle with distilled water and tighten the nozzle. Shake vigorously. Spray a fine mist on your comb and glide it through your styled hair to give it an inviting aroma, suggests Sally Cadwallader.

WHATSIT?

Q: This rusty old thing is 10 inches long. The top section has three prongs and the bottom section two. When closed, the five prongs are intertwined. What do you think it is?

A: This is a curling iron made between 1750 and 1840. The ends were heated and pressed over damp hair to form curls in wigs or natural hair. By the way, don't oil or polish your "rusty old things" because doing so will decrease their value.

Everything for Eyes

No matter whether yours are brown or blue, or a shade somewhere in between, your peepers can look perky with the right natural ingredients. Here are some simple homemade ways to restore that sparkle in your eyes.

The eyes have it. You've just come home from a big party and are ready to head for bed. The last thing you want to do is remove that stubborn mascara. Head to the kitchen for some super eye allies, says Sally Cadwallader. In a small bowl, combine 1 tablespoon castor oil, 1 tablespoon olive oil, and 2 teaspoons canola oil. Stir with a spoon. Dampen a cotton ball with the mixture and dab it on your mascara. The black lines will disappear without a struggle. Splash your face with lukewarm water and blot dry. Now you're ready to slide between the sheets.

Try a little skim milk magic. Need relief for tired eyes? Your answer is right inside your refrigerator, says Dr. Angela Stengler. Pour ¼ cup cold skim milk into a cereal bowl. Soak a clean washcloth in the milk, then wring it out and place it over your closed eyes for 10 minutes. Remove the washcloth and rinse your face with warm, then cool water, and your eyes will be refreshed.

GIVE YOUR EYELINER THE BIG CHILL

It smudges here and smudges there. Are you ready to toss your eyeliner out the window? Don't do it, says Susan Baker. When you need to make a fine line on your lid, place the eyeliner in your freezer for about 5 minutes before you use it. The cold air will harden the core of the pencil, and that means you can sharpen it cleanly. Then you'll be able to glide on an accenting line to showcase your eyes.

Sleep away wrinkles. You can minimize those laugh lines around your eyes with cocoa butter. Licensed aesthetician Stephanie Tourles says that you can skip those pricey cocoa butter lotions at salons and beauty shops and buy a raw stick of cocoa butter for about a dollar at your local drugstore. The best part is that "the cocoa butter stick smells like chocolate," Stephanie says. "I use it as a lip balm and rub the tube around my eyes before I go to bed at night. It is a creamy tan, smells heavenly, and works to moisturize my skin and fight wrinkles."

Luscious Lips

It's hard to pucker up when your lips are dry or chapped. Heat and cold, alcohol, even smoking can take a toll on your lips. So what's a poor little mouth to do? Heed our expert advice, and you'll soon have a kissably soft and smooth kisser.

Spread on the jelly. When it comes to keeping your lips soft and smoochable, heed the KISS principle: Keep it simple, sweetie. Good old petroleum jelly (one brand is Vaseline®) is one of the best balms going. It's inexpensive, and it works. Apply it before you go out in cold or dry weather and just before bed.

You can't lick 'em. It's cold and dry outside, and it's bone-dry inside. So what do you do? Lick your lips. But that's the worst thing you can do. As your saliva evaporates, it takes more precious moisture from your lips, which makes them drier, which causes you to lick them. It's a vicious cycle. Keep your tongue in your mouth and apply lip balm whenever you get the urge to lick.

Avoid exotics. If you're using lip balm or lip gloss with ingredients such as camphor or phenol, you may be doing your kisser more harm than good. Those ingredients can actually dry

MAKE it LAST

Make it stick

YOU HAVE a cup of coffee, and your lipstick ends up on the cup. You kiss someone goodbye, and it's on his cheek. Tired of having to reapply lipstick all the time? Now, I don't wear lipstick, but I know a few women who do. Here's their favorite way to keep their lips looking rosy. For a longer-lasting look, they simply dust their lips lightly with face powder before applying lipstick.

out your lips. Instead, shop for lip balms that include beneficial ingredients such as coconut oil and jojoba.

Fabulous Faces

We all want youthful-looking skin. But how can we get it? Forget the face-lifts. Our natural beauty experts are here to help you get great skin for pennies a day. Here are their simple facial scrubs, masks, and steams, which will clean and moisturize your skin from the neck up.

Opt for old-fashioned oats. For a cleansing weekly facial, pour ¼ cup oats into a coffee grinder. Pulse for about 15 seconds, or until the oats are finely ground to the consistency of grated Parmesan cheese. Then add 2 teaspoons water and stir to form a paste. Wash your face with lukewarm water and pat dry before applying a thin layer of the oatmeal paste. Start with your neck and work your way up to your forehead, staying away from the eye area. Leave the mask on for 10 to 20 minutes, then rinse with lukewarm water. Oatmeal removes dirt and oil without robbing your skin of its protective oils.

For the best breakfast treat for your face, stick with pure oats—not instant oatmeal, which contains sugar and other fillers, says Stephanie Tourles.

Try this steamy solution. All skin types need hydration, even oily ones. Water keeps skin looking youthful and helps wash away toxins and dirt buildup. So once a week, steam your face and lift your spirits with this easy four-step treatment.

1. Pour 3 cups boiling water into a large heat-resistant bowl.

2. Add your favorite herbal tea. Chamomile and green tea are

GOOD HEALTH EQUALS GOOD LOOKS

Some of the best friends of soft, healthy skin aren't available in fancy salons. Practicing good health habits can go a long way toward helping you look and feel years younger, says Dr. Mark Stengler, N. D., who offers this four-step skin care prescription.

1. Get ample sleep. Getting 6 to 8 hours of sleep every night does wonders for your skin. A lot of healing and mending within your skin's cells takes place while you snooze.

2. Eat nutritious foods. Like your car, your body needs high-octane fuel to operate optimally. Boost your intake of fresh fruits and vegetables (especially yellow, orange, red, and green ones), whole-grain breads, and low-fat meats. The nutrients from these foods will keep your skin looking younger.

3. Drink plenty of water. Never underestimate the power of H_2O. Drinking 1 quart a day will keep your skin hydrated and help it maintain its elasticity. And faithfully downing water, herbal tea, and other noncaffeinated beverages will help rid your skin and body of waste and toxins.

4. Exercise daily. Spend 20 to 30 minutes a day working up a sweat—walking, jogging, biking, or doing any other aerobic activity—and you will ensure that your heart pumps a healthy supply of blood to your skin to keep it supple and strong.

good choices, because they're both natural cleansers and germ killers. If you're using loose tea, add about 1 tablespoon. If you're using tea bags, 2 bags ought to do the job.

3. Drape a large towel over your head and lean forward over the bowl, keeping about a foot away. Stay in this position for 10 to 15 minutes to unclog dirty pores.

4. Pat your face dry with another soft towel, then rinse with lukewarm water. Don't rinse with hot or cold water, because these temperatures can damage the tiny capillaries in your face, says Dr. Mark Stengler.

Call in the 20-mule team. Not only does it give your laundry a boost, but borax can cleanse your face, too. Put about a teaspoon of borax laundry booster on a warm, damp washcloth and, using circular motions, gently clean your face. Don't forget your forehead. Then rinse with warm water and pat your face dry with a towel.

Attack acne with olive oil. Here's a strange-sounding remedy for acne. This cure has been handed down through the generations of Susan Baker's family. Her great-grandmother is credited with starting this first-thing-in-the-morning regimen.

In a small bowl, mix 3 tablespoons olive oil with about 2 teaspoons salt, or enough to make a paste. Apply the mixture to your face with your fingers. Leave it on for about 10 minutes before rinsing with lukewarm water. Your complexion should clear up within a few days.

Discover the fountain of youth. Wake up in the morning looking years younger just by using this pure, natural moisturizer. All of these products are available at health food stores.

Blend 2 tablespoons glycerin (optional), 2 tablespoons witch hazel (make sure it doesn't contain rubbing alcohol), 1 tablespoon

---

A HONEY OF A FACIAL

As a child, Stephanie Tourles looked forward to visiting her grandparents and coming home with quart jars of honey from their busy beehives. By the time she was a teenager, she was enjoying not only eating honey in homemade cookies and tea but also slathering it on her face as a skin tonic. Now a licensed aesthetician, Stephanie continues this sweet tradition once or twice a week.

First, she washes her face with lukewarm water and pats it dry with a clean towel. Then she dips her fingertips into the honey. Now comes the fun part. "I dot my face and neck with the honey, up and down like I'm playing the piano," she says. "The glow that comes over my skin is incredible. Honey is a natural moisturizer. And it's water-soluble, so after 5 minutes, it's easy to rinse off."

Stephanie is picky about the honey she uses for her face. "I recommend raw honey over processed honey," she says. "Both will work, but the honey you find in a supermarket has been heated, processed, and refined, taking away some of the minerals and vitamins."

---

rose water, 3 tablespoons honey and 3 tablespoons wheat germ oil together in a small bowl with a wooden spoon.

Rub this cream over your freshly washed face and leave it on overnight. In the morning, rinse and rejoice in your rejuvenated, supple-looking skin. Store the mixture in an airtight container in a cool, dry place. Use once a month.

Use a cuke cream. Of course you know that cucumbers add crispness to your salads, but they can be a treat for your face, too. Jonni McCoy, who lives in Colorado Springs, Colorado, and is the author of *Miserly Moms: Living on One Income in a Two Income Economy*, shares her favorite cucumber facial cream recipe. This batch makes a 2-month supply, says Jonni. You'll find beeswax and almond oil at your local health food store.

In a blender, puree 1 diced cucumber, then strain off the liquid using a mesh cloth or strainer. Melt ½ ounce beeswax or paraffin in a double boiler. Add the cucumber and ¼ cup almond oil and mix until smooth. Let cool completely before using.

Dab a light layer of this mixture on your face and let sit for 15 to 20 minutes, then rinse with lukewarm water. Store the cream in an airtight container in the refrigerator. Be sure to label it facial cream so that your kids won't think it's a dip for carrot and celery sticks.

Skin Care

Those dry, flaky cells clinging to your skin are oldies, not goodies. Every 20 days or so, the wafer-thin top layer of skin gets sloughed off and is replaced by a layer of younger, more vital cells. As we age, this natural shedding cycle slows down. The skin loses its elasticity, and wrinkles appear.

You can help your skin maintain its healthy radiance by exfoliating (sloughing off the surface layer of dead skin cells) at least once a week, says Dr. Angela Stengler. She and other natural beauty experts share their skin care secrets in this section.

Perform an evening ritual. Beautiful skin can be yours—if you're willing to spend a few minutes every night performing an ingeniously simple cleansing ritual. Add a couple of drops of essential oil (orange, spearmint, or rose) to your mild, inexpensive commercial skin cleanser and massage your body with a loofah to remove salt and dead skin buildup, says Stephanie Tourles. This cleansing routine is best done at night because your body boots out toxins through your skin as you sleep.

Hydrate from the inside. Winter is beauty's formidable foe. Indoor heat robs skin of its moisture, and outdoor winds and cold can leave your skin red and scaly. But you can fight back with flaxseed oil. Stir 1 to 2 teaspoons flaxseed oil into your salads and fresh or steamed vegetables. Flaxseed oil contains beneficial fats that moisturize skin, says Dr. Mark Stengler.

Ditch the deodorant. Keeping your family stocked with deodorant can cost you lots of money each month. But you can keep your family odor-free by skipping those expensive commercial products and switching to a homemade preparation. Here are three.

1. Milk of magnesia. Dab some of it on a clean cotton ball and apply it under each arm after you shower and towel-dry.

2. Cider vinegar. This refreshing tonic is also an odor fighter.

3. Cornstarch. It's not just for making gravy. It's also a terrific stand-in for commercial deodorant.

Help for Hands and Feet

Nothing zaps moisture and softness from your hands and feet faster than winter's icy winds and dry indoor heating. Dry air robs your skin of its natural protective barrier, which is made of water, oils, and a protein called keratin. This leaves your skin cracked, itchy, and wrinkly.

What's the answer? When the temperatures begin to fall, give your hands and feet a little extra attention with intensive moisturizing treatments. By paying special attention to your hands and feet, you can hydrate your entire body and feel calm and relaxed.

Heed this clip tip. If you've sworn off manicure parlors because you once wound up with a nasty nail fungus, be warned that these fungi can strike at home, too. But there is an ingeniously simple solution. Before you indulge in a well-deserved manicure or pedicure, submit your clippers to this easy cleaning regimen.

Just toss the clippers into your dishwasher with your dirty

YOU'RE SOAKING IN IT!

Remember those old commercials where women complained about dishpan hands? Well, you can turn the dreaded dishwashing chore into a spa treatment for your hands, says herbalist Susan Baker.

"Before you plunge into a sink full of hot water, apply shea butter moisturizer to your hands," Susan says. Shea butter comes from the nut of the African shea tree and is the main ingredient in many moisturizing creams. Slip on rubber gloves with cotton liners and do the dishes. The gloves will protect your hands against harsh detergents, and the warm water will open your pores, allowing the moisturizer to penetrate. Afterward, remove your gloves and pat your hands dry.

---

dishes. You'll kill all the germs and remove any buildup. No dishwasher? No problem. Set the clippers in a pot of boiling water (2 cups), then add ¼ cup ammonia to the bubbling brew. Allow this mixture to boil for 2 to 3 minutes, then remove your clippers, rinse with warm water, and dry thoroughly with a clean towel.

Serve a banana banquet at bedtime. Tame dry, cracked hands and feet with this fruity, ingenious solution offered by Susan Baker. In a small mixing bowl, use a wooden spoon to combine 1 ripe banana, ¼ cup honey, 2 tablespoons lemon juice, and 1 tablespoon softened margarine. Apply a thin layer of this mixture to your hands and feet once a week. Put on white cotton gloves and socks and go to bed. The clean, loose-fitting gloves and socks will allow the emollients to work into your skin rather than evaporate into the air while you sleep. In the morning, step into the shower and rinse off the mixture.

Stamp out stinky soles. Are you prone to foot odor? Not to worry—just try these two ingenious tips.

1. Try a sage solution . . . If your feet aren't smelling as sweet as you'd like, fight back with an herbal ally—sage. Just sprinkle a pinch of dried or fresh sage into your shoes before you slip them on. During the day, the herb will combat odor and sweat. You can stop foot odor while you sleep by mixing 2 drops sage essential oil with 1 tablespoon baking powder, then sprinkling the mixture into your sneakers or dress shoes.

2. . . . Or a mint lift. Keep your feet cool, dry, and odor-free with this recipe from Stephanie Tourles. All of the ingredients are available at your local health food store or drugstore.

Combine ½ cup baking soda, 2 tablespoons zinc oxide powder,

FABULOUS FOOT FEATS

As a naturopathic physician and the mother of two young children, Dr. Angela Stengler is constantly on her feet. But she never loses the spring in her stride, because she devotes 15 minutes a few times each week to her foot-reviving ritual. "It's a little bit of heaven," she says. "It takes so little time and costs so little." At the end of the day, after seeing patients and putting her children to bed, Dr. Stengler follows these four easy steps.

1. First, Dr. Stengler fills a small foot tub with warm water and drops in two peppermint tea bags. She soaks her tired feet for 10 minutes to let the peppermint refresh them, then she dries them with a towel.

2. Dr. Stengler cuts a fresh lemon in half and rubs the juice over her heels, her feet, and up to her ankles to slough off dull, dry skin.

3. She rinses her feet in the bathtub and rubs ¼ cup olive oil into her feet and toes. Meanwhile, her husband, Mark, moistens two bath towels and heats them in the microwave for 30 seconds.

4. Dr. Stengler wraps the warm towels around her feet and leaves them in place for 5 to 10 minutes. The heat hastens the absorption of the oil into her skin. Then she unwraps her feet and puts on a pair of clean socks.

2 tablespoons white cosmetic clay, ½ cup arrowroot and 1 teaspoon peppermint essential oil in a medium-size mixing bowl. Sprinkle 1 teaspoon of the mixture into your shoes and socks daily. Store the rest in a glass jar in a cool, dry place. Label the jar well.

Naturally Gorgeous Nails

Fabulous fingernails do more than look beautiful. They're also visible proof of good health. So strive to keep yours looking their best. Here are some expert tips for doing just that.

The do-it-yourself manicure. One of the easiest ways to care for your nails is to give yourself an at-home (but spa-quality) manicure and pedicure once a week. It costs only pennies compared to the $50 you might pay for the same treatments at a salon. Pay special attention to tidying up your cuticles, which can tear if they're dry, and filing and polishing your fingernails. Follow these six steps, courtesy of Stephanie Tourles, for the perfect manicure.

1. Start clean. Before you begin a manicure, wash your hands thoroughly and remove dirt from under your fingernails.

2. File away. When you file your fingernails, make sure to file from one edge of the nail to the center, then from the other edge back to the center. Always use smooth, long strokes. Avoid short, sawing motions, which can weaken or tear the nail.

annals of ingenuity

Polish with Purpose

It's not surprising that women have been painting their fingernails for a long time. And it shouldn't be a surprise that the first nail polish was invented by the ancient Chinese around 3000 B.C.

Back then, the favored ingredients of nail lacquer included beeswax, egg whites, gelatin, and gum arabic. And nail polish wasn't just a cosmetic affectation. In both China and Egypt, the colors you wore announced your social class to the world, and a woman caught wearing the wrong colors could be punished with death. Talk about a fashion faux pas!

MANICURE MUST-HAVES

Get off on the right foot—er, hand—by selecting the right manicure tools to keep your fingers and nails looking beautiful. Salon pro Susan Baker recommends these four tools.

1. Emery board. The most important tool in your nail care kit. Always file nails straight up at the sides; never file nails inward. The thickness of your emery board should match the thickness of your nails.

2. Nail buffer. Use this tool to lightly buff back and forth across the nail surface. Continue polishing until the nail is shiny and smooth.

3. Cuticle stick. The pointed end of this hardwood stick cleans under the nails thoroughly but gently. With the beveled end, you can gently push and shape your cuticles.

4. Cuticle trimmer. The stainless steel V tip trims away any stray strands of skin or ragged edges.

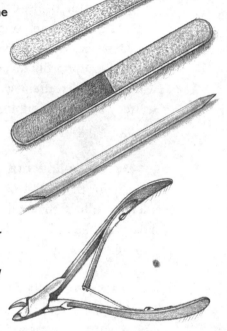

---

3. Buff for perfection. Buff away imperfections with gentle strokes. Always move in one direction.

4. Soak your nails. Soak your nails, cuticles, and fingers in warm soapy water to lock in moisture. Gently blot your hands dry with a towel.

5. Get pushy with your cuticles. Using a cuticle pusher or cutter, gently push the cuticle back under the skin of each finger. Cut the hangnails, which are really just dead skin, but *never* cut into the cuticle, because you risk damaging the nail or inviting infection.

6. Oil 'em up. Massage olive oil—a terrific all-natural moisturizer—into your hands, especially working it into the cuticles. Leave the oil on overnight, then wash it off in the morning.

Give your nails cold comfort. Tired of those annoying bubbles that form in your nail polish? The solution is ingenious, easy, and free, says cosmetologist Sally Cadwallader, who has been solving beauty problems since 1963. Just dip your hands in cold water, then dry them well before you apply nail polish. This strategy eliminates bubbles when you apply your polish, guaranteeing a smoother finish.

Get the yellow out. Susan Baker offers this quick and clever remedy for that yellowish tint that can form on fingernails. Slice a lemon in half, then rub each nail over the lemon. Do this once a day, and the yellow will fade in less than a week. Your fingertips will smell lemony fresh, too!

Treat your nails at night. Before you slip under the covers for the night, treat yourself to an overnight sensation: castor oil. Don't worry—we mean for your nails. This thick, inexpensive oil will strengthen your nail bed and keep your fingernails from cracking due to dry weather, says Stephanie Tourles.

Place a tiny dab of castor oil on each fingernail and rub it into your cuticle thoroughly so that there isn't any residue left over to soil your sheets. (Any extra oil can be rubbed into your elbows to keep them soft and moist.) Within a week or so, you should notice a major improvement in your nails. They will be healthy, pliable, strong, and shiny.

chapter 13

health and first-aid
hints

THESE DAYS, STAYING HEALTHY CAN BE quite a challenge. Invisible and plentiful, germs live on door handles, get exchanged during handshakes, and fly through the air when someone sneezes. But whether you're at home, at work, or on the road, there are dozens of ingenious ways to fortify yourself against the three Cs: colds, coughs, and congestion. And, of course, let's not forget the flu. And don't get us started on aches, pains, bumps, and bruises. Luckily, we've assembled a whole group of health experts who share their ingenious professional advice about all those common ailments and more. For instance, Mark Stengler, N.D., of La Jolla, California, offers tips about staying healthy by taking advantage of the remedies Mother Nature has to offer. Dale Anderson, M.D, a clinical assistant professor at the University of Minnesota Medical School in Minneapolis and a physician in Roseville, Minnesota, shares his advice for fighting the common cold and taking care of paper cuts. Karen Cichocki is a retired emergency room nurse from Dyer, Indiana. She'll help you shoo the sniffles with a homemade nasal spray. Jerry Huber is a certified massage therapist in San Francisco who explains how acupressure can remedy nausea and motion sickness.

In these pages, you'll meet more experts who offer dozens of other ingenious remedies for everything from colds and flu to backaches and blisters. But don't take our word for it—read on and take theirs.

Colds and Flu

Dr. Dale Anderson keeps colds and flu at arm's length by avoiding shaking hands with people as much as possible during cold season. When he does press the flesh, he heads to the nearest bathroom to wash his hands with warm soapy water. Of course, that's not to say Dr. Anderson isn't friendly. He just practices the wave. "Colds can pass easily from hand to hand, so during cold season, I greet folks as much as possible with a friendly wave of my hand, not a handshake," Dr. Anderson says. Here are some more uncommonly ingenious ways to battle the common cold.

Skip the pizza and beer. Certain foods and beverages can make you more prone to colds during the winter months. They include apple cider, applesauce, beer, cheese, vinegar, and wine—all of which worsen mold allergies and weaken your immune system. "Too often, I see patients at the urgent care clinic on

Saturday morning who had pizza, beer and salad with Italian dressing on Friday night," says Dr. Dale Anderson. "By Saturday morning, they are socked with a horrible viral cold complicated by mold allergies."

Grab the garlic. Yes, nature's pungent bulb packs quite a medicinal punch. During cold season, eat 1½ raw cloves a day. Or if you're worried about your breath, take 300 milligrams of enteric-coated garlic capsules three times a day to keep the sniffles at bay, says Dr. Mark Stengler. Garlic rates high in nature's medicine cabinet for its antibiotic and antiviral properties. After you eat the garlic, munch on a sprig of parsley, which will freshen your breath.

Drink flu-fighting tea. The next time you're fighting the flu, hasten your recovery by drinking this herbal tea at least twice a day. In a bowl, combine equal parts dried peppermint leaves, yarrow leaves, and lemon balm leaves. Add 2 teaspoons of the herbal blend to a cup of boiling water. Let steep for 5 to 10 minutes, then strain out the herbs and sip while the tea is warm.

End chills with ginger. When the flu gives you the chills, add a pinch of ground ginger to your food and drink. Ginger helps warm you up and keeps the blood flowing to all parts of your body. It also acts as a tonic, a circulatory stimulant, and an immune system booster, says Dr. Mark Stengler. And ginger con-

THE PROS KNOW

we'll drink to this remedy

A LITTLE ALCOHOL, specifically brandy, can help you fight a cold, says Dr. Dale Anderson. Make yourself a hot toddy before bedtime by adding 2 tablespoons brandy and 1 teaspoon honey to a cup of hot water. Stir and sip slowly.

Why brandy? "It's pure alcohol that contains no mold by-products," Dr. Anderson says. "It's a cold remedy that our grandmas have supported for years."

tains gingerols and shogaols, two compounds that soothe nausea and stomach upset.

CONTROLLING CONGESTION

Do you hab a code? Then you probably have some congestion, too. But don't worry—our experts will have you breathing easy in no time.

Spice it up. Unclog congestion quickly by sprinkling hot pepper flakes or ground red pepper onto your food. Hot spices help open clogged nasal passages by thinning mucus and making your nose run. So keep that tissue box handy!

that's • ingenious!

try grandma's cure

IF YOU'RE LOOKING for a natural way to break up congestion, head to the kitchen and grab some onions. Sauté 2 diced onions in a little vegetable oil over low heat until they're transparent. Let the onions cool, then spread them on your chest. Place plastic wrap over the onions, put a warm towel on top of the plastic wrap, and let sit for 30 minutes. Onions contain chemicals that stimulate blood flow, and that helps break up congestion and carry waste materials away so that you can breathe more easily.

Concoct your own nasal spray. When Karen Cichocki, a retired emergency room nurse from Dyer, Indiana, runs out of nasal spray, she doesn't dash off to the store. Instead, she makes a spray using ingredients from her own kitchen. This ingenious solution works in a pinch until she can get to the drugstore.

Add ½ teaspoon salt and 1 teaspoon baking soda to 1 cup lukewarm water. Pour this mixture into a child-size bulb syringe. Spray the solution into your nose a few times, then gently blow your nose to un-block your nasal passage.

Elevate your pillows. When you're suffering from the sniffles, you can increase your chances of an uninterrupted night's sleep by sleeping on your back with your head raised on two or three pillows.

COPING WITH COUGHS

Unpleasant as it may be, a coughing fit is your body's way of clearing mucous buildup and airborne irritants from your airways. Next time you get a throat-tickling dry cough or a phlegm-raising moist cough, try one of these ingenious remedies.

Send your hacking packing. Rein in a stubborn cough with this home remedy. Add 1 teaspoon each honey, horseradish, and Tabasco® to a glass of cool water. Stir well, then drink. This concoction won't win any prizes for its taste, but the powerful spices will stimulate your airways to secrete water, and that will thin the sticky mucous buildup that causes you to cough.

Make it thyme time. Relieve bronchial spasms caused by coughing attacks by sipping a cup of thyme tea two or three times a day. Steep ½ teaspoon dried thyme leaves in a cup of hot water for about 10 minutes, then strain and sip. Thyme is Mother Nature's expectorant, says Dr. Mark Stengler.

SOOTHING SORE THROATS

A sore throat can make you feel miserable. What's happening inside your throat is a drying of the mucous membranes that line your airways. Our experts offer these soothing solutions.

PUT THE KIBOSH ON COUGHS

Here's a simply ingenious way to calm a cough and boost your intake of vitamin A. Add a few drops of vegetable oil to a glass of fresh carrot juice and drink it up. Carrot juice is loaded with vitamin A, and when it's combined with vegetable oil, it fortifies your respiratory system and helps ease coughing episodes.

Drink ginger. Control a sore throat by drinking ginger-orange tea at least three times a day. Squeeze the juice of 1 orange into 1 cup boiling water. Add ¼ teaspoon grated fresh or ground ginger and ½ teaspoon honey. Let the mixture steep for 10 minutes, strain out the ginger, and sip slowly.

Think zinc. Stop the virus causing your sore throat by sucking on three to five zinc lozenges every day. Zinc reduces the severity of symptoms and speeds recovery. For best results, select zinc lozenges at your supermarket or drugstore that contain 5 to 15 milligrams of zinc gluconate.

Stomach Upsets

Vomiting and diarrhea have a variety of causes, including viral infections and emotional upsets. In minor cases, the problems usually don't last long and can be eased with the following tips. Keep in mind, though, that when vomiting and diarrhea last longer than a day or two, they can cause serious dehydration, especially in small children and elderly people. Our tips can help in the short term, but if the symptoms persist, it's time to see a doctor.

Diarrhea? Keep drinking. For benign cases of vomiting or diarrhea, drink up. That's the word from William Forgey, M.D., president of the Wilderness Medical Society in Gary, Indiana. The disconcerting side effects of food poisoning or viral illnesses are actually good signs, he says. "You're getting the toxins out of your system," Dr. Forgey explains. However, if vomiting or diarrhea continues for any length of time, you can quickly become dehydrated. In that case, your primary aim should be to rehydrate with a constant flow of water.

Clean, fresh water is definitely best, but almost any water will do in that kind of emergency. "Even if you suspect that it's the water that's making you sick, when you're losing water, you need to replace it with more water," Dr. Forgey says. So drink up.

Also drink orange juice or eat a banana. Both are high in potassium, a mineral that gets depleted in your body when you become dehydrated.

Stick to bland foods. When you're suffering from vomiting or diarrhea, fortify your weakened body with clear soups, boiled vegetables, white toast, and bananas. These foods are easy to digest and don't cause much intestinal action. Steer clear of fruit juices, especially cranberry, apple, and prune, all of which can worsen diarrhea. So can high-fiber foods such as raw vegetables or bran flakes.

Use acupressure. You can relieve minor nausea without medication by using a simple acupressure technique, says Dr. Mark Stengler. Find the acupressure point in the weblike area between your thumb and index finger, then use the thumb and index finger of your opposite hand to apply firm, deep pressure to that spot for about 3 minutes.

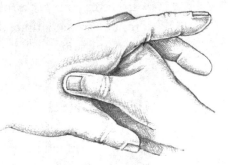

When nausea strikes, relieve it with this simple acupressure technique.

Aches and Pains

Ouch! Ow! Oooh! Anyway you say it, everyday aches and pains can make you feel less than 100 percent. Our clever experts offer oodles of creative ways to help your muscles work more effectively.

BACKACHES

Many of us take our backs for granted. Your back is always there when you need to pick up a heavy box, twist the torso to swing a golf club, or support you when you declare war on dandelions and start weeding. Here are some ways to ensure that back pain won't crimp your lifestyle.

Do the wall shimmy. Here's a quick and easy way to ease minor back pain. Stand about 18 inches from a wall with your knees slightly bent. Place your back flat against the wall and hold the pose for 30 seconds. Standing in this position allows your back muscles to stretch, says Dr. Dan Hamner.

Shorten your vacuum strides. Avoid making long lunges with your vacuum cleaner. All that bending and stretching forward taxes your back. Instead, suggests Dr. Dan Hamner, vacuum a foot or two at a time, then move to another location. Your back will thank you.

HEADACHES

Headaches are often caused by muscle tension or emotional stress. However, infections, allergies, head injuries, strokes, and even brain tumors also can cause head pain. If a headache is accompanied by nausea, vomiting, a fever, a stiff neck, or vision problems, see a doctor immediately. Otherwise, use these tips to help stop the throb of an everyday headache.

Halt a headache with your hands. When you're suffering from a tension headache, and the ibuprofen bottle is empty, take matters into your own hands with a reflexology treatment recommended by Jerry Huber.

Locate the fleshy web between your thumb and forefinger. This area will be sorer on one hand than the other, says Jerry, but you can increase the benefits by treating both sides. "There will probably be a knot there and a feeling of tightness," he says. "Inhale, push down into the sore spot for a count of three, and then exhale, releasing the pain you feel in your hand. On the next exhalation, press the spot and release the pain you feel in your head. And on your third exhalation, release the pain from both spots into the sunset." (See page 239 for an illustration of this techinque.)

Minimize it with mint. Next time you're suffering from a real throbber, try this clever remedy: Mix a few drops of peppermint essential oil with a few drops of vegetable oil in a small bowl. Dip your fingertips into the mixture and gently massage it into your forehead and temples for a few minutes. The menthol in the peppermint oil will act as a natural analgesic and comfort the nerves causing the headache.

that's • ingenious!

brush away back pain

ONE HABIT THAT contributes to back pain is bending over the sink to brush your teeth. Now, we're not going to suggest that you stop polishing your pearly whites, but we do have a simply ingenious way to do it. Just brush your teeth in the shower. (Be careful not to confuse the hair conditioner with the toothpaste, though.) That way, you can stand up straight and keep your back pain-free.

First Aid

It seems that when you need first aid the most, you're the least prepared. Chalk that up to the nature of emergencies: They happen without warning and tend to throw people into a panic. But panicking is the last thing you want to do when you're faced with trouble. Luckily, the best way to help in an emergency is also the simplest: Immediately call for help. This means dialing 911 from your home phone, a pay phone, a borrowed cell phone—any phone. Only after you've summoned the experts should you assess the scene and possibly offer assistance.

BROKEN BONES

A break or a crack in a bone is also known as a fracture. Although pain will prevent some movement of a broken bone, it's not necessarily true that "if you can move it, it's not broken." If you have any reason to suspect a broken bone, err on the side of caution with these tips, then get to an emergency room for diagnosis and further treatment as soon as possible.

Grab a book or a broomstick. Broken bones need to be stabilized, both to prevent further tissue damage and to provide some pain relief, so splint a break with what you have on hand. Ultimately, stabilization will probably come in the form of a cast of some kind, but for first-aid purposes, you'll need to focus on fashioning a makeshift splint. Look for something rigid that is approximately the size of the affected limb. A broomstick or a closed, full-size umbrella might work for a leg. A hardcover book, a folded newspaper, or even a magazine could suit an arm or a wrist until you can seek professional care, says Doug Levy, a retired emergency medical technician and trained firefighter in San Francisco.

Secure the splint.
After you've gently placed an injured limb on top of a makeshift splint, you'll need to secure it snugly but avoid a tight grip that can cut off circulation to that area. Fasten the splint in place with duct tape, torn strips of clothing, or even strong vines if that's all you can find. But be aware that you need to allow circulation to pass under the wrappings, says Tiffany Osborn, M.D., an emergency medicine physician at the R. Adams Cowley Shock Trauma Center at the University of Maryland Hospital in Baltimore and spokesperson for the American College of Emergency Physicians. "You will know if it's too tight because the foot or arm will get cold and numb. Test it by looking at the pink part of a fingernail or toenail. If you push there and it takes more than two seconds to regain color, the binding is too tight."

that's • ingenious!

crazy, man

A STRANGE BUT SANE remedy for those irritating paper cuts is to cover the slit with a dab of Krazy Glue®. This commercial product provides a protective layer and prevents infection from forming in minor cuts on your fingers, says Dr. Dale Anderson. Just be careful to use only a tiny drop or two, and *never* use it on your face, especially around your eyes.

BURNS

Effective burn treatment requires knowledge of the three degrees: Third-degree burns are the most severe and affect the full thickness of the skin. They can also go beyond the skin into underlying tissues. Third-degree burns are serious, but because the nerves have been damaged, they usually aren't painful. Second-degree burns affect partial skin thickness; these burns are moist and painful and will develop blisters pretty quickly. Some severe sunburns can be second degree burns. First-degree burns are red and painful but dry. Most first-degree burns, such as mild sunburns, will be fine within 24 hours.

Never try to treat a third-degree burn on your own. Instead, seek professional treatment right away. First- and second-degree burns can benefit from these self-care tips.

---

annals of ingenuity

THE KINDEST CUT

t he year is 1920. The place is New Brunswick, New Jersey. Josephine and Earle Dickson are newlyweds with a problem. It seems that Josephine is no Julia Child in the kitchen. Oh, she gets the meals on the table all right, but in the process of doing so, she ends up with lots of nicks, cuts, and burns. After a while, hubby Earle, a cotton buyer at Johnson & Johnson, gets tired of dressing her wounds and comes up with a solution.

He lays down an adhesive strip and spaces little squares of cotton along it, then covers it with fabric to create a whole strip of ready-made bandages that Josephine can apply herself. The bigwigs at Johnson & Johnson love the idea and promote Earle to vice president. (We presume that his raise was big enough for Josephine to hire a cook and get out of the kitchen.)

Douse it with vinegar. Whether you burn yourself cooking or spending too much time in the sun, you can soothe the pain by pouring vinegar on the hot spots. Why does it work? "Vinegar contains acetic acid, which counteracts the damage to your skin," says Dr. Dan Hamner. "The damage turns the burned part of your skin alkaline. The acetic acid in vinegar restores your body's pH balance."

Chill the burn. When it comes to minor burns, think cool thoughts and act immediately. If you spill hot coffee on your arm or singe your sleeve in a campfire, immediately remove anything touching the burned area. That's because skin can continue to burn when it's touching something hot, says Dr. Tiffany Osborn. Then you need to douse or soak the burned area with cold, clean water as quickly as possible to decrease tissue damage.

Make aloe your pal-o. If you have access to an aloe plant, it's the best source for treating a burn, says Victoria Hamman, N.D., a naturopathic physician in San Francisco. Snip off a thick leaf and split it open. Scoop out the cool green gel inside and coat the burn with it. Apply some gel three or four times a day until the burn heals. To hasten the process, add a drop of lavender oil to the aloe gel. Teaming aloe with lavender helps to relieve pain, reduce swelling and redness, and protect against infection.

Stop! Don't pop! Second-degree burns produce blisters relatively quickly, but let them be. "Resist the urge to pop blisters," says Dr. Tiffany Osborn. Breaking a blister will expose the tender skin beneath and make infection more likely. Wash and dry the area gently, then cover it with a loose dressing.

INSECT BITES AND STINGS

Here's the real buzz on insect bites and stings: Most times they're more uncomfortable than dangerous. Still, who wants to be shooing mosquitoes and other winged bugs while enjoying a nice walk through the woods? Here are some simply ingenious ways to stop the stinging and nibbling.

Banish bugs with a homegrown tonic. Create a homemade insect repellent from these essential oils, which you'll find at most health food stores.

In a small spray bottle, combine 8 drops cedar, 5 drops eucalyptus, 4 drops lavender, 2 drops rosemary, 2 drops juniper, 1 drop peppermint, 1 drop cinnamon and 1 drop clove essential oils with ¼ cup vegetable oil and spritz yourself before you head outside. The aroma of this mixture will encourage bugs to seek their snacks elsewhere. And don't forget to pack the bottle when you go on a long hike or an overnight camping trip.

ESSENTIALS FOR AT-HOME EMERGENCIES

One of the best housewarming gifts you can give—or get—is a well-stocked first-aid kit. You can purchase ready-made kits on the Internet or at medical supply stores. Sizes and prices range from small, inexpensive portable kits to pricey wall-mounted models. Choose one with the size of your family in mind. Or make your own, using the basic guidelines here. And don't let your supplies gather dust. Check your first-aid kit regularly and replace items whenever you run out or before they expire. According to the American Medical Association's *Handbook of First-Aid and Emergency Care,* here are the basics of a good home first-aid kit. Feel free to add extra items you need to care for family members with special health problems.

- Adhesive bandages in various sizes
- Alcohol swabs
- Antihistamine tablets (to treat allergic reactions)
- Bottle of iodine solution
- Bottle of 3 percent hydrogen peroxide
- Butterfly bandages
- Individually wrapped, large nonstick gauze pads
- Pain killer (ibuprofen or acetaminophen)
- Rolled elastic bandage (2 to 3 inches wide)
- Roll of 1-inch-wide adhesive tape
- Roll of 3-inch-wide gauze bandage
- Safety pins
- Scissors
- Syrup of ipecac (to induce vomiting)
- Tube of 1 percent hydrocortisone cream
- Tweezers

Take your vitamins. The next time you get stung by a bee, tame the pain and shrink the swelling with ingredients from your kitchen cupboard. Just dab the sting with a mixture of castor oil and the oil from one vitamin E capsule. "Castor oil contains vitamins A and D, which stimulate your immune system and reduce the swelling," says Dr. Dan Hamner. "Vitamin E is a fat-soluble vitamin that protects your skin."

Stop the sting with baking soda. You can put an end to the throbbing pain of an insect bite or sting with a thick paste of baking soda and water. Clean the area with warm water and soap, then apply the paste to the sting or bite. (A paste of meat tenderizer and water works well, too.) Leave the paste on for 15 to 20 minutes, then wash it off. The alkalinity of the baking soda and meat tenderizer has a cooling effect that neutralizes the acid of the sting.

Ease the itch. When a sting or bite is itchy, dab it with lemon juice, vinegar, or onion juice. All will relieve the itch naturally.

SPLINTERS, RASHES, AND BLISTERS

Sometimes it really is the little things that count—especially when those little things are slivers of wood, ankle-high plant leaves, or injuries affecting the square inch of flesh covering your heel. Splinters, rashes, and blisters may seem minor, but they can stop you in your tracks. The good news is that with just a little know-how and our ingenious expert tips, you can keep on truckin'.

SEEK MEDICAL HELP!

If you find yourself with someone who is having an allergic reaction to an insect bite or sting, seek medical help immediately. Symptoms range from numbness or cramping, to difficulty breathing or swallowing, to bouts of nausea and vomiting, to the appearance of hives.

---

wrap your blister

"BE INVENTIVE WHEN it comes to treating an established blister," says Dr. William Forgey. If you must keep moving in the same footwear, try using something thin and slick to ease the friction, such as a bit of cellophane from a gum package. Place the plastic right over the blister and use your sock to hold it in place. Then get to a place where you can remove or at least change your shoes.

Seek a sticky solution. If you've ever walked barefoot on an old boardwalk, you know that splinters can be painful. And while they're rarely life threatening, deep ones can become infected, and that can spell big trouble. One easy way to remove a splinter is to use something sticky. Duct tape or even clear cellophane tape can pull protruding splinters out, says Dr. Victoria Hamman. "Soak the area in very warm water first to expand and loosen things up a bit," she recommends. Anytime you remove a splinter, do so as carefully as possible to prevent it from breaking off in the skin.

Stop the itch with salt. When it comes to treating poison ivy, any type of wet dressing can help ease the itch, says Dr. William Forgey. Wrap a damp bandana or even a wet piece of clothing around the affected area. If you have table salt available, sprinkle that onto the dressing before applying it. "Salt helps dry out a weeping rash," Dr. Forgey says.

Got milk? Use it. You can ease the itch and soothe the swelling of a rash with a food you probably have right in your refrigerator. Dip a clean washcloth in milk (whole, low fat, or skim, it makes no difference), then place it directly on the rash for 10 minutes. Repeat a couple of times a day.

SPRAINS AND STRAINS

A sprain can—and usually does—occur unexpectedly. You trip and land on your wrist, or you take a step and turn your ankle. Ouch! Ligaments that stretch or tear leave nasty calling cards: black-and-blue bruising, swelling, tenderness, and pain. Our experts offer some ideas for sidestepping sprains and strains.

Practice steady footing. Veteran hikers rely on walking sticks or trekking poles to avoid sprains or fractures while stepping through the woods. The next time you take a hike, step carefully over fallen logs and around wet leaves, wet rocks, moss, and any slippery terrain that can cause you to sprain or break an ankle or wrist.

Make sure the shoe fits. A surprisingly common cause of many ankle sprains is worn-out shoes. Shoes that wear out at the front or along the heel create less-than-stable footing. So when your shoes show signs of wear, replace them, says Dr. Dale Anderson.

RICE is nice. When it comes to minor strains and sprains, RICE is the answer. RICE stands for rest, ice, compression, and elevation—the four components of treatment for many injuries.

SPRAIN OR STRAIN?

You wake up after a run, and your calf is unusually sore. You trip on the curb and twist your ankle. Is it a strain or a sprain? If you don't know the difference, you're not alone. Simply put, a sprain is a wrenching or twisting of a joint that results in an injury—stretching or tearing—to the ligaments (the tissues that connect bones). A strain is simply the overstretching of a muscle.

---

1. Rest. Get off that injured foot or stop using that injured wrist or finger.

2. Ice. Ice reduces swelling and promotes healing. During the first 48 hours after an injury, wrap the area with a bag containing ice (or a package of frozen vegetables) for 20 minutes at a time, then remove the ice for 40 minutes.

3. Compression. Wrap the injury (but not so tightly that you cut off the circulation) with a bandage.

4. Elevation. Keep the injured area elevated.

WOUND MANAGEMENT

You need to clean and bandage a wound to prevent infection. But what if you don't have a complete first-aid kit available? Just refer to the following expert wound management tips.

Put water under pressure. "Proper cleansing is the most important step in effective wound management, especially in an outdoor situation," says Dr. Tiffany Osborn. That means using water pressure to flush bacteria from the wound. If you don't have access to a faucet or hose, pour the water from a cup. Even better, says Dr. Osborn, pour the water into a clean plastic bag, make a small hole in one corner, and aim the jet of water at the wound while you squeeze the bag.

Battle bacteria with beer. Ever hook yourself while out fishing? If you're like many folks, you probably packed a nice lunch and some cold beverages but forgot the first-aid kit. No

---

PENNY FOR YOUR . . . NOSEBLEED?

The next time you get a nosebleed, tilt your head back, grab hold of your nose, and pinch it slightly closed. Or place a penny just above your upper lip and press firmly to stop the bleeding. "Either way, you're putting pressure on the capillary bed inside your nose, which should stop the bleeding within a couple of minutes," says Dr. Dan Hamner.

---

problem, says Dr. Dan Hamner, a sports medicine physician. Just open a cold bottle or can of beer and pour the suds directly on the wound. The ingredients in beer are antibacterial agents and will keep the wound free from infection until you can get to shore and apply an antibacterial ointment.

Seal the gap. A gaping wound needs to be held shut to prevent further damage and keep it from getting dirty again. If you don't have a butterfly bandage on hand, you can use duct tape to hold the edges of a wound together temporarily, says Dr. Tiffany Osborn. If a wound needs duct tape to keep it closed, that means you need stitches—so get to an emergency department right away.

In a pinch, you can use duct tape to close a wound.

Sacrifice a clean shirt. If you don't have sterile gauze, you can use any piece of clean, dry fabric, such as a T-shirt, to bandage a wound. Tear off a suitable-size strip of fabric and wrap it around the wound, Dr. Tiffany Osborn advises.

chapter 14

hobbies, sports, and
g a m e s

TO THOSE WHO WOULD SAY that the key to a happy life is to eat more ice cream, we'd add a corollary: Spend more time doing the things you love. Not that work and chores can't be fulfilling, but isn't it time you got out that needlepoint kit you bought 18 months ago? Or spent an afternoon shooting baskets with the neighborhood kids? Or took a turn at a more unusual pastime—creating art with glue, a wedding invitation, and clear glass dessert plates? The important thing is that you take a break and pursue something you really enjoy.

After you've made up your mind to make time for relaxation, check out the following pages for dozens of ways to enjoy that time even more. Along the way, you'll meet our band of ingenious experts. There's softball coach Bubba Teeters of Lake Worth, Florida, who will help you improve your swing at the next church softball game. Dot Richardson, M.D., of Orlando, Florida, explains why warming up before the big game is so important. She ought to know—not only is she an Olympic softball gold medal winner, but she's an orthopedic surgeon, too. We cover other sports as well. Bowlers will want to check out Lisa Fine's tips for knocking down the pins. Lisa is a veteran bowler from Sevierville, Tennessee. Tennis buffs will enjoy Bob Byrd's advice about saving money on lessons. Bob is a retired high school tennis coach in Indianapolis, Indiana. For outdoor enthusiasts, we have words of wisdom from fishing expert Mike Finley from North Hills, California, and outdoorswoman Margy Floyd from Costa Mesa, California.

Of course, you don't have to be outside to have fun. When you're feeling crafty, dig into the second half of this chapter. That's where you'll find Knoxville, Tennessee, art director Tom Russell's ingenious decoupage tips and ideas for using up craft supplies from yarn to shellac. Finally, we take on indoor gardening, offering some ways to make your houseplants happier and healthier.

Sports and Recreation

Maybe you abandoned your dream of playing in the WNBA. Perhaps you just never were the type who found herself serving up the winning point or sinking a tournament-clinching putt. But sports still have plenty to offer. They're a great way to get that weight-bearing exercise or cardiovascular workout your doctor is always going on about without joining a posh health club.

Whether it's tennis, softball, or shuffleboard, if you do something that's actually fun, you're much more likely to stay active. And casual sports—a game of tennis with your nephew, croquet at the family reunion—are great ways to bond.

There's one other thing to keep in mind. Sports might be more enjoyable for you today than they were when you were faced with a jury of your peers in grade school gym class. "I'm a much better athlete today than I ever was as a teenager," says 49-year-old Chuck Kennedy, an attorney in Watchung, New Jersey. "I actually enjoy playing on my corporate softball team, and we do pretty well." Here's another reason you might enjoy sports today more than you ever thought possible: You've read these great tips from our truly ingenious athletes. Batter up!

BASEBALL AND SOFTBALL

It starts out innocently enough—a family gathering, some friends getting together in the park, a company picnic. And the next thing you know, you're up at bat, all eyes on you, with visions of Charlie Brown dancing in your head. Don't hyperventilate. We've rounded up some experts whose ingenious advice will help you get safely to first base or stab that ground ball.

Coil like a cobra. Most nights, you'll find Bubba Teeters at a softball diamond. If he isn't coaching, he's umpiring the sport he loves. In fact, he exchanged wedding vows with his wife, Joanie, on a softball field. Although he coaches preteens as well as players well past their 40th birthdays, he always stresses fundamentals and drills.

His advice when you're in the batter's box? Keep your hands nice and loose around the bat. As the pitcher releases the ball, coil like a snake and strike the ball in front of you. "Power comes from your hips, so you need to pivot your hips when you swing," Bubba says. "Your hands should be close to your right ear (if you're right-handed), then extend your arms out straight for a nice, level swing."

WRAP YOUR BAT

When the temperature drops below 50°F, wrap your aluminum bat in an old cotton T-shirt to keep it from getting too cold. "Cold temperatures can crack the bat," says Bubba Teeters. "And the ball won't come off a cold bat very well."

Keep that elbow up. If you don't play much softball or baseball, remember one thing when it's your turn to bat. "Keep your back elbow up while you swing," says Wade Slate, an 8-year Little League coach from Knoxville, Tennessee, who now just plays for fun. "If you drop your back elbow, you're much more likely to swing up under the ball and miss or make a loop and swing around on top of the ball and just beat it into the ground." Need practice? Work ahead of time with a bat and an old tennis ball, which is much less likely to shatter the neighbor's window.

Stay on your toes. When fielding a ground ball, stay on your toes. As the ball comes toward you, tap the ground with your glove to keep the ball from squirting through the gap between your legs. Keep your throwing hand just above your glove so that you can cup the ball into the glove if it should pop out.

BOWLING FOR . . . FUN

You paid to rent shoes and a lane, so you should at least try to have fun, but wouldn't it be nice to knock down some pins, too? Here are some simply ingenious ways to do just that.

Don't throw the ball. "Try rolling the ball, not throwing it," says 16-year bowling league veteran Lisa Fine. It sounds obvious,

gold medal know-how

SECOND BASEMAN and orthopedic surgeon Dot Richardson is 40, but she remains fit, injury-free, and at the top of her game. In fact, she was a starter for the U.S. Olympic softball squads in 1996 and 2000. What's her secret to softball longevity?

"Whether you're playing at the Olympic level or in a local recreational league, young or old, you should spend at least twenty minutes stretching every part of your body to increase your chances of optimal performance and reduce your risk of injury," Dr. Richardson says. "Start with your head and neck, then gradually work your way down to your heels."

She also spends a few minutes doing 40-foot sprints—running forward, backward, and side to side—to awaken her fast-twitch muscles so that she can maintain her legendary base running speed. One warm-up drill she calls the Frankenstein walk involves walking with her legs straight up and out. She brings her right leg forward with a straight knee, then her left leg. With each stride, she stretches and warms her hamstring muscles.

but it's not always easy. "First, look for the wooden arrows that are inlaid in the floor a few feet from the end of the bowling lane," Lisa advises. "Find the one in the center. Then roll the ball so that it will slide over the arrow one or two to the right or left of the center arrow. That should make your ball hit the 'pocket' between the front pin and one of the two pins behind it. That's how you make a strike—or at least knock down a lot of pins."

Reach for the sky. A big part of bowling (or any sport, for that matter) happens after you let go of the ball, says Lisa Fine. It's called follow-through, and it will make the ball travel in a straighter path to the pins. "After you release the ball, follow through with your palm facing up, lifting your hand in an arc toward the sky," Lisa says. No one will look at you funny—that's how all the best bowlers get strikes.

Don't get left holding the ball. Another tip from the pros for the occasional bowler is not to stick your fingers in the holes of your ball and tote it around before you actually bowl. Why? You'll tire your arm and make your fingers sweaty—which will make the ball stick to your fingers and careen wildly into the gutter when you release it.

Lighten your load. One drawback to being the occasional bowler is the bowling balls. Typically, bowling alleys have very lightweight balls for tots or heavy castoffs from league bowlers. What most adult women need, at least in the beginning, is a ball in the 8- to 10-pound range. So stop by the thrift store before you set out for your next bowling date. A used ball shouldn't cost more than a couple of dollars, which is a bargain if it will allow you to knock down a few pins. And if you live in a small town or a small suburban area—the one-alley town, if you will—just ask the alley owner if you can leave your ball there for the next time you come in. It won't hurt if other people use it, too.

MAYBE THEY SHOULD CALL IT YANKEE BOWLING

In every crowd, there are bowlers and there are people who can't bowl very well. Inevitably, members of the two camps will get together for a night out at the bowling alley. Want to make things more fun for everyone? "Try Scotch bowling," says Lisa Fine. "You form teams of two, putting a strong bowler with someone who's not as experienced. Each team member bowls every other ball for a single score." That way, if the weaker member leaves an impossible spare or split, the stronger member is responsible for picking it up. The bonus (and the reason it's called Scotch bowling) is that you pay for only one game per two bowlers, and that will please any frugal Yankee.

TENNIS, ANYONE?

"You can get a great workout playing tennis for just an hour," says Bob Byrd, who coached high school tennis for 10 years, even though he didn't take up the sport himself until age 34. "It's not high impact, and people prone to knee and ankle injuries can ordinarily play. And unlike golf, it's great if you have a family, because you're done in an hour." Here is some more of Bob's ingenious advice.

Avoid the high-cost lesson racket. You know the old saying that goes, "Don't worry that we're cold in the winter, we'll have plenty of heat in the summer"? That's sort of the mentality to apply if you want to learn to play tennis at a reasonable price, says Bob. "Try to learn to play tennis in the warmer months, even though it can be real hot," he says. "That's when you can go outdoors and avoid the high racket club fees—and their typical requirement that you join for an entire year." Check out the local parks department, high school, or community college for low-cost tennis lessons, and consider group lessons to reduce your cost further.

Bigger is better. Picture yourself trying to race someone wearing new track shoes while you're wearing work boots. That's what it's like when you attempt to economize by playing tennis with an old wooden racket. "There is

---

annals of ingenuity

SPHAIRISTIKE, ANYONE?

how's that? Well, sphairistike—known to us as tennis—is what retired British army officer Major Walter Wingfield called the game he invented in the early 1870s. Maybe he was putting on airs (sphairistike is Greek for "ball playing"). More likely, though, he was acknowledging that his game was based on a similar game played in ancient Greece.

Wingfield may have "invented" the game, but perhaps it is Arthur Balfour, Wingfield's friend and future prime minister of England, who deserves the credit for popularizing the game. It was only after Balfour suggested renaming sphairistike lawn tennis did the game really catch on.

set your strings right

HELP YOUR TENNIS game by making sure your racket strings are set at the right tension for your style of play. Officials from the United States Racquet Stringers Association offer these string and racket facts.

• **Lower string tension generates more power.**

• **Higher string tension generates more ball control.**

• **A heavy racket frame generates more power and fewer vibrations than a lightweight frame.**

• **A larger frame is less prone to twisting and offers a larger sweet spot than a smaller frame.**

• **Rackets should be restrung based on how many times a week you play. If you play twice a week, schedule the restringing every 6 months. If you play 4 times a week, have your racket restrung every 3 months.**

no point in even trying," Bob says. "The new rackets are just so much lighter. The heads are amazingly large, and the sweet spot is so big that it feels good even if you hit the ball slightly off center." Bob likes graphite composite or titanium rackets. "You want the midsize or oversize head, and stick to name brands, such as Prince®, Head®, or Wilson®," he advises.

FISHING

Mike Finley the attorney likes the challenge of debating a case in the courtroom. Mike Finley the fisherman loves the challenge of trying to hook a strong, wily, and swift striped bass at a freshwater lake. Known as "Dr. Mike" to the folks who visit his Web site (http://mike_esq.tripod.com/mikesfishingtips/), he loves to share his inside fishing tips. So grab your pole, a worm (or an old candy wrapper), and get ready to catch some fish.

PLAY HOOKY WITH GARLIC

Bass and trout flock to certain scents that you and I would find less than appealing. You can use that fact to your advantage by mixing 2 tablespoons each cod liver oil and garlic powder with 1 teaspoon salt in a small container. Coat your lure's hooks with this blend. The aroma is irresistible to these fish, says Mike Finley.

Attract 'em with trash. Most bait fish shine and shimmer when they move, catching some of the sun's rays. That dancing light is irresistible to many freshwater fish, such as bass and bluegills. Mimic the bait fish look by using aluminum foil candy wrappers or the shiny insides of an old potato chip bag as a fishing lure. "To a bass, the candy wrapper looks like a bait fish, and they will be attracted to it," Mike says.

Operate on fish time. Fish don't wear wristwatches, but their routines are clocklike. The best time to catch striped bass is at night right after sundown or in the morning right before dawn. Mike says that the bass's eyes adjust more quickly to changes in light conditions than do the bait fish's, so pick those times to drop your lure into the water. And wear polarized sunglasses to help you see underwater better.

Catch crickets with chips. Live crickets are considered a delicacy by most bluegills. You could buy crickets at a bait shop or pet store, but it's cheaper to catch your own at home, Mike says. Just buy a cricket trap for a couple of dollars at a pet store. Add a few pieces of lettuce and potato chips to the trap to lure crickets. Set the traps at night and retrieve them in the early morning before ants discover the site. The traps are reusable.

HIKING AND CAMPING

Margy Floyd grew up in a camping and hiking family in southern California. When she isn't managing an indoor rock-climbing gym in Costa Mesa, California, she's likely scaling a mountain. In fact, she's climbed all 13 of California's 14,000-footers. Here are some of her most ingenious tips.

Pack your pack in order. You can save yourself time and frustration by packing with a purpose when you head out for a hike or backpacking expedition, says Margy Floyd. Put your sleeping bag at the bottom of your pack, then dedicate the main compartment to the heaviest items, such as your tent, food, and cooking gear. Place your "must-haves"—maps, guides, camera, sunscreen, rain gear, and pocketknife—in the top of the backpack. Even better, store your clothing and food in different-colored sacks inside your pack so that you can quickly retrieve them.

Don't leave home without 'em. Whether you're planning a day hike or a weekend trek, there are some items you should always pack. Here they are.

First-aid kit. Because you just never know.

Freeze-dried food, dried fruit, or energy bars. In case you need to be out longer than you planned.

Iodine tablets. To purify water from lakes, rivers, and streams. (People with thyroid conditions should not use iodine products to purify water. Rather, they should carry a water filter that doesn't use iodine. If you're not sure, check with your doctor.)

Lighter or matches tucked inside a waterproof pouch. In case you have to build a fire.

Water bottle. Never leave for a hike without plenty of water. People can survive weeks without food, but only a couple of days without water.

Tarp. Just in case you need to build an emergency shelter.

that's · ingenious!

get your bearings

NOT SURE WHETHER you're heading east or south? Here are some simply ingenious ways to help you get your bearings the next time you're in the heart of the wilderness. But a word of warning: Nothing beats having a map and a compass and knowing how to use them.

- Anthills are usually located on the south sides of trees and other objects.
- Moss usually grows on the north sides of trees, especially those exposed to sunlight.
- Most trees tend to lean eastward unless there are prevailing wind factors. Notable exceptions: Poplars and willows generally slant southward.
- Woodpeckers prefer to peck into the east sides of trees.

Make sure your sleeping bag measures up. The ideal sleeping bag provides 3 to 6 inches of toe wiggle room. Less than that, and you're in for a night of toe cramping. More than that and you risk cold toes, because your body will have to work overtime to heat that extra space. If you plan to be out during the cold months, always select a sleeping bag rated for 10°F lower than the lowest temperature you might encounter.

Dress for success. Seasoned outdoors people have a saying: "Cotton kills." That's because cotton is a poor insulator when dry and an absolutely useless one when wet. So leave your blue jeans at home when you head out for a hike and opt instead for lightweight, water-resistant clothing made from so-called technical fabrics such as Coolmax®, polypropylene, or Polarfleece®. Also, dress in layers so that you can add or shed clothing as the temperature drops or rises.

Hobbies

Have fun and get personal. That's designer Tom Russell's advice for any craft—quilting, sewing, ceramics, paint by numbers, you name it. "I do crafts because they're relaxing and fun," he says, "but they also give me a chance to make designer items look exactly how I want them to—with my designs, my colors, and the patterns I'm already using in my house."

An avid machine quilter and crafter, Tom doesn't get so carried away by personal expression that he forgets the other advantage of his hobbies: mucho money saved. "I couldn't even afford designer frames or handmade quilts unless I made them myself," he says. "I'm amazed at what people will pay hundreds of dollars for at a home store, when they could make their own at home."

Tom, a program guide art director for a cable television house and garden network, also knows timesaving shortcuts and how to get the best hobby and crafting supplies at the lowest prices. And he knows when you can get away with inexpensive substitutes and when you should use only the best. He and other experts in their hobbies offer this assortment of ingenious ways to get the most out of whatever hobby you choose. All you have to do to save time and money and to get better-than-professional results is read on.

THE DEAL ON DECOUPAGE

"If it isn't moving, you can decoupage it," says Tom Russell, and he's exaggerating only a little. "You can really get creative with decoupage as long as you realize that once it's there, it's there— you can't get it wet, and it's very tough to remove." Tom has experimented with decoupage far beyond what you see in the pages of the home and garden magazine he designs. Here's his advice for ways to make designer-look projects at a fraction of the cost you'd pay for the finished products.

Try these unusual projects. If you've already mastered the basics of decoupage, don't put away that brush just yet. There are lots of ways to enjoy this hobby and use up the economy-size jar of Mod-Podge® to get the best value for your hobby dollar. While you're humming happily as you work with scissors and glue, you'll also be creating low-cost accessories that express your personal style and keepsake-quality gifts that brides, new mothers, friends, and family will treasure for years to come. Try these.

1. Hello, doily! If you have a small round-top stool that's ready for the trash, consider painting it a dark color, then topping it with a paper doily—which you decoupage to be a permanent fixture. It makes a great end table for a Victorian-style room.

2. Turn the tables. Experiment with reverse decoupage on clear glass plates. This is an inexpensive, elegant way to display special paper mementos, such as wedding invitations or graduation announcements. "Essentially, you're attaching the elements to the back of the plate so that they can be viewed from the front," says Tom Russell. "With the chemicals in the finish and the fact that it can't get near water, the plates are meant only for viewing, not eating."

To do this so-called reverse decoupage, place the plate facedown, then arrange your cutouts, saturated with glue and also facedown, on the back of the plate. To make the background look more pulled together, cover the decoupaged images with a layer of Chinese rice paper, which you can purchase at a craft store or via the Internet. Saturate the rice paper with decoupage glue, too, and attach it to

WHATSIT?

Q: This accordion-like object has eight small metal feet. Can you guess what it is?

A: It's a yarn winder. It wound yarn that came from the spinning wheel into skeins, which were later unwound to weave on a loom.

THREE CREATIVE DECOUPAGE PROJECTS

There's something addictive about decoupage. "It's a relaxing, fun hobby, plus you end up with beautiful objects," says Tom Russell. It also just might be one of the hottest crafts going right now.

But once you've finished every frame and shoebox in the house, what next? Quit eyeing your husband's briefcase and consider these fresh ideas that people will actually appreciate.

1. Cut out fish shapes from patterned kraft paper and decoupage them onto a plain paper or fabric lampshade. Use a small hole punch to put three or four holes around the bottom edge of the shade and dangle a few fishing lures (sans hooks) from them, attached with fishing line or florist's wire. This one is perfect for a cabin.

2. Create a new mom's memory book before a baby shower. Gather a copy of the shower invitation and handwritten snippets of parenting advice from people who will attend. Attach them to the front of a photo album or scrapbook with acid-free pages, and consider adding some photocopies of photos of the expectant couple—or perhaps their own baby pictures.

3. Photocopy pages from antique housekeeping books and decoupage them to the walls of the laundry room, on top of wallpaper or in lieu of wallpaper. You can repeat the same pattern over and over or not, as you wish.

the back of the plate, on top of the other images. Then finish the back of the plate with a few more coats of decoupage glue.

NEEDLECRAFTS

"And she even sews her own clothes" has become a tribute to a person's all-around resourcefulness. So we can assume that people who sew have lots of resourceful ways to do it faster, cheaper, or more creatively—as do our friends who wield needles of any kind to knit, crochet, or embroider. Want some great ideas without going to a sewing circle or quilting bee? Pull up a chair.

Make a place for your pins. Just because your passion is sewing doesn't mean you actually get to sew very often. That's sad because you don't get to enjoy yourself as often as you'd like. But it's even sadder because the longer you go between projects, the more likely your sewing supplies are to disappear. Anyone seen the pincushion? If the answer is no, head for the bathroom. Grab a fresh bar or ball of soap to use as a makeshift pincushion. And if your "real" pincushion ever shows up, you can always use the soap for its intended purpose.

Gather what you sew. Forget woolgathering; it's fabric gathering that's tough. Here's an ingenious shortcut from Lisa Price, editor of a sewing and craft Web site in Knoxville, Tennessee, that guarantees seamstress-quality gathers.

First, go find the family kite. Actually, you don't need the kite, just kite string or something similar. Heavy-duty button cord works well, too. Cut a piece a little longer than the length of the fabric you need to gather. Place it along the edge, leaving just a half inch or so hanging from each side. Then sew a zigzag machine stitch right over the string (try to center it in the zigzag) and right through the fabric. When you're done, hold one end of the string tight and pull the other through the zigzag seam. Voilà, a perfect gather!

Make a simple gather with kite string.

USING HOBBY LEFTOVERS

Is there anything more frustrating than having leftover hobby supplies that are still useful but not worth saving? The best thing to do, of course, is to buy precisely the amount of, say, gold leaf or embroidery yarn required for your project. But when that's not possible (and let's face it, that's never possible), try to use the leftovers quickly, before you forget what you have or before they deteriorate to the point where they're not usable. Stumped for ways to use up your leftover hobby supplies? Here are some ingenious alternatives.

Use up scrap yarn. Yarn is one of those things that just accumulates—like mildew in the shower. If you use up your scraps, you'll save space and waste less money. Even better, once you're done with the remnants of the last project, you can buy fresh, fun yarn in brand-new colors for your next dream project with a clear conscience. Here are two ways to achieve that yarn-free state.

1. Feather a nest. If you have only a couple of feet of yarn, put it out for nesting birds in the spring. Cut it into 3- to 4-inch lengths, stash it in an old mesh bag (like one that onions come in), and dangle it from a tree or bush in an area protected from cats.

2. Give it to those who aren't knit-picky. Got so much yarn that you'd have to have condors in the neighborhood to use it all for nests? See if someone at the local senior citizens center or nursing home might need the supplies.

Make a bookmark. Here's an elegant and fun way to use up those miscellaneous strands of embroidery thread before they end up in a snarl at the bottom of your work basket, says Trish McCollum, an art instructor at St. Joseph's Elementary school in Fountain City, Tennessee.

1. Cut or find a square or rectangle piece of sturdy poster board that's no larger than 4 by 6 inches and no smaller than 2 by

3 inches. There's no need to rush out and buy poster board. The cardboard under an individually wrapped cupcake is perfect, or you can cut a piece from a cereal box. This is your form.

2. Working along the two short edges, cut quarter-inch notches at quarter-inch intervals. Each notch should match perfectly a notch on the opposite edge. Tape the end of a long piece of embroidery thread (at least 15 times as long as the card) to the back of the card. Then wrap the thread around the card lengthwise, threading it through the facing notches as if you were coiling a rope—until you have a series of threads that resemble guitar strings. Tape down the other end of the thread on the back.

3. Use a needle and other scraps of embroidery thread to weave the bookmark. Tie one end of the thread to one of the vertical threads on the card, in the bottom corner. Thread the other end through an embroidery needle, then draw the needle across the threads—under, over, under—one row. At the end of the row, come back weaving over, under, over. Gently push the rows together so they'll hold their shape. (Remember those pot holders you used to weave as a child? It's pretty much the same, only more delicate.) When you exhaust one scrap of thread, tie the next to its end and keep going.

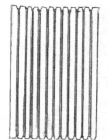

Cut notches on the top and bottom of the cardboard and wrap the thread around it lengthwise (left). Use a needle to carefully weave your bookmark (right).

4. When you have woven the entire bookmark, tie off the thread, then snip the loops that hold the weaving to the card, one at a time, and carefully double-tie their ends so your work doesn't unravel.

Get fruity with your shellac. What happens when you're finished with that woodworking project but there's a bit of shellac left over? Well, you're not supposed to shellac birdhouses (the birds won't roost there), and what are the odds that you'll have a dollhouse dining room table that needs exactly that shade? Instead, how about preserving some fruit for arrangements and centerpieces? Here's how.

1. Choose perfectly formed pieces of fruit and make sure they're completely dry.

2. Give each piece several coats of shellac. Let the shellac dry completely between coats, and stop when you can no longer feel the surface of the fruit if you run your finger over the shellac. You're also striving for that nice, even, translucent, glossy surface (no drips) that will make the fruit look well-polished but not fake.

After the last coat dries, you'll have "artificial" fruit that will last indefinitely. Don't try this with squishy fruits such as cherries or kiwifruit. Granny Smith apples, lemons, and oranges work well. Also, make sure the fruit is out of reach of children, so they won't bite into it and get a stomachache.

INDOOR GARDENING

Here's an easy way to tell which type of plant is which: Evergreens are the ones that stay green all the time. Deciduous plants lose their leaves in the fall. And the ones that lose their leaves as soon as you bring them indoors? Those are houseplants.

But that doesn't have to be true. You can keep plants alive in the great indoors just by following a bit of expert advice. And you don't have to stop at possessing one philodendron that made it through an entire calendar year. Indoor gardening can be a fun and varied hobby. Here are some tips to get you started and to keep you interested in this, er, growing hobby.

Give plants their space. It's true—some plants really do like to live in cramped quarters. Cacti like to be potbound, as do

African violets and dozens of varieties of green plants. But don't take this small-pot idea too far. Always choose a pot that allows for about a half inch between the top of the soil and the rim of the pot. That way, you'll be able to get in there with the watering can without the water splashing off the leaves and never reaching the roots. Yes, it's worrisome that the plant won't be packed in if it prefers the rootbound state. But, if the water runs all over the coffee table every time you water a plant, it probably won't last long anyway. So at least give the little green guy some chance of survival with a pot that will accept water.

Make a multiplant planter. Ever wonder how florists keep those beautiful planters with a variety of greenery and blooms flourishing? They have a deep, dark secret you can adopt. See, those plants aren't really growing in the planter. They're growing in their own individual pots. Florists arrange the individual pots inside the planter, fill in between them with rocks or soil, and then cover up their work with moss (widely available at craft stores). Here are the advantages of this approach: You get a nice grouping effect, you can give each plant the water and fertilizer it requires, and you can easily remove any plants that don't perform.

Brew up some drainage. Almost all houseplants need good drainage. They like to drink water, but the roots will rot if they sit in it. Traditionally, indoor gardeners put gravel at the bottom of pots for drainage, and that's a good idea. But they also typically put potting soil right on top, and that's not such a good idea, because the soil will eventually flush down into the rocks, and sooner or later the rock-soil mixture will start to hold water. To prevent that, place a coffee filter between the rocks and the soil, with the filter lip facing up. You can also place another coffee filter flat beneath the rocks to keep the smaller ones from slipping through the drainage holes.

PART 3

YARD AND

garden

Imagine this: It's a sunny day. You're gathered
with your family for a backyard barbecue.
The grass is green—and completely weed
free. The birds are singing, your flower
garden is a glorious explosion of color. Just
before you serve the salad, you pluck a red,

ripe tomato from the vine and slice it up. Sounds idyllic, doesn't it?

Our ingenious experts, a cagey bunch with years of experience, will help you achieve that idyll. For instance, our landscaping pros will explain how to build a stone wall that will last for years and offer an easy way to make your driveway skid proof. Our lawn and garden experts will help you keep your lawn green and make your flower and vegetable gardens worthy of a magazine cover. And if you're interested in inviting wildlife to your backyard, well, we've devoted an entire chapter to attracting garden good guys.

We end this section with a chapter dedicated to offering safe ways to rid your property of the pesky pests who want to peck holes in your siding, nosh on your garden, or (ahem) just use it as a latrine.

chapter 15

low-cost landscape
features

YOUR BACKYARD SHOULD BE A HAVEN, a place where you can put the world and all of your worries on hold. That's what we'd all like, anyway. But if that description doesn't quite fit your yard, try picturing it with evergreen hedges or a fence that blocks the sound of passing cars. Or imagine that your chain-link fence has been transformed with morning glories. Now add a redwood deck, or perhaps a rose-covered arbor, or maybe even a herringbone pattern brick path leading to a water garden. Suddenly, your yard is more than just the space between property lines.

Sounds glorious, doesn't it? Well, all it takes is a little imagination, some determination, and the ingenious advice of our experts, including Joe Murphy, a masonry pro from Swarthmore, Pennsylvania, who shares his expert advice about driveways and walkways. Landscaper Steph Sickles of Arlington, Massachusetts, offers ingenious tips about walls and fences—both manmade and natural. Veteran contractor Kevin MacIntyre of North Reading, Massachusetts, chips in with his know-how about decks. Finally, Bill Underhill, manager of the aquatics department at Hyannis Country Garden in Hyannis, Massachusetts, offers the lowdown on water gardens.

A word of caution: Before you undertake any project involving digging or building, contact your city hall and utility companies to find out about local building codes and permits, and to make sure you're avoiding utility lines.

But enough introduction. It's time to get your tools together and get to work!

Driveways and Walkways

If you're planning a major project involving concrete—whether it's laying a new driveway or building a walkway with brick and mortar—the best advice Joe Murphy can give you is to hire a pro. "If you don't have experience working with concrete and you try to tackle a big job, you're probably going to make some big mistakes," says Joe. "And it's going to cost you more to have those fixed than it would have cost to hire someone to do the job in the first place."

Joe knows: He's a mason who built and repaired sidewalks and brick walls for the city of Philadelphia for a dozen years. He also spent time (and earned pretty good money) fixing the mistakes of do-it-your-selfers who took on concrete jobs they weren't capable of handling. However, there are plenty of driveway and walkway

---

MAKE it LAST

Steer clear of gravel

IF YOU WANT to lay down a driveway that lasts, you might want to think twice about using gravel. At about $1 per square foot for a 2-inch layer, it is the cheapest option available. But sometimes you get what you pay for.

The drawbacks? Gravel scatters easily, your car tires will eventually sink ruts into it, and weeds have a heyday. If you live in a cold climate, there's another thing: When you try to plow or shovel snow off of it, you might just leave half of your driveway in your lawn.

---

projects that anyone can do. Here are some simple and ingenious tips that will help make them even easier.

DRIVEWAY AND WALKWAY REPAIRS

There's no sense fixing cracks in your driveway or walkway if the patches will just crack again in a couple of months. And we guarantee that they will unless you follow these simple steps.

Check the temperature. Is there a chill in the air? If so, it's best to wait until the temperature outside is at least 60°F before you begin a repair project. Any colder and the repair material won't cure.

Start clean. "When you're repairing cracks in a driveway or walkway, whether it's concrete or asphalt, always clear the cracks of any plants or debris," says masonry pro Joe Murphy. Otherwise, a plant could grow right through your patch.

Seal the deal. After you patch a driveway crack, make sure to seal the repaired area. "That way, moisture won't get into the concrete and create another crack," says Joe. There are a number of commercial sealers on the market, but you can also make your own at home. Just prepare a mixture of equal parts linseed oil and mineral spirits. Keep in mind, however, that this homemade sealer will darken the concrete.

Spray your patch. Want to strengthen your patching compound when you're repairing a crack in concrete? It's easy: Just mist the compound with water after you apply it, then cover it with 4-mil construction-grade polyethylene sheeting for about a week. "That will extend the curing time and strengthen the patch," says Joe Murphy.

WINNING THE UPHILL BATTLE

Tired of sliding down your driveway or landing on your backside every time it snows? Here are three ways to improve your footing and your tires' traction.

Add sand before it snows. Next time you apply a blacktop sealer to your driveway, finish it off by sprinkling a little coarse sand on top. You might never slip again.

Stick with safe salt. When it snows, steer clear of sodium chloride-based ice melt products on driveways and walkways if you have an adjacent lawn. Not only does sodium chloride damage grass, but it also damages the mortar in walkways and driveways. Calcium chloride is friendlier to plants and mortar.

Reach for kitty litter. On a snowy day, you can apply a mixture of sand and clay kitty litter to your driveway and walkways.

WALKWAY KNOW-HOW

If you plan to lay a brick walkway in sand, there are a few things you need to know before you get started. First, you have to figure out how many bricks you'll need. "The rule of thumb is five bricks per square foot, which allows you some leeway for the waste that occurs when you cut bricks," says Joe Murphy.

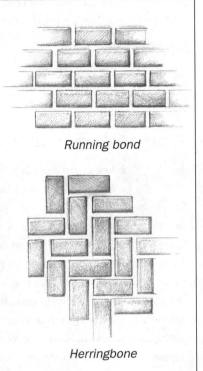

Running bond

Herringbone

You also need to decide what kind of brick pattern you're going to use. Keep in mind that some patterns, such as herringbone, are complicated but require minimal cutting. Others, such as the horizontal running bond pattern, are simple to lay down but require lots of cutting.

As for the type of bricks to use, that depends on where you live. "If winters are harsh in your area of the country, you'll want to use only paving bricks that are rated for severe weather," Joe says. If your winters are mild, you can use a less durable brick, which will be less expensive. Remember to leave plenty of elbowroom along your walkway, keeping the edges at least 2 feet away from any trees, large plants, or walls.

The sand gives you traction, the clay absorbs the water as the ice melts, and neither will damage plants or driveways.

Stone Walls

Stone walls can last for hundreds of years—if they're built right. If they're built wrong . . . well, just ask landscaper Steph Sickles what can happen.

"I had a customer who had a cinder block and mortar retaining wall built at the bottom of a hill on his property," Steph says. "The wall was about thirty feet long and five feet high and once stood straight. But after years of water flowing through the soil and down the hill, the wall teetered at a one-hundred-and thirty-five-degree angle. The only things keeping the wall from toppling were the grass roots that had wrapped around the cinder blocks."

The home owner neglected to include weep holes in the wall to let moisture drain through. He had to pay someone to tear down the wall and rebuild it. In that same town, less than half a mile away, there are stone walls that are as solid now as they were when they were built more than 200 years ago by the colonists. If you follow our ingenious expert tips, maybe someone will be admiring your wall generations from now.

Look for low- or no-cost stone sources. You've decided to build a stone wall. Great. So where do you get the stones? Well, you could purchase them from a stone supplier, but there are at least four less expensive sources.

1. Check out your own property. You may have a gold mine of stones out in the back 40. And unlike purchased stones, these will look natural in your landscape—as if the wall grew there all by itself.

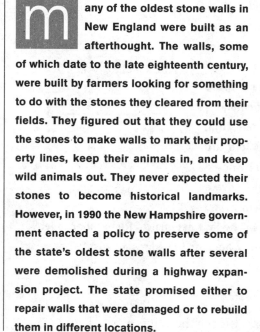

annals of ingenuity

ROCKS FOR THE AGES

many of the oldest stone walls in New England were built as an afterthought. The walls, some of which date to the late eighteenth century, were built by farmers looking for something to do with the stones they cleared from their fields. They figured out that they could use the stones to make walls to mark their property lines, keep their animals in, and keep wild animals out. They never expected their stones to become historical landmarks. However, in 1990 the New Hampshire government enacted a policy to preserve some of the state's oldest stone walls after several were demolished during a highway expansion project. The state promised either to repair walls that were damaged or to rebuild them in different locations.

HOW MUCH STONE DOES IT TAKE TO BUILD A WALL?

You have it all planned out: a lovely stone wall running through your property. But how do you determine how much stone you'll need? Just use this ingenious formula.

Multiply the thickness of the wall by its height and then by its length—all in feet. That will give you the number of cubic feet in the wall. One ton of stones equals 12 to 16 cubic feet.

So let's say that you want your new wall to be 1 foot thick, 2 feet tall, and 100 feet long. That's 1 foot x 2 feet x 100 feet, which equals 200 cubic feet. Next, divide 200 by 16 and by 12 to get an idea of how much stone you'll need: 200 ÷ 16 = 12.50 and 200 ÷ 12 = 16.67. So you'll need between 12.50 and 16.67 tons of stones for the wall you want to build.

Stones are sometimes sold by the cubic yard. To get that figure, divide the cubic feet by 27. Sometimes they're sold by the pallet, which usually equals 20 cubic feet, or 1.5 tons.

---

2. Visit a quarry and ask about its waste, which usually comprises shale and other sedimentary rock perfect for your stone wall.

3. Try a construction site where there has been some demolition or excavation going on.

4. Contact a loam company, which sells dirt after removing the rocks from it. They'll probably be happy to let you take away some of their stones.

Solve the stone wall puzzle. Building a stone wall is kind of like putting together a three-dimensional puzzle: You need the right pieces to fit into the right spots. In fact, to build a wall correctly, you need six specific types of stones. Here's what they are and how they fit into the puzzle.

1. Cornerstones. Stones with two fairly flat faces will give your wall sharp, clean corners.

2. Tie stones. For strength and stability, you'll want some stones that are long enough to span the width of the wall and rest on two or more smaller stones.

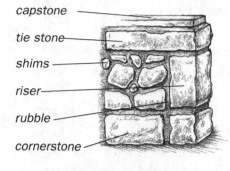

capstone
tie stone
shims
riser
rubble
cornerstone

3. Capstones. Broad, flat stones on your top layer will give your wall a relatively even surface.

4. Risers. Stones that are tall enough to reach up through two layers of smaller stones will break up horizontal lines in your wall and improve its appearance.

5. Shims. Small rocks and stones will fill gaps and stabilize the bigger stones.

6. Rubble. Broken stones can be used for filler in the middle of the wall.

Two stones over one and one stone over two is the principle to remember when you're building a stone wall.

Use a one-two punch. To build a sturdy wall, follow this principle: two stones over one and one stone over two. Your wall will have a layered, overlapping design that will maximize both strength and appearance.

Keep it dry. Dry stone walls usually outlast walls made with mortar because they're more flexible and will settle and flex as the soil underneath them shifts. However, you'll need to create good drainage underneath the wall to keep it from frost heaving as the ground freezes and thaws, or it could eventually topple over. Here's how.

Mark the ground where you're going to build the wall, then dig a trench in that spot that is 8 inches deep and wide enough to accommodate your wall. Fill the trench with 4 inches of gravel. Place your first layer of stones on the gravel, for perfect drainage.

Batter your wall. Any wall higher than 2 feet should be battered—that is, its base should be wider than its top. The wall should slope outward 1½ to 2 inches from top to bottom for every vertical foot. For instance, a wall that's 3 feet high should be 4½ to 6 inches wider at the base than at the top.

You can build an ingenious gauge to measure the batter of your wall as you work. First, cut two 1-by-2s that are equal to the wall's final height and nail them together at one end. Next, pull them apart at the other end and insert a spacer that is 1½ to 2 inches long for every foot that the wall is tall. Again, if your wall is 3 feet high, your spacer should be 4½ to 6 inches long. Your gauge should resemble a triangle or the letter *V*.

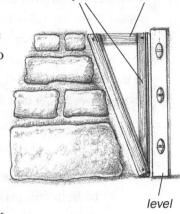

1-by-2s   spacer

level

You'll know whether the wall's batter is correct if one leg of the gauge is plumb (perfectly vertical) when you hold the other leg against the wall. Use a level to test whether the leg is plumb.

Terrific Terraces

Yards with steep slopes can seem like so much wasted land. But that doesn't have to be the case if you know how to create a terrace that gives you several garden areas in small steps rather than one big garden. Terraces also prevent erosion by allowing water to soak into the ground instead of running downhill—and taking the soil with it.

Wood works well. The best material for building a terrace is landscape timbers. They're cheaper than masonry materials such as bricks or cinder blocks, and they're a whole lot easier to work with.

TERRACE ALTERNATIVES

Terraces are just one way to keep a slope from eroding. Another option is to plant grass. If your slope is too steep to mow, you might consider planting a hardy ground cover such as juniper, pachysandra, English ivy, or vinca (periwinkle). If you don't want terraces but do want garden beds on your slopes, plant beds of perennials separated by strips of grass. The perennials will help reduce erosion once they're established, and the grass strips will catch any soil that runs off the beds. (Remember to plant the grass strips wide enough so that you can run your lawn mower over them.)

Make sure they're high enough. Here's an ingenious way to help you plan your terraces. The height of your terrace walls should be determined by the steepness of the slope. The terraces have to be high enough for the land between them to be nearly level. The higher the walls, the more pressure is on them, and the more important it becomes to secure them and to make sure the ground drains properly.

To figure out how high your walls need to be, you need to figure out the slope's rise (the slope's height at its highest point) and run (the entire length of the slope). Let's say your rise is 6 feet, your run is 15 feet, and you want to build 3 terraces. Now divide both the rise and the run by 3. Based on those figures, you can build three 5-foot-long terraces, each with 2-foot-high walls. Keep in mind that the taller the wall, the less stable it will be.

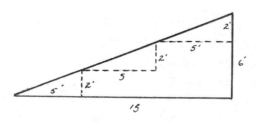

So how do you use this information? Once you know the rise and run of your slope, you can decide how big your terraces are going to be, how many terraces you want, and how high you want your walls to be.

Fabulous Fences

Fences and their natural alternatives, such as hedges and other shrubbery, can do more than just establish boundaries and make good neighbors. They can increase your privacy, reduce wind and traffic noise, keep out trespassers—four-footed as well as two-footed—and block unattractive views. "Before you build a fence or plant a hedge, keep in mind what function it's supposed to serve," says Steph Sickles. "That will help you decide what to build or plant, and where on your property to do it." Read on for our everyday experts' ingenious fencing ideas.

Save on stringers. Let's say you're building a wooden privacy fence and want to use 2-by-4s for the stringers (the hori-

---

VINES ARE FINE FOR FENCING

One way to transform your chain-link fence from an eyesore to an eye-popping attraction is to grow a showy vine on it. Following are six vines that will grow in most climates, mature in one season, and quickly provide plenty of leaves and flowers to camouflage that not-so-pretty fence around your yard. Grow one plant for roughly every 3 feet (length) of fence. Remember that these vines are all annuals. They'll die at season's end, so you'll need to replant them every year. (For a more permanent cover, plant perennial vines such as clematis and climbing roses with your annuals. They'll fill in after a couple of years.)

1. Sweet peas
2. Black-eyed Susan vine *(Thunbergia alata)*
3. Purple bell vine *(Rhodochiton atrosanguineus)*
4. Morning glories *(Ipomoea species)*
5. Hyacinth bean *(Dolichos lablab)*
6. Climbing nasturtium *(Tropaeolum majus)*

---

zontal pieces of wood that hold the pickets in place). Want to save a bit of cash? Here's an ingenious way to do just that: Buy 2-by-6s instead and cut each one down the middle to make two 2-by-3s. You'll need only half as many pieces of wood to get the job done.

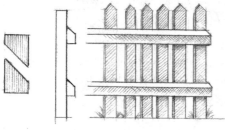

Cutting picket fence stringers at a 45-degree angle (far left) will increase security around your home.

Cut your stringers for security. When you make the cuts in your stringers, instead of cutting straight, make the cuts at a 45-degree angle. Attach the wood to the fence so that the angled edge is at the top and facing away from the pickets. That'll make it more difficult for someone to get a good foothold if they're trying to climb your the fence.

Be a good neighbor—to yourself. Before you build that lovely picket fence in your front yard, keep in mind that most wooden fences have two distinctive sides, a front (very pretty) and a back (not so attractive). If you build your fence with the front facing the street or the neighbor's yard, you're going to see the back of your fence every time you look out your window or step into your yard. If that prospect bothers you, consider a "good neighbor" fence—a picket fence that's constructed so that it looks the same from both sides. (Note that it's illegal in some communities to put the "back side" of a fence facing the road or your neighbors, so check with city hall.)

NATURE'S FENCING

You know, nothing says you have to put up a picket or hurricane fence. Mother Nature has provided us with lots of options. And let's face it, they're a lot prettier than manmade fences.

A WORD ON WHACKERS

Those string trimmers for weed control might be convenient and fun to use, but they can do a real job on fences—wood, metal, even natural fencing such as hedges and shrubbery. They chip the paint and gouge the wood, leading to rust or rot and a shorter life span for your fence.

But there is an ingenious solution: "Your best bet is to lay some stone around the base of your fence so that you don't have to worry about trimming the grass around it," says Steph Sickles.

Plant a natural "No Trespassing" sign. Want to discourage trespassers from entering your yard, but don't relish the thought of installing an ugly security fence? Take landscaper Steph Sickles's advice and plant nature's barbed wire: barberry. "It's a nice purple color, it grows easily, and it has big thorns," Steph says. Other prickly hedges include rugosa roses and trifoliate orange.

Be bamboozled. Bamboo is another natural fence option. But be careful, says Steph Sickles. Bamboo can quickly take over your yard. "You have to keep it maintained," he says. "I'm always getting calls from people asking me, 'How do I get rid of this stuff?' The answer is, with a lot of digging and hacking. But there is a simple and ingenious solution to the problem of marauding bamboo. Rather than planting it directly in the ground, simply grow it in long, narrow planters. Of course, you can sink the planters into the ground to make them more stable. Problem solved!"

Decide on deciduous shrubs. Deciduous shrubs work hard from spring through fall, then go dormant over the winter.

During the winter, they provide an impenetrable hedge of stems and shelter for visiting birds. But if you're looking for natural fencing that will provide color, shade, and privacy during the growing season, they can't be beat. Here are six favorites.

1. Forsythia (*Forsythia* species)

2. Lilac (*Syringa* species)

3. Privet (*Ligustrum* species)

4. Rugosa rose *(Rosa rugosa)*

5. Shrubby dogwoods

6. Spirea (*Spiraea* species)

Try an evergreen screen. Evergreen shrubs are a timeless favorite when it comes to adding year-round privacy from passersby or a screen to shield your yard from the wind. Here are seven that work especially well.

1. Arborvitae *(Thuja plicata)*

2. Boxwood *(Buxus sempervirens)*

3. Hemlock *(Tsuga canadensis)*

4. Holly *(Ilex aquifolium* or *I. opaca)*

5. Juniper (*Juniperus* species)

6. Rhododendron

7. Yew *(Taxus baccata, T. cuspidata* or *T. media)*

Shed Savvy

Your lawn mower and garden tools need someplace to live, too, right? Might as well be a shed. And when it comes to sheds, your options are varied: You could build your own from scratch; you could hire someone to build one; you could buy a kit and assemble it yourself; or you could buy a premade shed made of wood, metal, or vinyl. Each method and material has its pluses and minuses.

Wood, for example, is usually the most attractive material, and you can paint it to match your house. On the downside, wood is

---

BUILD A CLEVER COVER-UP

What do you do when your property is too small for your landscaping plans? Steph Sickles had a customer who solved that problem in an ingenious way. He wanted an arbor, but he didn't have enough space for one in his yard. Instead, he built it over his driveway. "He planted wisteria around it," says Steph. "So now in the summer, he has a carport with leaves and flowers that shade his car from the sun."

---

pricier than the other options, and if you don't use rot-resistant cedar or redwood, it will be susceptible to insect infestation and rot. Here are some other points to keep in mind when building or selecting a shed.

Give yourself easy access. If your shed is going to be big—say, 10-by-20-feet—position the doors in the middle of one of the long walls. If you put the doors in one of the short walls, you may have a hard time getting to anything that you've stored in the back of the shed.

Build a window on the world. Your shed needs to breathe, says veteran contractor Kevin MacIntyre. "You want airflow, because it could get really hot in there, and that'll make your wood warp. So make sure there are ridge vents or some kind of vents in the shed's gables.

"If you're storing a lawn mower or any other gas-powered equipment in your shed, this is especially important because you need to be sure the fumes can escape. When I built sheds, I'd build them with windows and screens. They gave more light and extra ventilation. Of course, windows are also going to reduce your storage space, so it's a trade-off."

Decks Done Right

Ah, the deck—an American classic. It's where you barbecue, enjoy cocktails, and watch sunsets while swatting mosquitoes on summer evenings. But when you're building a deck, there are so many questions: How big? What kind of wood? How to care for it? We're here to help with some nifty tips and hints, courtesy of Kevin MacIntyre, a retired contractor.

BUILDING A DECK

As with all construction projects, there's a right way and a lot of wrong ways to build a deck. And then there are easier (and downright ingenious) ways to build it right. Here is some advice to help you get started.

THE PROS KNOW

predrill your holes

EVER WONDER HOW experienced carpenters never seem to split the wood that they're nailing? It's not just because they know how to handle a hammer. It's also because they know how to use a drill.

"If you try to drive a nail through the end of a one-by-six floorboard, chances are it's going to split immediately or eventually," says Kevin MacIntyre. "The easiest way to keep that from happening is to predrill the holes."

How big is big enough? Not sure how big you want to build your deck? Let the lumber help you decide. "Lumber is cut in lengths of eight, ten, twelve, and sixteen feet," says Kevin MacIntyre. "Plan your deck to accommodate those sizes. You don't want to build a deck that's seventeen feet long, because you're going to spend a lot of extra money for that extra foot, and you're going to be left with a lot of leftover scrap wood."

Keep in mind that the floorboards of your deck should overhang the frame at least an inch or so on all sides. So, if you use 16-foot lengths of lumber, the frame shouldn't be any longer than 15 feet 10 inches.

288

DON'T BE RED-FACED OVER ROSES

One sure way to make your deck or any woodworking project look as though it were done by an amateur is to be careless with a hammer and nails," says Kevin MacIntyre. "For finish work such as the floorboards or railings on a deck, always use a nail set (a tool used for driving nails) with the last couple of hammer swings so that you don't leave an indentation in the wood. Professional carpenters call those indentations roses, and they like to say, 'Save the roses for Valentine's Day.'"

It takes pour planning. The first step many people take when they build a deck is to pour the concrete on which the posts are going to rest. Uh-oh, says Kevin MacIntyre. "That's a big mistake. A base isn't very big, but the post needs to rest right in the middle of it. If you're off by just a couple of inches, either you're going to have to move the post into a position that's not symmetrical, or it's not going to sit correctly on the base. Either way, it's going to look bad."

Kevin suggests a simply ingenious solution: Build the deck first, then pour the cement. In other words, when you build the deck, you should have temporary posts (2-by-4s) holding it up. Once it's finished and you know exactly where the real posts are going to rest, you can pour the concrete. After it cures, just attach the permanent posts.

CARE AND MAINTENANCE

Your deck needs a little TLC every now and then. Read on to find out how to take care of it so that it will always be there for you.

Steer clear of latex. Don't use latex paint on your deck. "If you're going to stain the wood, use an oil-based stain. It will penetrate the wood better," says Kevin MacIntyre. "Latex paint will just peel."

Floss between your . . . boards. You can make your deck last a whole lot longer just by using a putty knife. No, we're not suggesting that you scrape the deck down, only that you regularly clean out any pebbles, dirt, or leaves that get caught in the spaces between the floorboards. If the debris is left there, it will allow water to pool and could eventually cause the wood to rot.

Wait until a cool wind blows. For weeks, you've been dreading the job of stripping and restaining the deck. Now that you have the time to do it, it's mid-August and the temperature is above 80°F before you've even finished breakfast. That's too hot to do the job. Your best bet is to wait until the weather cools. The ideal time to work with wood strippers and cleaners is when it's cool and overcast. Bright sun and high heat will quickly dry out the chemicals. Besides, you don't want to be swooning from the heat and the chemicals as you do this labor-intensive work. Better go to the beach instead. (Tell your spouse we said it was okay.)

Seal that deck. Should you seal your deck? Absolutely! The obvious reason is to keep the wood from rotting. But sealants also keep wood from splintering. And they'll protect your deck from dirt, mold, and algae, all of which will build up on an unsealed deck, making it slippery and dangerous to walk on.

Reach for the bleach. Before you buy an expensive deck-washing formula, you should know that the active ingredient in most such products is bleach. In fact, you can make your own deck-washing solution by mixing 1 part bleach with 4 parts water. When using a deck wash, whether store-bought or homemade, try not to get it on any nearby plants. Bleach can kill them.

ROOM WITH A GARDEN VIEW

M y water garden nearly resulted in some costly renovations for my next-door neighbor, and it had nothing to do with flooding," says Roger Neal of Tewksbury, Massachusetts. "One day a couple of years ago, my neighbor was having her house built, and she was standing where her kitchen eventually would be, looking through the framing into my yard. She saw my water garden, with its five-foot-high waterfall, colorful koi, and vibrant plants, and she immediately called the home builder. She wanted to change the building plans to add a window to her bedroom, which overlooks my water garden."

Water Gardens That Work

Bill Underhill manages the aquatics department of Hyannis Country Garden in Hyannis, Massachusetts, and has held a Master of Ponds certificate from the International Waterlily and Water Gardening Society for many years. He finds it funny when people tell him they want their water garden to be natural—not to have any pumps or filtration systems. "There's no such thing as a natural water garden," he says. "It's manmade. When you dig a hole, put a liner in it, and fill it with water, it's not natural."

You'll need to buy some equipment, says Bill, but there are ways to keep down costs—and to make sure the money you do spend isn't wasted. Here are some of Bill's expert tips to help you get your water garden off to a great start.

Seek the high ground. If you're looking for the best place in your yard for a water garden, avoid the lowest land. Rainwater always flows downhill, and it generally brings pesticides, fertilizers, and other hazards with it. You don't want these pollutants ending up in your garden, where they're likely to kill your plants and fish.

291

Don't make it in the shade. You'll also want to avoid that lovely shaded area under your trees when you're siting your water garden. The leaves that drop during the summer and fall will land in the water. Then they'll decay and get icky. And they'll raise the water's acidity and make your fish sick. Stick to an open area with clear skies.

WHATSIT?

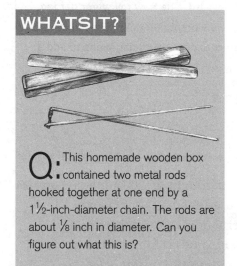

Q: This homemade wooden box contained two metal rods hooked together at one end by a 1½-inch-diameter chain. The rods are about ⅛ inch in diameter. Can you figure out what this is?

A: This appears to be a pair of rods used for finding water underground. Dowsers are apt to use anything to claim to find water, from a lilac branch to brass rods. This box and rods were probably made by a man who was proud of his ability to find water and who wanted his tools to be the best.

Read this liner note. Before you line your new pond with plastic, line it with newspaper. Come again? Well, a generous half-inch layer of newsprint will protect your plastic liner from damage by sharp rocks. And once you've laid out the plastic, the newspaper will slowly decompose into a cushy layer of mulch. It will also hold water should your liner ever spring a leak.

Green around the gills? Don't panic. Don't worry too much if your water garden looks a bit green come spring. That's the time of year when pond algae "blooms" (which is to say, really gets growing), and when it does, it'll turn the water green. Just check your filter to make sure the water is circulating as it should. If everything is okay, the water should clear up in a couple of weeks.

Never use an algicide to get rid of the algae—unless you also want to get rid of your fish. The algicide triggers a process that quickly kills off the algae, but it uses all the oxygen in the water in the process.

As Good as Gold(fish)

When it comes to stocking a water garden, Bill Underhill prefers goldfish over their larger, showier, and much costlier cousins, koi. "Goldfish usually don't bother plants, but watch out with koi," Bill says. "They're messy, and they like to eat plants, especially floating plants when they get big." Within 3 years, he says, koi will grow as long as 16 inches. "So you better enjoy your plants those first three years, because you might not have some of them too much longer," he warns. If you have koi, says Bill, choose broad-leaved plants such as cattails, water irises, and lotuses, which resist their attacks better than narrow-leaved and floating plants.

Just add salt. Sometimes waterfalls in water gardens get covered with a slimy coating of algae. "It's not going to hurt your garden, but it does look ugly," says Bill Underhill. There's a simple, ingenious way to get rid of the algae, though. Bill suggests shutting down the waterfall, sprinkling some non-iodized kosher salt over it, and covering it with a tarp for about 10 hours. "The salt will break down the algae," Bill says. Why the tarp? "You don't want the sun baking the salt on the waterfall," he explains.

If you don't have or don't want to bother with the tarp, you could perform this salt treatment overnight, when sunlight won't be problem. After the salt has had a chance to do its work, rinse off the waterfall with a hose. "The fish will eat up the algae that fall off the waterfall, and the extra salt in the water won't hurt them," Bill says.

lush lawns and
flowers

IF YOU'RE READING THIS, you're probably a gardener. Perhaps you're a dabbler. Maybe you're someone for whom gardening is a consuming passion. But we'd bet that no matter what your level of interest, you'd like to do it better, faster, or less expensively.

Well, you're in luck, because in this chapter, our experts share their ingenious ways to help you do just that: Make your lawns, landscape, and flower gardens look even better in the most economical, efficient, and downright ingenious ways. For instance, Sally Cunningham, a gardening writer, Cooperative Extension agent, and dedicated organic gardener from East Aurora, New York, shows you how to make windbreaks from discarded Christmas trees and clothesline. Rochelle Smith, horticulture/agriculture educator with the Orleans County Cornell Cooperative Extension in Orleans County, New York, helps out with, among other ideas, a simple and ingenious way to measure how much water your trees are getting.

Among our lawn care experts are Nick Caggiano, a groundskeeper for a minor league baseball stadium in Nashua, New Hampshire; and Bob Dembek, a golf course superintendent in Stow, Massachusetts. When you want fun recycling ideas for the lawn and garden, turn to the last few pages of this chapter. That's where you'll find East Aurora, New York, landscaper Peggy Giermek's ingenious—and adorable—way to stake your trees.

There's a lot more, too, from tips about conserving water to advice about mulching. And whether you read this chapter during planting season or as the leaves begin to fall, we guarantee that you'll find something you can do today to help keep your lawn and garden gorgeous.

Seasonal Tips for the Garden

Part of the appeal of gardening is that its rhythm follows that of the seasons. We start in early spring, planning, making purchases, and preparing the garden area. From that early stage, we move on to those jobs that feel like *real* gardening: planting and tending our flowers and landscapes. In summer, we water, deadhead flowers, and try to stay ahead of pests. Then, all too soon, it's autumn, when we clean up the yard, maybe plant bulbs or other plants, and prepare for winter.

But how do we best use our gardening time during each season—especially if our time is limited (and whose isn't)? That's a question new and not-so-new gardeners ask again and again. Our garden experts offer some ingenious advice about these seasonal tasks that will help you make the most of your gardening time.

SPRING IS IN THE AIR

Gardeners can sense spring in the air long before it's time to plant in the garden. But we hold back, knowing that it's not quite time to plant anything except trees and shrubs. That doesn't mean there's nothing to do. On the contrary, there are plenty of odd jobs to keep us busy in early spring: pruning, gathering yard waste, and preparing to compost, among others. And once the soil thaws, we can occupy ourselves pulling weeds, planting trees and shrubs, and dividing perennials. Of course, if you're human and didn't sharpen your tools during the winter (when the experts advised you to), you can do that, too, before planting time rolls around.

Prune your trees. Springtime is the right time to prune most trees and shrubs, because they're still dormant. Exceptions are spring-flowering plants such as lilacs and forsythias, since you might lose the beautiful blooms. Also, maple trees and some others ooze lots of sap (or bleed) when you prune them in March, so some folks prefer not to prune them until early summer.

When you do prune, be sure to learn the proper technique. Never make the mistake of "topping" a tree (cutting the main trunk to shorten it). It's disfiguring and often fatal. And when you prune shrubs, don't trim all the branches evenly into a ball or flat-topped shape (unless you're designing topiary). That leads to spindly, leggy growth with all the foliage on top.

Break the wind with brush. "March really does come in like a lion where I live," says Sally Cunningham. "That's the time of year I wish my property had more evergreens, which make terrific windbreaks. I do like the deciduous trees and shrubs that are

bang the trunk slowly

"I HAD A WISTERIA for several years that wouldn't bloom, no matter what tricks I tried—and I know a few, because I've worked in the floral and landscaping business," says Jim Ouellet of Exeter, New Hampshire.

"For four years, this wisteria wouldn't budge, and I was about to give up, when I remembered a tip I'd heard a long time ago from an old pro. That spring, I got out a rubber mallet and banged it against the trunk—not out of frustration, but to wake up the plant. I did this several times a week for about three weeks, then put away the mallet and waited. In fact, I had to wait another year, because shocking the plant like this actually generates growth for the following year. Sure enough, the following spring saw a few blooms. But I kept knocking. The year after that, my wisteria burst into bloom." (Note: This technique also works for lilac bushes. If you don't have a rubber mallet, wrap a towel around a regular hammer to keep the hammer from damaging the bark.)

already on the windward side of the back flower garden, but they don't have leaves in spring, when the wind blows hardest and destroys the beautiful spring tulips."

To solve the problem, Sally builds a windbreak that saves her blooming bulbs and pleases birds that are hungry and preparing to nest. Here's how you can do the same.

First, find some mature trees on the windward side of the area you want to protect. If you don't have trees well-placed for this purpose, drive 6-foot stakes into the soil every 8 feet or so. Weave about 100 feet of clothesline loosely around the tree trunks just above a branch and at least 4 feet off the ground. Be sure to pad the contact points between rope and trunks. Pieces of hose, fabric, or mittens will do.

PLANT A WINNER

Front yard gardens are different from those in backyards," says Sally Cunningham. She ought to know, because she instructs judges how to evaluate entries in Buffalo's annual Buffalo in Bloom gardening contest. "In backyard gardens, you can experiment, Sally says, "But the front is for the world to see, so plan it that way."

Here are Sally's tips for planting a winning garden.

1. Choose carefully. Pick a color scheme that features only two or three colors and stick to it.

2. Use fewer varieties. Limit the variety of plants, but use a lot of each kind. Some of the most eye-catching front gardens use only three or four types of annuals or perennials, but in masses.

3. Focus. Choose a dramatic focal point, whether it's built-in (a great front door or an ornamental gate) or added (a statue, fountain, trellis, or bench).

4. Don't be afraid to repeat yourself. Repeat or echo the plant groups and colors near the street, close to the house, and in hanging baskets or containers. That ties all the elements together.

5. Keep it simple. Overly fussy details and subtle textures don't have curb appeal. Simplicity is the way to go.

Entwine all the discarded Christmas trees you can find in the ropes. (Some town highway departments will drop trees off in your driveway if you tell them you're interested.) You can also use fallen tree limbs, large brush, and dead shrubs that have been put on the street when people start winter cleanup or after a big windstorm. Your new "hedgerow" is also a handy place to stick the smaller brush that's all over the yard at the end of winter. The yard will look neater, the wind will be buffered, and you might even have a chance to sit in a sheltered spot to absorb that early-spring sunshine.

Don't waste your waste. It's a typical scene on a spring weekend afternoon: home owners pruning shrubs and raking their yards, then sending the waste to the curb as trash.

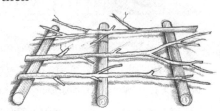

"Wasting that so-called waste is such a waste," says Sally Cunningham. "Every bit of brush, leaves, dead annuals, and perennial prunings can and should be used. It's easy to make a compost pile at the back of your lot with smaller items, such as discarded flowering plants and old leaves. The

Your brush pile doesn't need to be messy. Start it with several logs or 4-by-4s then arrange your brush on top.

easiest thing to do with large brush is make a brush pile—and it doesn't have to look messy or ugly."

Why would you *want* a brush pile on your property? It's a gold mine for wildlife of all kinds, providing a safe haven for hiding, breeding, and raising young. It's a food source, a shelter, and a spot to perch and survey the kingdom. And eventually the brush pile will break down and add humus to your soil.

"But don't just dump the brush in a messy heap," Sally advises. For a brush pile to be useful to pheasants, turkeys, or whatever animals live near you, it needs a base. "You can make one by lining up two sets of large-diameter logs, 4-by-4s, or even cinder blocks parallel to each other and 1 to 2 feet apart. Top the logs with a crisscrossing layer of coarse branches or logs. That layer makes the best hiding places and tunnels for Peter Rabbit or Phyllis Pheasant."

Let some plants sleep late. Sometimes perennial gardeners give up on plants too soon. When they don't reappear in spring with all the rest, some gardeners assume that those plants are dead. Other gardeners are so eager to get into the garden that they start working before everything has had a chance to show up.

MAKE it LAST

Do away with drooping blooms

THE LABEL on your petunias, geraniums, or verbena (or other new annual) says, "Grow in sun." You follow directions, so you dutifully place them in the sun. Only now they're drooping to beat the band.

It may be helpful to know that those plants need to "grow in sun" in the spring months. During the dog days of summer, they are better off in the shade. So cut them back a bit, maintain them, and keep them watered—but out of the strong sun—and they'll last a lot longer.

That's no good, because the gardener ends up stepping on or digging up perfectly viable plants that are simply late sleepers.

Examples of classic late sleepers include balloon flower (*Platycodon* species) and butterfly weed (*Asclepias* species). Other plants, such as hardy hibiscus (*H. moscheutos*) and butterfly bush (*Buddleia*), show dead sticks and twigs from last year's growth, and it's really hard to tell what's alive.

To avoid damaging these late sleepers, exercise patience and a little ingenuity. Once they do wake up, mark where they are so that you won't be wondering about them again next spring.

Beautify your brush pile. Keep your brush pile from looking messy: Decorate it with a climbing rose, Virginia creeper (*Parthenocissus quinquefolia*), or any attractive vine appropriate to the site and your climate. If you want a permanent barrier between your lot and the wind (or your neighbor's lot), create a long, continuous brush pile ornamented with a pretty vine. Discuss your plans with your neighbor. After all, good fences make good neighbors only if both agree on the kind of fence.

THE GOOD OLD SUMMERTIME

Summer is when most gardeners actually get to spend time enjoying their lawns and gardens. It's the season for picnicking, barbecuing, playing, and just hanging around. But summer is also when most of the planting, weeding, watering, and working on flower gardens and lawns gets done. Here are some simply ingenious ways to make the most of your summer gardening and outdoor time.

Save your gray water. Folks who have wells and people with city water who care about conservation often come up with ingenious ways to collect so-called gray water—water left over after you wash dishes or take a bath—and get it out to the garden where it can do some more good. Here are some of the best suggestions.

1. Check around the house for basins or buckets that fit into your kitchen and bathroom sinks, then wash vegetables, hands, delicate laundry, and dishes—even brush your teeth—over the bucket rather than let all the water run down the drain. When the container is full, tote it out to the garden. Of course, you shouldn't use water that contains any harsh cleaners.

2. Keep a container near an outside door to catch the falling rain. Ideally, that container will have wheels or sit on a cart with

---

HANG TIME

Here's a beautifully ingenious way to display your new blooming annuals so that they'll get maximum flowering time and avoid the sun. Hang the baskets from tree limbs in your yard. Tie them up with pretty ribbon or colorful rope at varying heights. Not only will they beautify the tree, but they'll need less attention and droop less, because the tree will shade them.

MULCHING DO'S AND DON'TS

Mulching is simply a matter of tossing some wood chips on your garden, right? Not so fast. Mulching certainly isn't brain surgery, but there are some do's and one big don't to keep in mind.

DO

- To keep the moisture where it's needed and to block the growth of weeds, mulch where your trees' and shrubs' roots are.
- Spread a layer of mulch 3 to 4 inches deep, starting a few inches out from the trunk and continuing past the dripline, or farthest branches.
- Shredded bark, wood chips, chopped leaves, and compost make good mulch.

DON'T

- Somewhere along the line, so-called volcano or Vesuvius mulching became popular. That's the practice of mounding mulch up the tree trunk in a cone-shaped pile. But it's a bad habit, say horticulturists and arborists. Mulch piled against the tree will rot, encourage fungal disease, and eventually damage or kill the tree. Rather, pull the mulch away from the tree trunk to the point where the rootball begins. If your tree was planted properly, the top ½ to 1 inch of the root crown—the spot where the bark meets the roots—should be visible.

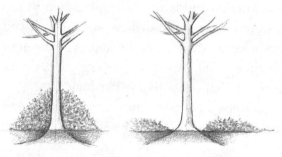

Piling mulch against the tree (left) does more harm than good. Instead, start the mulch a few inches out from the trunk (right).

wheels if you plan to move it. Think seriously about the size of the container you use. Water is heavy—a pint weighs a pound.

3. More than one home owner has rigged a siphon system to move water from an upstairs bathtub to the flowerbeds below.

Water wisely. Water is the one do-or-die requirement plants have. Unfortunately, it can be the hardest thing to provide. Sometimes you're just too hot and tired to water the plants. Other times you're having too much fun swimming or barbecuing to bother. Maybe you have well water and have to save it for yourself, your family, and your pets. Perhaps your property is so large and you have so many flowerbeds that you just can't keep up. Don't worry; our experts have raised watering to an art form. Here are some of their secrets.

Do the cancan. To many of us, the words "watering can" mean a familiar long-necked bucket. But to Rochelle Smith, a horticulture/agriculture educator in Orleans County, New York, a watering can is *really* small and helps gardeners answer the question, How much water is enough?

"We're always telling people to be sure that their trees and perennials get an inch of water a week," Rochelle says. "Yet even after all the years I spent with my professional landscape company, I wouldn't try to guess how many inches of rain has fallen or how much water the sprinkler has pumped out."

Rochelle suggests an ingenious way to measure how much water your plants have received. Save some tuna or cat food cans, wash them well, and then sink them into the soil so that the top of each can is just below the surface. Site them under the dripline of your trees (that's where the feeder roots are) and

THE PROS KNOW

the autumn planting season

SPRING IS THE SEASON for planting, right? Well, yes, but it's not the *only* time. Many perennials, shrubs, and trees can be planted in autumn, too. Some gardeners even prefer autumn planting because it gives them—and their plants—a head start come spring. And let's face it, gardeners usually have a lot more time on their hands in autumn than in spring. A good rule of thumb is to plant perennials until about mid-October in the Northeast. Trees and shrubs can often succeed if planted even later.

scatter them throughout the garden. Then, next time you water, you can measure. "Those little cans are about an inch deep, so you'll know exactly when the soil has received an inch of water," Rochelle says. "Hey, just because it's easy to do with homemade material doesn't mean it's not good science!"

Mulch more to water less. Summer is when spring-planted trees, shrubs, and perennials are in imminent danger of death by desiccation, or drying out. Trees and shrubs need up to 30 gallons of water a week to grow roots and become established. Some experts say that if the soil is dry to a depth of 6 inches, your tree is at risk or may already be suffering.

Watering is the obvious answer, but water isn't always available. Luckily, there's something you can do that will make a big difference: mulch. It holds in moisture and greatly reduces the amount of water your plants will need each week.

AUTUMN AND EARLY WINTER

When school opens and the leaves begin to fall, it can feel like the gardening season is over. But it's not, say our ingenious experts. Depending on where you live, the arrival of autumn may mean that you have many more weeks to work in your garden and yard. And the work you do then is at least as important as the chores you perform in the summer. Autumn is when you determine how well your lawn, perennials, shrubs, trees, and soil will survive the winter and whether you'll enjoy blooming bulbs next spring. Here are some ingenious ways to make sure your autumn leads to a spectacular spring.

Better late than never. Most of the spring-blooming bulbs we know and love need to be planted in autumn. In fact, bulbs get the best head start if they're planted in September or October. But here's good news: Don't fret too much if you miss that October cutoff date. Although bulbs planted in late autumn may develop small flowers or only foliage during the first season, you can plant them up until the ground freezes.

Improve your soil. Take advantage of autumn's cooler days to gather organic material—leaves, straw, pulled-out annuals, garden debris—and start a compost pile.

Much ado about mulching. After the ground freezes, mulch your perennials, bulbs, shrubs, and trees to help the soil retain moisture, equalize its temperature, and prevent roots from heaving out of the ground during freeze-and-thaw cycles. Three to 4 inches of mulch is a good rule of thumb.

THE **P**ROS **K**NOW

water well before winter

WE KNOW, you don't want your pipes or hose to freeze, but don't put that garden hose away just yet. Keep it handy up until the ground freezes. That way, you can easily water anything you planted during the past year, especially recently planted trees and shrubs. Keep in mind, says Sally Cunningham, that plants need to enter the winter season well-watered to avoid winter damage or death due to dried-out roots.

For Lawns Only

Cornell University in Ithaca, New York, is well-known for its horticultural research. A primary topic of research is what home owners should do for their lawns and when. At the end of the day, the researchers and the home owners have the same goal: lush, thick lawns, achieved with as little effort, money, fertilizers, seed, and pesticides as possible.

"In lawn care, you have to do your homework," says Sally Cunningham. "Cornell University teaches master gardeners to start with the soil. Test it, amend it if necessary, and then plant the right seed for your site."

Once you have a good lawn established, it's the maintenance that counts. How and when you mow, fertilize, and water make all the difference.

MOWING

Mowing is one of those chores that has to be done. Having access to a teenager solves only one problem—who's going to do it. But that still leaves a host of unanswered questions—unanswered until now, anyway.

Give your mower the once-over. Sharpen your mower blades and check the accuracy of your mower height before you cut your lawn for the first time in spring. Then cut the grass when it's 2½ to 3½ inches high, and never cut off more than one-third of the height at one time.

Sleep in. The best time to mow your lawn is early evening, because the grass has more time to recover before it has to face the daytime heat.

Cut, then recut. Mulching mowers are terrific, because they cut and recut grass clippings before dropping them back onto the lawn. If you own a side-discharge mower, you can duplicate the action of a mulching mower by cutting your lawn in such a way that

WHATSIT?

Q: The head of this nasty-looking device is sandwiched between two plates, into which the tapered tines are set. There is an outer row of 15 tines (about 11 inches long) and an inner row of 14 tines (about 9½ inches long). The overall length is 12 inches, the head is 5½ inches wide, the butt is 1¾ inches in diameter, and there is a ⅜-inch hole drilled through the handle. Any idea what it is?

A: It's a rippling comb, used in raising flax for making linen. After the flax was pulled and dried, the best method for removing the seeds was to pull the fibers through this comb until all the seeds fell off.

the clippings get thrown onto the uncut grass. That way, as you continue to cut the lawn, you'll be giving the clippings an extra cut or two.

Don't bother raking grass. Now that you've mowed your lawn, what should you do with the clippings? Nothing. Just leave them where they are. Here are five reasons why.

1. Clippings are a great source of moisture for your lawn. In fact, they're made up of about 90 percent water.

2. Clippings are a good source of nutrients—as good as most fertilizers. "If you return your clippings to the soil, over the course of a year of mowing, you'll add two pounds of nitrogen per one thousand square feet," says Bill Winter. "That's all the nitrogen you need for a low-maintenance lawn. Even for a high-maintenance lawn, you don't need any more than four pounds per square feet a year."

3. Clippings don't create thatch. Thatch comes from dead stems and roots and can choke your grass.

4. Even if you did rake your clippings and bag them, you might have trouble getting rid of them. Yard waste accounts for as much as half of what's discarded into some landfills, so many city and town dumps no longer accept grass clippings.

---

annals of ingenuity

BUDDING GENIUS

if you're like lots of folks, you sometimes daydream at work. Fortunately for us, that's how Edwin Budding spent some of his time. Budding worked at a textile mill in England in the early nineteenth century, and he apparently spent a lot of time thinking about lawns.

Up until 1830, grass was cut with a scythe by hand, which, as you can imagine, was a time- and labor-consuming process. Some large estates required 50 men just to keep up the lawns. While working at the mill, Budding was inspired by a machine that sheared the nap on velvet to give it a smooth finish. He knew that if grass was trapped between two blades the way the velvet nap was, it would be easier to cut. He set to work designing a contraption to do just that. On August 31, 1830, Budding was granted a patent on his invention, which he called "a machine for mowing lawns, etc." To us, it's the good old rotary mower.

THE LONG AND SHORT OF MOWING

People often cut their lawns short, leaving their grass less than 2 inches tall. That's a big mistake for a variety of reasons. Here are five reasons to leave your lawn 2½ to 3 inches tall.

1. The bigger the blade, the bigger the target for sunlight. "Think of the grass blade as a solar panel that creates energy for the plant through photosynthesis," says groundskeeper Nick Caggiano. "A two-and-a-half-inch blade will collect a lot more energy than a one-inch blade will."

2. The higher the grass, the cooler the soil. The soil under a 3-inch lawn can be as much as 10 degrees cooler than the soil under a 1½-inch lawn, says lawn care expert Bill Winter of Russell's Garden Center in Wayland, Massachusetts. As the soil warms, the organic material that the grass feeds on starts to break down.

3. By keeping your grass high and your soil cool, you'll prevent needed moisture from evaporating from the ground.

4. Grass that isn't cut too short is less stressed and can grow a better root system, which means less watering all season.

5. Taller grass shades the soil and helps prevent weed seeds from germinating.

5. Think of all the time and money you'll save by not bagging. A half-acre lawn can yield nearly 3 tons of clippings each growing season. That's 465 one-bushel bags that you won't have to buy and about 7 hours that you can spend enjoying your lawn rather than working on it.

Don't leave your leaves. Leaves are a great source of nutrients for a compost pile, but it's not a good idea to leave them on your lawn after they fall from trees. A thick layer of leaves can smother your grass if left on all winter, although it's okay to leave small amounts on the lawn after you've shredded them with a lawn mower.

WATERING

Of course you know that your lawn needs to be watered. But how much and when? It's no surprise that our ingenious experts have the answers.

Water early in the day. Water is a precious resource, so you don't want to waste any. One way to conserve it (and make sure your lawn gets enough) is to water early in the day. That way, the sun won't evaporate the water before it reaches the roots.

Don't water at night. The problem with watering at night isn't evaporation, but disease. "If you water at night, the grass will stay wet during the night, when it's cool, and that's going to give you fungi," says groundskeeper Nick Caggiano. Nick handles field maintenance for Holman Stadium in Nashua, New Hampshire, which hosts the Nashua Pride's minor league baseball games. "It's like taking a wet sneaker and throwing it in the closet," he says. "It never dries out."

Water well for deep roots. The deeper your lawn's roots, the better it can handle stress caused by drought, insects, or disease. One way to promote deep roots is to saturate the lawn when you water it. "You're not doing any good if you just run the hose

---

AFTER THE FLOOD, AERATE

Flooding that leaves your backyard underwater for long periods of time can damage your lawn by choking off the oxygen that the grass needs. Most types of grass can handle a couple of days underwater, but just in case, it's a good idea to aerate the ground after the water recedes. Aerating helps get oxygen back into the soil.

across the lawn for a couple of minutes," says Nick Caggiano. "You should water long enough so that the soil is moist six to eight inches down. The roots will grow longer when there is water deeper down."

FERTILIZING

Lawns can't live by sun and water alone. To grow strong, your grass will probably need a snack now and then and perhaps some other supplements.

Know your pH. Some home owners and even some lawn pros have a tradition of liming their lawns every spring—without necessarily having a good reason. Lime raises the soil's pH, which is a measurement of the soil's acidity. Most lawns do best when the soil's pH falls between 6.8 and 7.2. If the pH is significantly outside that range, the grass won't grow—but some weeds will thrive.

First things first: Whether you're starting a new lawn or caring for an existing one, you need to test your soil's pH. Most Cooperative Extension offices offer the service—along with good advice. Test kits are also available at many garden centers.

If your soil's pH turns out to be high (above 7.2), you'll get advice about how to treat it with a sulfur product. If it's low (below 6.8), you'll need to

that's • ingenious!

wanted: moss

NOT EVERYBODY wants to get rid of moss. In fact, some folks take elaborate steps to get that mossy, antique look on their garden walls, flowerpots, and statuary. Here's how you can get it, too.

Mix equal amounts of moss and buttermilk in a blender, then paint the mixture anywhere you want the moss to grow. It's that simple—and ingenious!

READ THE LABEL

Before you buy a bag of fertilizer, be sure to read the label so that you know what you're getting. Most labels include the letters N, P, and K. The N stands for nitrogen, which promotes leaf growth and gives you a green lawn. The P stands for phosphorus, which helps roots develop. And the K is for potassium, which increases the plants' tolerance of stress. The numbers that correspond to the letters refer to the percentage of each element in the fertilizer mix. For instance, a 10-18-10 combination means that the bag is 10 percent nitrogen, 18 percent phosphorus, and 10 percent potassium.

---

add lime. The good news is that soil pH can be changed. The bad news is that if you've been one of those regular limers, it might take a few seasons.

Remember that timing is everything. If you decide to fertilize your lawn, you'll have some choices to make: not only what kind, but when to use it. If you want your lawn to be the greenest, densest carpet in the neighborhood and don't mind a high-maintenance project, you might fertilize three times a year. Otherwise, once a year is probably sufficient.

Turfgrass specialists and extension agents from Cornell University say that correct timing is important, too. For instance, if you fertilize once a year and live in the Northeast, the best time is right around Labor Day. That way, you're helping the plants develop strong root systems, which will carry them through the winter. If you choose the three-a-year treatment, fertilize in late spring (around Memorial Day), late summer (around Labor Day), and late autumn (around Thanksgiving). Of course, folks who live elsewhere in the United States can get expert advice from their local Cooperative Extension agent.

stake your trees with gloves

WHENEVER A ROPE or cord touches a tree trunk, there could be damage to the all-important cambium layer, just under the outer bark. It's the part that carries all the nutrients and water—rather like your blood vessels—to keep the tree alive. So whether you are staking a just-planted tree in a windy place or roping a tree for some other reason (such as the windbreak on page 296), soften the contact with that trunk. Here's one easy way.

"Maybe it's because landscapers used to be mostly men and not moms," says Peggy Giermek, owner of Nature Calls Landscaping in East Aurora, New York, "but jamming rope through pieces of garden hose seems like a difficult way to make padded tree stakes." Instead, she suggests using discarded children's gloves and mittens. "Just poke a hole in the tips of the pinkie and the thumb (where there's often a hole anyway) and thread the rope from the wrist opening through the hole in the finger," Peggy says. "This ingenious technique works even better if you use two lengths of twine or rope, threading one through the wrist and ring finger and the other through the wrist and thumb. Place the glove around the trunk of the tree you're staking, with the finger and thumb above and below the branch." Thick wool or padded ski mittens work best.

Discarded mittens and gloves make terrific padded tree stakes.

312

DON'T COUNT YOUR SEEDS

The labels on grass seed bags or boxes can be deceptive, because they tell you the percentage *by weight* of a particular seed in the mix. But different seeds have different weights. For instance, bluegrass seed is lighter than rye seed, so a mixture of 50-50 bluegrass and rye actually contains more bluegrass seed than rye seed.

Make a date to fertilize your lawn. While you have your date book out, make a note that you should *not* fertilize your lawn in mid-autumn. Growth then is weak and susceptible to disease, such as snow mold fungus. Early and middle spring are out, too, because you're going to get a natural growth spurt at that time anyway. Adding fertilizer to the mix just means that you'll have to mow every 3 days because the grass will grow so fast.

Work with your worms. Yes, worms are good for the soil and good for your lawn. They act as natural aerators and produce worm castings, which are great fertilizer. However, the little wigglers can be an annoyance, because when it rains, they have to bore through the soil to come up for air. "They make those little volcanoes when they come to the surface," says Bill Winter. "But that shouldn't be a problem unless you're cutting your grass too short." Whatever you do, don't try to flatten those little volcanoes with a heavy roller. That will compact the soil, and that's bad for the grass, because it will prevent air, water, and moisture from reaching the roots.

Look for telltale moss. If there's moss growing in your yard instead of grass, it could be trying to tell you something. Moss means that your lawn needs to be reinvigorated—reseeded

313

or fertilized—and the soil improved. Moss grows wherever there's poor competition, and a weak lawn in infertile soil just can't fight those moss spores.

The answer is to rake up the moss, improve the soil, and reseed. If the lawn is still fairly thick, just remove the moss and fertilize.

Do your math homework. Nitrogen is the key ingredient in fertilizer, especially for established lawns. Lawn care expert Bill Winter recommends using 1 pound of nitrogen for each 1,000 square feet of lawn. So if you buy a 50-pound bag with a 10-18-10 rating, nitrogen accounts for 10 percent, or 5 pounds, of the fertilizer, and that's enough to cover 5,000 square feet of lawn.

Opt for slow-release nitrogen. Always use a fertilizer containing slow-release nitrogen, as opposed to the water-soluble kind. Water-soluble nitrogen will immediately give you a green lawn and a big growth spurt, but the color will quickly fade, and a quick growth spurt can weaken the grass and leave it susceptible to disease and insects.

Fill your plugs with sand. Early spring is a good time to aerate your soil, because the ground gets compacted during the winter, making it more difficult for fertilizer to penetrate or for seed to take hold. When Bob Dembek, the golf course superintendent at Stow Acres Country Club in Stow, Massachusetts, aerates his course, he fills the plugs with sand, which is very porous and can be penetrated easily. Each time he aerates, Bob removes the plugs at different depths. "That prevents the formation of what's called a cultivation pan—a solid layer of ground that water and roots won't be able to penetrate," he explains.

veggies, herbs, and
fruit

HOW DO YOU SUPPORT THE SPRAWLING TOMATO VINES, weed around your onions, and keep the herbs from flopping? How do you save money on raised beds and soil building? And how on earth do apple tree owners keep those branches spread out and low so the fruit is easy to pick? Our garden experts are happy to share their secrets—along with some ingenious angles you won't find anywhere else.

For instance, Joanne Tanner, a Master Gardener from Orchard Park, New York, with years of experience in all matters gardenening, reveals her ingenious ways to put scrap computer paper and Velcro® to work in the compost pile. Sally Cunningham, a gardening writer and Cooperative Extension agent in East Aurora, New York, makes a living helping everyday folks with their gardens and gardening questions. She shares her ideas for recycling old shelving and plastic utensils. And Craig Vogel, a gardener from Eden, New York, reveals how to make an onion hoe, which makes quick work of weeding the narrow area between onion sets. These experts and others will show you how to have the most ingenious garden on the block.

Ingenious Ideas for the Whole Garden

From making a hammock for your melons to building raised beds—out of old feedbags, no less—our experts have come up with many ways to improve your garden.

RECYCLING IN AND AROUND THE GARDEN

Nature is the ultimate recycler. Whether it's autumn leaves, rabbit droppings, or a fallen oak tree, everything eventually gets recycled. Smart gardeners mimic that process by composting kitchen scraps. Home owners do the same thing when they leave grass clippings on the lawn to decompose.

But composting isn't the only kind of recycling going on around the garden. Long before the birth of the environmental movement, gardeners and farmers reused and recycled common, everyday objects from city homes and country farms. Some did it out of frugality, some out of necessity, and others because of lack of time or energy to go to town for store-bought supplies. For many it was—and is—a matter of common sense: Why buy a new item when there's a perfectly useful replacement lying around? And why throw something away that might just come in handy tomorrow?

Our expert gardeners offer dozens of ways to turn found objects into handy gardening helpers and many more creative solutions to everyday problems. Once you start thinking the way they do, you may surprise yourself by inventing brand new ways to recycle previously used "stuff"—and realizing how little you actually need to buy.

Save your feed bags. If you buy mulch, pet food, or live-stock feed in 50-pound bags (or if you have access to the feed bags that a local horse owner or farmer throws out), start collecting them. Those bags have lots of uses in the garden. Here are three.

1. Lay a foundation. Feed bags make a great foundation for garden paths. Lay down the bags, then heap stones, sawdust, or wood chip mulch on top of them. The bags block out light and add a barrier that slows down weed growth.

2. Mulch 'em. Paper feed bags (and only paper) make superior landscape fabric because they eventually decompose and provide organic matter for the earthworms, microorganisms, and other soil critters that help your garden. Before that happens, though, they block weeds and keep the soil evenly moist—in short, every-thing that mulch does, but for free. And there's another bonus:

MAKE it LAST

Cut old tools down to size

WHEN A TOOL HANDLE breaks or cracks, or when you decide to replace an old hoe or rake with a more ergonomic model, hold on to the old one. Cut the handle down to 12 inches, sand the end to make it smooth, and use the newly created tool when you're sitting, kneeling, or squatting in the garden. The best news is that your new hand tool will probably be stronger and more solid than a purpose-built model.

Using feed bags allows you to use much less mulch than you otherwise would—only 2 to 3 inches instead of 4 to 5.

Lay out the bags with a 5-inch overlap anywhere you want to mulch. If you like, spread compost or scatter alfalfa pellets under the bags to boost the soil's nutrition. Put wood chips or whatever mulch you have over the top to dress up the area.

3. Bolster a bed. You can use any kind of mulch or feed bag to construct the sides of a raised garden bed. Stuff the bags with organic matter of any kind—or even the clumps of clay and rocks that you want out of the garden—and lay them end to end. You'll need about 12 stuffed bags to form a 4- by 12-foot garden bed. Fill the center of the bed with soil and compost, and you're ready to garden.

The bag bolsters are free substitutes for expensive landscape timbers, which are heavy and hard to handle. This method also allows you to avoid using telephone poles, railroad ties, or pressure-treated wood, all of which present questions about health and safety. Maybe this bagged-up bed isn't beautiful, but it's practical, and the price is right.

Benefit from old boards. In rural areas where there are barns and in urban areas with old homes, you might come across old, unpainted boards put out on the street as trash. (If you're recycling-minded, ask for the boards whenever you see a demolition in progress.) Grab them. Because they're already weathered and unlikely to warp or bow when they get wet, they're especially useful in the garden. Here are four ingenious and practical uses for them.

1. Walk the planks. Put the boards to use as movable planks in the garden. They'll help disperse your weight and keep you from compacting the soil when it's damp.

2. Lay them down the garden path. If the boards are sturdy enough, use them as a permanent garden path.

plant a take-along garden

IF SPRING PLANTING TIME is slow to arrive in your area, you might appreciate an ingenious, whimsical planter that lets you plant and harvest greens away from the cold wind and rain. A child's wagon makes a perfect portable garden. It's easy to pull from place to place, and it's just deep enough for shallow-rooted crops such as lettuce, spinach, and mesclun (the pricey mixed salad greens sold in stores these days).

First, make sure the wagon has drainage. If it's old and about to be discarded, drill some small holes in the bottom; otherwise, add a layer of gravel. If the sides of the wagon seem too low, build them up by placing a 4- to 6-inch wall of wire mesh, plywood, thick cardboard, or gutter guard against them. Fill the wagon with potting soil, then plant your greens. As they grow, you can pull the wagon into the early-spring sunshine, into the garage during hard rainfalls, and right up to the door when you want to cut some for salad.

3. Build a bed. Put old boards to work as sides for raised beds. Just nail them together, and you're ready to go.

4. Anchor row covers. Those old boards are terrific as weights to hold down row covers.

There are many uses for the boards, and it feels good to recycle the wood. There is one caution, however: Don't scavenge treated or painted wood, which may have lead or other contaminants in it. Even if the paint is water-based, paint chips don't look nice falling into the soil.

Make a hammock for your vine crops. Old stockings and panty hose are perfect for tying up tomatoes or vines, but that's not where their usefulness ends. They can also support melons or other vine crops when they get too heavy for the vines. Make a hammock by tying both ends of a stocking leg to a stake and then supporting the vegetable in the sling to take the weight off the stem. The hose will stretch as the fruit grows.

Turn shelves into row covers. Sally Cunningham is a gardening writer and extension agent who collects ingenious recycling ideas for the garden. "Watch the roadsides on trash days and peruse yard sales for stackable shelving," she says. "It has so many uses in the garden—not to mention its possibilities as actual shelving for garden storage. My favorite use for them is for row cover support."

Row covers are a kind of fabric sold for frost protection, pest prevention, warmth, or shade. Reemay is the best-known brand. "I find that the hoops sold to hold up the row cover tunnels are too short or too low for easy access to the crops," Sally says. "But then I found that I could separate stackable shelves and use each unit in place of a hoop. I place the shelf, one every five feet or so, so that it straddles the row, then I drape the row cover over them, and I have a perfect tunnel that's easy to peek under." Another benefit of using shelves is that you can prevent the row cover from blowing away by placing boards or rocks on top of each shelf.

For real pest protection, such as what you'd need to avert cabbageworms on cabbage family crops, Sally suggests securing the row cover with rocks, boards, or the long pins sold for that purpose.

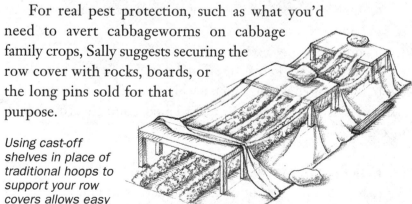

Using cast-off shelves in place of traditional hoops to support your row covers allows easy access to plants.

There is one last use for the shelves later in the season, says Sally. "After the row covers come off, I leave the shelves where they are and place flats, window boxes, or pots of flowers and herbs on them. The flowers, particularly those in the daisy and aster family, such as calendulas, cosmos, and marigolds, provide nectar for many beneficial insects. Especially when they're off the ground on the shelves, the flowers might lure some spined soldier bugs or their lady beetle girlfriends. Now you have row covers and predatory insects helping to protect your crops."

annals of ingenuity

GIVE THANKS FOR HAULING HELP

t he next time you're hauling a load of compost all the way to the far side of your yard, take a minute to thank Chuko Liang, the prime minister of Shu Han, a kingdom in medieval China.

Folks who knew him (and even some who didn't) said that Chuko had a mind that "surpassed the gods." Whether that's true or not, we can't say. But we do know that Chuko is said to have invented that ingenious garden laborsaving device, the wheelbarrow. As for Chuko's gardening skills, we can't speculate about those either. He invented the wheelbarrow to haul around war supplies.

Turn sheets into tomato tarps. The evening the weatherman predicts a frost is not the time to start searching frantically for some way to protect your precious tomato plants. Instead, keep a stack of old sheets at the ready in your barn, garage, or toolshed. When frost is forecast, place the sheets over your tomato cages and anchor them at the bottom with rocks.

Collect clothespins. Wooden or plastic clothespins are indispensable in the garden. They come in handy when you need to attach a row cover to its hoop in a windy area or to attach sheets to your tomato cage when frost is coming.

Roll out the (old) carpet. Even old carpet scraps can be put to good use in the garden. Here are three nifty ideas.

use your utensils

SALLY CUNNINGHAM is a recycling fanatic. So she was especially pleased to notice the cleanup crew at a large gardeners' picnic bagging the used plastic forks, spoons, and knives and collecting the heavy paper coffee cups.

"I told the crew I thought it was a great idea to reuse the plastic," Sally says. "After all, it cleans up perfectly well in the dishwasher. That's when one of the guys turned to me and said with a perfect deadpan, 'Oh, I don't even wash them—I just reuse them.' I was relieved to learn that he uses them not in the kitchen, but in the garden." Here's how.

Spoons and knives. Use these to label crop varieties, to mark where you finished seeding a section of row, or to stretch string when marking out straight lines. Write on the utensils with magic marker, or dip the knife ends in nail polish to color-code varieties or flower colors.

Forks. Some gardeners say that you can never collect enough forks. For one thing, they're terrific for transplanting seedlings: Stick a fork, tines down, in the soil next to large seeds such as squash, pumpkins, or radishes when you plant them. When it's time to thin or transplant the seedlings, just use the fork to gently lift the little clumps of roots. And they're also come in handy for lifting plants out of flats. Forks are also useful when you're starting seeds. Stick forks, tines down, in the flats of seedlings, then drape plastic wrap over the top to form a little greenhouse. The plastic holds in moisture while the seedlings grow, and you won't have to buy the expensive plastic lids that are sold for this purpose.

Paper coffee cups. Cut off and discard the bottom of each cup. Place the cup cuffs around seedlings such as beans, broccoli, or peppers to protect them from cutworms. Sink the cups into the soil about ½ inch. Paper cups are organic and will decompose over time, so there's no need to remove them.

IT'S CURTAINS FOR YOUR PLANTS

I f those old sheer curtains are too beat-up to use inside the house, put them to work in your garden. Use them as lightweight shade cloths in the summer to protect spinach or lettuce from strong sunlight. Those crops tend to bolt as the sun comes on strong. A double thickness of tinted sheers makes an especially good shade cloth.

Sheers can also be used as row covers to prevent pests such as cabbage butterflies from laying eggs that produce cabbageworms.

---

1. Cover bare spots. Use old carpet scraps to cover bare patches of garden during the winter. Spread leaves, manure, shredded paper, or straw under the carpet, where it will decompose and feed your soil. The carpet keeps weeds from growing and spreading more seeds before frost and prevents their emergence in the spring. And when you remove the carpet, the soil beneath will be friable and ready to plant.

2. Make a path. Strips of carpet also make great foundations for garden paths.

3. Discourage the deer. Lay 6-foot-wide pieces of carpet around the perimeter of your garden. Deer don't like to step on carpet and will steer clear of it—and your vegetables.

COMPOSTING: RECYCLING TO THE EXTREME

Black gold—that's what gardeners call compost. Its properties are considered magical by many. Not only does compost feed microorganisms in the soil, improve soil texture, help it hold moisture, and fight plant diseases, but it's also the ultimate way to recycle. Intrigued? We thought you might be. Here are some ingenious ways to get started.

323

It doesn't have to be expensive. Page through any up-scale gardening catalog, and you're liable to see some pretty expensive composting systems. Well, here's good news: You don't need any of them. You can build your own compost container from any number of items, including discarded pallets (also known as skids), chicken wire, old window screens, old dog kennels—whatever you find or invent. There are only two rules: (1) The container should be 3 feet wide and 3 feet deep, and (2) air must be able to penetrate and circulate in the container.

It doesn't have to smell bad. If your compost is a little, um, fragrant, you have what's called an anaerobic condition, which is decomposition without oxygen. To eliminate the odor, you need to do two things. First, turn the compost to get more air in there. Second, add material with a high carbon content, such as shredded newspaper, sawdust, twigs, or even wood chips.

It doesn't have to attract animals. Some folks pooh-pooh the idea of composting because they fear that it will attract unwanted animals. When done correctly, it won't. Never add animal products—such as meat, bones, fat, and butter—to your compost. Salad dressing and other oily nonanimal products are out, too. And if you add fragrant foods, bury them at least a foot deep to prevent animals from discovering them and digging them up.

Get a little help from your worms. Vermicomposting—composting with the aid of red wiggler worms—

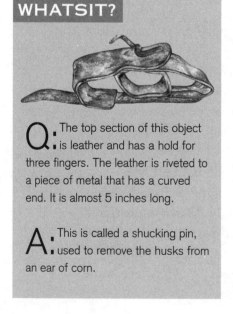

WHATSIT?

Q: The top section of this object is leather and has a hold for three fingers. The leather is riveted to a piece of metal that has a curved end. It is almost 5 inches long.

A: This is called a shucking pin, used to remove the husks from an ear of corn.

MAKE YOUR COMPOST BEAUTIFUL

A compost bin or pile doesn't have to be a backyard eyesore. In fact, there are dozens of ways to make one look pretty darned good. Here are three of Sally Cunningham's favorites to get you started.

1. Add flower boxes. If your compost bin is constructed from pallets or other material that gives it thick sides, line the top with planter boxes filled with pretty flowers.

2. Or flowering vines. If your compost bin has chicken wire sides, plant flowering vines all around it. They'll climb on the wire and brighten the site.

3. Surround it with plants. Plant tomatoes, pumpkins, or sunflowers all around a compost pile.

Once your imagination gets cranking, you might find it hard to stop—and your neighbors might not even know you have a compost bin.

---

is becoming more popular these days. Adding worms to your compost mix adds worm castings, which have rich nutrients needed by plants. Vermicomposting is also popular because it can be done indoors and generally takes up less space than conventional composting. Want to hear more? Here are some quick tips to get you started.

1. Try this tired tip. Old tires make fine worm bins for vermiculture—raising worms, that is. Stack the tires and toss in shredded paper, coffee grounds, red wiggler worms, and your compostable kitchen scraps. Stacked tires are also terrific for growing potatoes. And since they retain lots of heat, they're good for peppers, eggplant, and tomatoes, too.

2. Make a meal for your composting worms. Gardeners who like to make worm compost report that the favorite bedding choice of red wigglers—the kind of worms used in composting bins—is shredded paper. Add some coffee grounds and the

computing for compost

MASTER GARDENER JOANNE TANNER has an ingenious way to recycle—and help her garden at the same time.

"I once worked in an office where we used the kind of computer paper with perforated edges that feed the paper through the printer," Joanne says. "Normally, we'd tear off those edges after the paper went through the printer, but I never threw them away. In fact, I asked everyone in the office to collect them so that I could take them home to use in my compost. The paper was perfect because it was uncoated and, since it was full of holes, decomposed quickly.

"If you don't use a feeder-type printer at your office or home, get yourself a paper shredder. For less than thirty dollars, you can shred your discarded paper for use in the compost. But don't stop there. Instead of giving your old newspapers to the recycling center, shred them in your paper shredder, too!"

According to compost pros, paper you add to your compost should be uncoated (that means no glossy magazine paper). And since paper is slow to decompose, limit the amount you add. Too much paper may cause your compost to "cook" slowly. If that occurs, just add some high-nitrogen ingredients, such as grass clippings or manure.

occasional fruit or vegetable scrap, and you have your own mini-compost factory.

3. Don't dig up the backyard! Don't make the mistake of putting good old night crawlers in your vermicompost bin. The worms used in vermicomposting are called redworms or red wigglers, and you can find them at many garden supply stores or in some gardening catalogs.

IMPROVISING IN AND AROUND THE GARDEN

Recycling is just one of the ways that gardeners reveal their ingenuity. Most gardeners use their resourcefulness and native problem-solving skills just about every time they step outside. After all, sometimes things don't go as planned (a tool breaks, or the one you have isn't quite right), and you simply must improvise.

Come to think of it, enjoying those moments when our ingenuity and resourcefulness shine might be one of the reasons we garden in the first place. When you're able to solve a problem creatively and work with what you have, there's a feeling of competence and satisfaction. And doesn't everybody need a straightforward sense of accomplishment once in a while?

Well, here's your chance. Next time you find yourself in the middle of a project, lacking the perfect something, check out these tips. You just might find what you're looking for.

Make an onion hoe. If you grow onions, you know why you might need a hoe with a special blade—about finger size, only sharp, pointed, and strong. Onions hate weed competition, and fungal disease or rot can worsen if moisture-holding weeds are growing between onion plants. That means it's important to catch the sprouting weeds early, even while the onion roots are still

---

A TERRIFIC IDEA FOR PEANUTS

A package just arrived from your favorite mail-order outlet, and the box is chock-full of packing peanuts. Now you *could* throw them away, but that would be a waste. Instead, put them to use in your garden. Pour some polystyrene packing peanuts (not the kind that dissolve) into the bottom of a pot when you plant or transplant a plant. The peanuts add drainage just as gravel or stones do, but they're a lot lighter.

327

fragile and shallow. The problem is that the weeds sprout between the onion sets, which are often only an inch or two apart, so you have to reach straight down between the plants to avoid knocking them down. Some gardeners use old table forks to scratch out the weeds, but they're wide, short, and clumsy. There is a better way.

Craig Vogel, a builder and gardener from Eden, New York, constructed an onion hoe—one he can use standing up—from an old broom handle and a steel shelf bracket. "It's easy to make," Craig says. "And I haven't seen the equivalent in a garden store. Most shelf brackets are just about one-half inch wide and sturdy, so the hoe should never break, and the weight of the tool pulled around the onion sets is enough to dislodge the weeds. And if you bump a few onions, so what? I just plant them close enough that a few early thinnings won't hurt."

To make your own hoe, screw the bracket to the broom handle so that the L faces out, with one side flat against the handle on one end. If you prefer, make a hoe with a 1-foot-long handle that you can use while sitting or kneeling. To use the hoe, just drag it gently between the onions. It also works around carrots, asparagus, or any other fine, closely planted crop.

A homemade onion hoe makes weeding between onion sets a breeze.

Hold your garden together with Velcro®. Joanne Tanner grows food and flowers at home, works with her husband in their home business, and volunteers hundreds of hours each year gardening with kids in Buffalo. "I need every shortcut I can find," she says. One of Joanne's favorite finds is Velcro®, which is available at any fabric store. It comes in handy all over the garden, and it's easier to deal with than rope or strips of cloth.

"Use double-sided Velcro® tape, sometimes called Velstrap

HERD YOUR HOSE

If you have to drag a hose around your garden, you know how easy it is to knock down plants. But our gardening experts have come up with three ingenious hose guards you can make yourself. Place any of them at the ends of rows or wherever the hose has to turn a corner.

1. Rocks. To be effective, a rock must be large and have a lip or ledge that juts outward enough for a heavy hose to get caught under it. The rock also must be heavy enough that yanking the hose won't budge the rock.

2. Plumber's discards. Watch the curb on trash day or ask your plumber for U-shaped or 45-degree-angle pieces of pipe and anchor them in the soil. Don't use straight sections of pipe that are shorter than 4 feet long around the garden, because you could seriously hurt yourself if you fell on one.

3. Cans and other containers. Find plastic containers or cans that are 5 inches or more wide and about 4 inches deep. Purchase long nails or spikes at least 3 inches longer than the containers are deep. Place a container upside down and hammer a nail through the bottom, sinking it all the way into the soil.

(not the two-piece kind), to hold tomatoes and pole beans to their stakes," Joanne advises. "I use Velcro® to train pickling cukes, clematis, and mandevilla vine to a trellis. Velcro® holds more firmly than string and can be repositioned or removed when necessary. And the wide band is gentler to stems than wire.

"Once, when some hollyhocks I had transplanted were drooping from the stress of being moved, I kept them straight by looping Velcro® firmly around each stalk and a bamboo stake until they could get through the shock, and stand on their own again."

For Herbs Only

What makes an herb an herb? By one definition, an herb is any plant that's useful—be it as a seasoning, a medicine, a fragrance or cosmetic, or an ingredient in other products such as dyes, rope, or fabrics. One of the reasons that herbs are so popular with home gardeners is that they're easy to grow. One of the reasons that our ingenious experts are so popular is that their hints and tips make herbs even easier to grow. And that makes them twice as useful.

Cut herbs early and often. Most herbs thrive when they're regularly harvested, so cut chives, basil, or oregano a couple inches from the ground often (as you would lettuce when you are harvesting salad greens) and use the extra bits in salads or other dishes. Perennial herbs such as lavender become woody if you let them grow unchecked, so regularly cut them back to 2 inches and enjoy the new, softer growth.

Don't let them bolt. If you're going to use herbs for fragrance, flavor, or oils, be sure to harvest them before the flowers appear. That's when the herbs' essence will be most fragrant and rich. Early morning, just as the dew is drying, is the best time of day to cut herbs you want to use for fragrant oils.

Start from seeds. It takes less patience to buy herb sets than it is to plant seeds in your garden. But some herbs—fennel and dill, to name two—have taproots and won't do well if you transplant them. For those herbs, experts advise direct seeding. Six to 8 weeks before the last frost date, sprinkle the seeds (watch for freebies from last year's plants, since both dill and fennel self-seed easily) on well-drained soil with good air circulation. Cover the seeds with a light layer of sand.

> ## DON'T LOVE YOUR HERBS TO DEATH
>
> Gardeners are often generous types who nurture their plants by watering and fertilizing them well and enriching their soil. Unfortunately, lavishing all that attention on your herbs isn't the best way to get them to produce. In fact, it's smarter to be miserly with food and water.
>
> Many culinary and ornamental herbs—coriander, lavender, oregano, and sage, to name a few—originally came from the Mediterranean. There, those herbs grow in sunny, sandy, dry sites, usually on hillsides, with perfect drainage. That's why adding lots of organic matter, watering regularly, and supplying extra nitrogen—great for most veggies—leads only to root rot, floppy succulent growth, and lack of flowering when it comes to herbs.

For Fruit Only

Fruit can be a challenge for the home gardener to grow, especially in an environmentally friendly way. After all, most fruit is so sweet and juicy that birds, insects, raccoons, and even the family dog just love it. And each fruit has its own unique needs and management issues. But our garden experts agree that growing fruit at home is worth the trouble. If you succeed, not only will you save on those high grocery store prices, but you'll also get to savor the incredibly delicious, irreplaceable taste of a sun-warmed berry, cherry, or apple from your own backyard. Here's an assortment of tips to help you make the most of your fruit-growing endeavors.

Weight down your apple trees. Apple growers go to great lengths to weight down the branches of their trees. They do it for a couple of reasons. First, lower branches mean fruit that's easier to reach. Second, the more the branches spread, the easier it is for sunlight to penetrate the tree—and more photosynthesis (the way

Hay! Protect Your Strawberries!

Mulch your strawberry plants with clean hay or straw. Not only will the hay or straw keep the weeds down, but it also will help protect those delicate berries and keep them clean.

tree leaves absorb sunlight and create sugars) means more apples. However, getting those branches low and spread often involves heavy (even ugly) objects such as cement blocks and ropes.

One apple grower we know created a traffic-stopping display that solved the problem. He gathered lots of brightly colored children's sand pails, filled them with rocks and sand, and hung them at various levels on the tree, weighting down the branches. If sand pails don't appeal to your sense of aesthetics, consider using Easter baskets. They're cheap and easy to find. And to go one step further, why not plant some flowering annuals in the containers, making a sweet scene even prettier?

Follow this berry good advice. Does anyone *not* like berries? Whether you're planting blueberries, raspberries, or strawberries, we have some ingenious tips for you.

Choose blueberries. New to growing berries? Try blueberries. They're a fairly foolproof, pest-proof fruit crop. Just keep in mind that the soil must be acid, or the bushes won't produce much fruit. Test your soil's pH. (Kits are available from many garden centers or from your local Cooperative Extension Service office.) If the pH is close to 5.5, your blueberries will produce well. If the soil is alkaline—a pH higher than 7—don't even think about growing blueberries. You can amend the soil pH over time, but it will probably be more trouble than those few boxes of blueberries are worth to you.

If your soil isn't perfect, keep in mind that blueberries make wonderful ornamental shrubs for the home landscape, so you might enjoy them even if the fruit doesn't amount to much.

Research before you plant raspberries. If you're planting new raspberry brambles, take care not to put them where you planted

seed standing up

SOME FOLKS NEED TO WORK without bending when they garden. Luckily, many tools—hoes and rakes, for instance—already have long handles and make some tasks easier. Seeding, however, is another story. It's one of the great pleasures of gardening, but it can be frustrating for folks who have trouble bending. After all, it's nearly impossible to get neat rows when you're dropping seeds from several feet above the target. Precision is impossible, and if the seeds germinate, the seedlings will be spaced erratically.

Help is on the way in the form of this ingenious, homemade seeding tool designed by Danny Papadatos, who lived and worked in Buffalo. Danny came up with this tool as part of a horticulture therapy project for seniors and others with special needs. Here's how to make your own.

Start with a piece of polyvinyl chloride (PVC) tubing that's long enough to reach from your waist to a couple of inches above the ground—3 to 4 feet long, depending on your height. Fit the small end of a large (6-inch-diameter) kitchen funnel into one end of the tube and secure it with some duct tape or a clamp from the hardware store.

Once you've prepared your planting area by digging the trenches or holes, you can easily move along the rows, putting seeds in the funnel one at a time. They'll slide right through the tube and come out exactly where you choose.

potatoes, tomatoes, eggplant, strawberries, or any other bramble crops up to 4 years prior. Those plants can carry a virus called verticillium wilt, which is deadly to raspberries.

Pick flowers to increase your strawberry yield. We know that this suggestion will be hard to follow, but trust us. When you plant June-bearing strawberries, remove the flowers they produce during the first growing season. In the long run, it will benefit you and the plants. Removing the flowers will promote root and runner growth, and that will mean even more berries for you the following year.

Banish black knot from your cherries and plums. Many home owners are appalled to find bumpy, irregular growths—like oddly shaped lumps of charcoal—on the branches of their lovely cherry or plum trees. Instead of taking a tree back to the nursery for a refund, gardening writer and Cooperative Extension agent Sally Cunningham suggests taking a walk in the woods.

"No, not just to calm down," Sally says. "It's to check out the wild cherry trees. Black knot is a fungal disease of plum and cherry trees. It's typically found on wild cherry trees in nearby woods. To have a healthy plum or cherry tree—for fruit or ornamental beauty—you'll have to get rid of the diseased wild ones."

The only way to cure black knot is to remove the cankers. Cut off any branches with growths a few inches from the knots, and disinfect your pruning shears (with rubbing alcohol or a solution of 1 part bleach to 5 parts water) between cuts. If the tree is too disfigured to keep, get rid of it and replace it with a different kind of tree. If you're determined to continue with cherries and plums, take that walk!

chapter 18

garden good
g u y s

WE YANKEES LOVE THE NATURAL WORLD. Maybe it has something to do with our colonist roots. Back in the old days, our
ancestors relied on nature to provide them with food, water, and
shelter—and they were grateful for it. And most of us appreciate
the fact that we share the planet with many creatures, whether we
live in the country, the suburbs, or the city.

Our experts are no different, and they've incorporated that
appreciation into their methods for drawing more beneficial birds,
mammals, amphibians, and insects closer to their homes. For

instance, Tom Moore, a biologist who works in Suwanee, Georgia, will tell you how to create a safe habitat for the creatures great and small that visit your yard. Steve Grinley, owner of Bird Watcher's Supply & Gift in Newburyport, Massachusetts, helps out by offering a simply ingenious idea for a free alternative to an expensive store-bought bird feeder.

There's a lot more, too. We'll show you how to make snug houses for rabbits and toads, and how to attract the beneficial insects that will keep those less desirable creepy crawlers from eating your greenery.

WHATSIT?

Q: It looks a little like a beehive, but it's made from a lightweight metal. It has two detachable halves that slip apart easily, but when they're put together, they form a sort of cage. What is it?

A: It's a cricket cage. Before horse races and gambling casinos, the Chinese bet on cricket races. They used to have cricket meets, complete with lore about famous crickets. Chinese ladies liked crickets and kept them in cages in their bedrooms. Male crickets sang during the night, and cricket song in the home was a sign of good luck.

Bird Basics

First things first, says Tom Moore. To attract birds (and other animal visitors) to your yard, you need to create an inviting habitat—an environment in which animals can find food and shelter. That's a scientist's way of saying, "If you build it, they will come." And water is at the top of the list.

"Birds are attracted to clean water even more than to bird food," says Jen Roediger of Nature's Outpost, a bird-watchers' supply shop in North Hampton, New Hampshire.

Water also will draw the attention of mammals, such as rabbits and deer, and amphibians, such as toads. "By attracting amphibians such as tree frogs and spring peepers, you can add wildlife night sounds to enjoy in the spring," says wildlife biologist John Scott of

Sandwich, Massachusetts. (You'll find more ways to attract toads later in this chapter.) Here are some of our experts' ingenious suggestions for feeding, watering, and sheltering your feathered friends.

FOOD AND WATER

Birds are just like any other animal. To live they need food and water. Here are some ingenious ways to provide both.

Wet their whistles. It's easy to provide water for birds. You just set a shallow dish on a rock wall or fence post or hang it from a branch. But don't be careless about the container you use. Here are a couple of tips from Georgia biologist Tom Moore and the folks at Nature's Outpost in North Hampton, New Hampshire.

1. Make sure it's shallow. "Remember that most birds can't swim, so they really need a wading pool," says Tom Moore. A shallow dish is better than a deep bowl.

2. Add some stepping-stones. An easy way to help keep visiting birds from slipping into a water source and drowning is to scatter a few pebbles around the bottom of the dish or pan, say the folks at Nature's Outpost. The birds can use the pebbles as stepping-stones on which to perch, lean, and drink. Or they can use

---

DARK DISHES FOR DARK DAYS

When the temperature dips below freezing, that ice in your birdbath won't do your feathered friends any good—they don't ice-skate. Steve Grinley has a simple and clever way to make sure your neighborhood birds always have fresh water: Choose a dark dish. "A dark dish absorbs sunlight more readily and will stay warmer, resisting freezing during colder weather," he says.

the pebbles as a refuge if they slip off the edge of the dish while drinking.

3. Keep it clean. It's a good idea to replenish the water regularly and clean the dish at least once a week. That will keep your feathered friends from contracting an illness from tainted water.

Ring the dinner bell. After water, food is the next item on your list of must-haves for attracting birds. But that doesn't mean you have to spend big bucks on a bird feeder. "Turn a garbage can lid upside-down and fill it with seed," recommends Steve Grinley. "Or use an old serving tray."

Many birds, such as cardinals, juncos, towhees, sparrows, and mourning doves, are ground feeders, which means they prefer to eat their food from, well, the ground. In fact, these birds will often wait for food to spill from a feeder. By placing a garbage can lid or a tray on the ground, you not only save money, but you also set a table that ground-feeding birds prefer.

Here are some snack ideas that will appeal to most birds, along with some hints about attracting specific species to your yard.

1. Grow a berry good snack. "Birds love edible berries," notes biologist Tom Moore. So plant berry-producing bushes and trees in your yard if you want to lure more birds. The best part? You don't need to keep refilling a berry bush the way you do a feeder—nature does that for you. "Try blueberries, hawthorns, and holly," Tom suggests. "In fact, because it's an evergreen, holly is great. It provides food and shelter."

2. Serve suet in winter. Keep your winter birds well-fed with suet, but don't buy it—make it yourself, suggest the folks at Nature's Outpost. Head to the meat market and ask for 2 to 3 pounds of beef, lamb, or pork fat. Bring it home, melt it in a saucepan over low heat, and transfer it to a bowl. Add sunflower seeds and millet (available at the supermarket, feed store, or hardware store) and mix well.

> ## MAKE it LAST
> # Store your seed
>
> YOU WANT TO keep birdseed around, but you don't want the local vermin to eat it. Just store the seed in a small metal trash can with a tight-fitting lid. It'll protect the seed from moisture and hungry nonbird critters.

While the mixture is still soft, form it into several orange-size balls, then allow it to return to its original consistency. Hang each ball from a tree branch in an onion or string bag. Store the unused balls in your fridge or freezer. (They tend to soften or melt if they warm up.) Your suet cakes will provide a good source of fat and protein for birds during the cold months.

If you don't have the time or inclination to prepare a suet mixture, just place the animal fat in an onion or string bag and hang it from a tree branch as is, suggests Steve Grinley. Birds will still get the protein they need from the plain fat.

Give them the salt of the (h)earth. Each winter and spring, birds are hit by cars while they're trying to pick up salt particles and minerals from roads. You can save a few feathered friends—and keep them closer to your house—by offering them a humane alternative.

In a large bucket, combine 1 cup table salt with 1 cup wood ashes and enough water to dissolve the mixture. (You will have to stir it.) Pour the mixture over a large rock, log, or stump in your yard. When the water evaporates, salt and ash crystals will form and attract hungry birds. Keep in mind that you can use wood ashes from your fireplace as long as they don't contain any residue from artificial logs, colored wrapping paper, or coated paper.

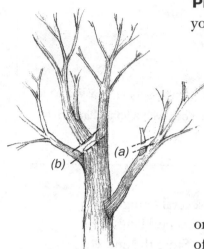

Pruning apple trees properly will produce more fruit.

Prune your trees. If you have apple trees on your property, you can increase their fruit by pruning them, says wildlife biologist John Scott. "Pruning releases more fruit, providing more food for local wildlife," he says.

To get the most from your pruning, use a pruning saw or shears to remove any dead limbs and branches as close to the living branch as possible (a). If a tree has multiple trunks, choose the largest and most vigorous to save and remove the others (b). Remove about one-third of the remaining live growth by cutting off 1 to 2 feet from the ends of side branches or vertical shoots. But don't remove the short spur branches, because these will bear fruit.

Don't deadhead your flowers. You can attract some birds to your property by letting your spring and summer flowers go to seed. Chickadees, goldfinches, sparrows, and titmice, are seed eaters that will enjoy the seeds of flowers such as asters and sunflowers, says Steve Grinley. You'll not only create less work for yourself, but you'll also be providing birds with their favorite meal.

Sow tree seeds. If you want to attract birds that lunch on seeds—chickadees, goldfinches, sparrows, titmice, and others—

FEEDER FACT

Planning to add a bird feeder to your lawn? Make sure to site it at least 4 feet from any windows. That way, birds will be less likely to collide with your windows and be injured or killed.

try planting an ash, oak, or hickory tree. These trees are hardy and long-lived and will provide your birds with food and your yard with welcome shade.

Offer orioles oranges. Wouldn't you love to see the bright orange of orioles in your backyard? Feed them oranges, say Jen Roediger and Steve Grinley. Here's a perfectly ingenious two-step way to do just that.

1. Hammer a nail into a tree, fence post, or log, then slice a fresh orange in half. Impale one half on the nail.

2. "Place fresh orange slices in the tray of your bird feeder or hang several slices from a tree branch in an onion bag or string bag," Steve suggests. Be sure to save a slice or two to munch on while you watch the birds.

Similarly, you can attract small mammals with a feeder made with nails and a board, notes John Scott. "Drive several large nails into a wooden board, then nail or screw the board to a pole or tree," John explains. "Impale apples, pears, or dried ears of corn on the nail." Your new feeder will likely attract raccoons, opossums, gray squirrels, chipmunks, and skunks. If you don't want those visitors to wander into your home, keep the feeder well away from the house.

Tempt tanagers with fruit salad. Want to attract scarlet tanagers to your yard? Here's a treat that's bound to whet their

THE PROS KNOW

give everlasting protection

JUST AS YOU wouldn't enjoy your picnic snack on a bench surrounded by hungry bears, many birds prefer to enjoy their meal well out of harm's way. Here's an ingenious way to give them cover.

"Small birds, such as chickadees, nuthatches, and wrens, will seek shelter as they feed," says Jen Roediger. They don't sit at the feeder to eat. Instead, these birds travel back and forth from a feeder, plucking a seed and taking it back to a safe bush or high tree branch. Planting evergreen bushes—yew, rhododendron, boxwood, juniper, holly, and the like—near your bird feeder will increase the chances that these birds will use the feeder.

appetites. Cut up an apple or a banana and mix it with a handful of raisins. Tear a slice or two of white bread into small pieces, add it to the fruit, and toss the mixture with 1 tablespoon sugar. Spread the treat in a dish or tray and serve it to your tanagers at ground level.

SHELTER

After water and food, birds will be on the lookout for a place to call home. That doesn't always mean a birdhouse. Following are some simply ingenious ways to provide your feathered friends with a safe and comfortable place to bunk for the season.

Accommodate cavity nesters. "Bluebirds, chickadees, nuthatches, and wrens are cavity nesters," explains Steve Grinley. "When you see dead branches and logs lying around, leave them alone or move them to a protected spot in your yard where you can see them but you won't trip over them or hit them with the lawn mower." These dead branches and logs also are havens for frogs and toads, as long as there is a nearby water source.

Provide a safe haven. When birds that nest in small trees or shrubs produce offspring, the babies may be vulnerable to cats and other predators. You can easily increase their safety by wrapping the sides of the tree or shrub with chicken wire or netting, leaving enough space open for the parents to fly in and out to feed and care for their young. And for goodness' sake, if *you* have an outdoor cat, do your best to keep her away from those bushes.

Hang a winter home. You're accustomed to hanging birdhouses in the spring to attract birds during nesting and breeding season, but how about during the winter? Tom Moore explains that birds such as bluebirds, cardinals, and chickadees, which don't migrate south for the winter, still need shelter. So sometime in the

HOME, HOME IN THE TREE

One sure way to attract birds to your yard is to put up a birdhouse. But keep in mind that any birdhouse you hang will be more appealing to birds if you follow these basic tips.

- **Provide adequate ventilation.** Whether you buy or build a birdhouse, make sure it has air vents to keep it cool and well-ventilated. You can also keep the house from becoming too hot by orienting the entrance to either the north or the east.
- **Put off pruning.** If it's appropriate for the trees on your property, wait until late summer or early autumn to prune. Many birds like to nest in dead or thick branches.
- **Don't crowd them.** Birds don't enjoy overcrowding any more than people do, so don't put all your birdhouses in one tree. Spread them out, with no more than one house per tree.

fall, take down your birdhouses, clean them, and then rehang them so that your little feathered friends can snuggle up together to keep warm on a cold winter's night. You'll not only enjoy having their company during the winter, but you'll be doing your bit to help them survive the cold.

Other Good Guys

Catching sight of a deer, a rabbit, or even a toad is a wonderful reminder that we're not the only ones who live in our communities. If you're missing out on seeing your four-footed neighbors, here are some ingenious ways to invite them over.

Set out a winter buffet. Most animals, such as deer and rabbits, have a tough time finding food during the winter months,

BUILD A SNOWMAN

Here's an ingenious way to amuse the kids and feed the birds (and other wild animals) during the winter. Build a snowman! Stick a raw carrot in the middle of his face for a nose—the deer will love it. Slice a raw apple in half for his eyes—birds and deer will nibble on it. Press a half circle of peanuts, walnuts, or other nuts into a smile—birds and deer will pluck at those treats. Finally, place a hat with a flattened top on your snowman's head and fill the brim and top with any type of birdseed—your feathered friends are sure to stop by for a snack. As the treats are eaten, replenish them. Your snack-laden snowman will provide lots of entertainment for humans and wildlife alike.

says Tom Moore. Here's an easy way to help them out. "Collect acorns during the fall, arrange them on a cookie sheet to dry, and then store them in a bucket," Tom suggests. "During the winter, scatter them on the ground or snow for forage." The animals will appreciate the meal, and you'll enjoy watching them eat.

Plant bushes for the bunnies. Although most types of rabbits do not hibernate during the winter, they do dig burrows in safe spots and experience periods of inactivity, coming out for a bit of foraging and frolicking. According to Tom Moore, you can assist in your cottontails' house-hunting efforts by planting evergreens such as boxwoods, laurels, rhododendrons, or yews on your property. These bushes provide shelter from wind, cold, and predators beneath their thick foliage, allowing bunnies to take a safe winter nap.

Don't tidy up your garden. You've probably heard a famous gardener or two recommend cutting back the stalks of perennials—daffodils, tulips, daylilies, and the like—that are past flowering. The idea is that it will keep your garden looking neater. "Don't do it!" says Jim Ouellet of Exeter, New Hampshire. Jim is the former owner of The Blossom Shop in Kensington, New Hampshire. "Those stalks provide nutrients to the plant throughout the winter," he says. "But that's not all; they provide shelter for birds, chipmunks, mice, rabbits, and toads. So leave those stalks right where they are. In fact, you can even add clumps of grass, dead flowers, and fallen leaves around the bases of those plants to increase the warmth and protection of the hideaway. When spring arrives, birds can use what's left of the plants to build their nests.

Attract bats to your belfry (and your backyard). Here's the good news about bats: They pollinate flowers and distribute seeds. And each bat consumes about half its weight in insects—mosquitoes and midges among them—every night. So what's not to love? Okay, so they can get into the attic or nest under the eaves or in the chimney of your house. But if you're thinking rabies, according to the experts at Bat Conservation International, the risk of contracting rabies from bats is small. Here's how to attract bats to your yard without inviting them to move in with you.

1. Buy or build a bat house. You can purchase one for a reasonable price at most places birdhouses are sold. Mount it at least 10 to 15 feet away from your house. Bats like to be up high and are partial to damp areas—lakes, streams, marshes, or even an area of your backyard that seems to be damp most of the time. (That's where mosquitoes hang out as well.) Bats also like to be near fruit trees. If you decide to build your own bat house, look for detailed directions in a library book or ask your local garden center if it might have a free instruction sheet.

Once you've built and mounted your house, be patient. It may take several months for the new residents to settle in. But when they do, you can enjoy the fruits of your labor: fewer bugs to bug you.

open a home depot for wildlife

"BIRDS AND SMALL MAMMALS can always use help building their nests," says biologist Tom Moore. You can lend them a helping hand—and make them feel welcome—by leaving nesting materials where they can find them easily—say, scattered around a tree trunk, under a bush, or near a fallen log. Here are seven nesting materials that will be especially appreciated.

1. Bits of wool (How about those pills you picked off that old sweater?)

2. Dryer lint

3. Fallen leaves

4. Grass clippings

5. Horse hair (If you live near a barn, ask to visit when the horses' manes and tails are pulled, and you'll probably take home a plastic bag full of hair.)

6. Pet hair (Say, doesn't your dog or cat need a good brushing right about now?)

7. Shredded cotton balls

2. Grow late (night) bloomers. Bats feed at night, so you can make your yard more appealing to them by growing plants that appeal to insects during the night. Good choices include bachelor's buttons, bitter cress, fireweed, four-o'clocks, goldenrod, lavender, phlox, sage, spearmint, sweet william, and thyme.

3. Light up the night. If you can do so without annoying your neighbors, place a mercury vapor light on a pole or tree away from your home. The light will attract loads of insects, and the insects will attract the bats.

Build a toad abode. Toads are wonderful insect eaters and are a delight to have around your garden. They also live for several years, so once you attract them, you will have natural bug control for more than one season. Toads are ideal for damp areas in your yard or garden that are breeding grounds for mosquitoes.

That's because toads love damp areas, too. You can encourage a toad to take up residence in a particular area by building it a house, says Tom Moore. Here's how.

"Take a clay flowerpot and cut a door hole out of the lip with a jigsaw or similar tool," Tom says. "Then set the pot upside down in a protected area, and you've got yourself a toad house." Your toad (or toads, depending on how many move in) will live in its flowerpot during the warm months, then burrow under a tree root or punky log to hibernate during the winter. In the spring, it will return to breed—and eat more bugs.

BRING ON THE BENEFICIAL BUGS

Bugs? Beneficial? Well, yes, actually. The insect world is loaded with creepy crawlers that gardeners and nongardeners alike are thrilled to have around. Some are friendly bugs that eat the not-so-friendly bugs that eat your plants. Others pitch in by pollinating plants. Still others are just pretty to look at. Here are some ways to attract beneficial insects to your garden and lawn, along with some tips that will help you recognize them.

> *annals of ingenuity*
>
> ### BENEFICIAL BUGS: THE EARLY YEARS
>
> When it comes to understanding and making use of beneficial insects, we again must look to the ancient Chinese. More than 1,600 years ago, the Chinese raised and sold yellow citrus ants to eat the insects that destroyed their mandarin orange crops.

Don't buy bugs. You could purchase beneficials such as ladybugs and praying mantises from some garden supply stores, by mail order, or over the Internet, but unless the conditions in your garden are just right, those insects might not stick around long enough to do much good.

A better idea is to contact your local Cooperative Extension agent and find out which beneficials are already indigenous to

WHAT'S IN A NAME?

Moth or butterfly—how can you tell the difference? And does it matter? Well, it helps to know, because although you probably want to attract butterflies to your garden, you don't want moths chomping on your cashmere sweaters in the attic or closet while you dine on a barbecued burger some summer evening.

Wildlife biologist John Scott offers a few simple tips for distinguishing between these two winged creatures.

Butterflies	Moths
Fly during the day	Fly during the night
Rest with their wings held up and together	Rest with their wings folded flat
Have "clubbed" antennae	Have featherlike antennae

your area and then do what you can to make your lawn and garden more appealing to them.

Supplement their diet. Sally Cunningham, an extension educator and gardening writer from East Aurora, New York, says that many beneficial insects prefer herbs over all other plants when the insects they feed on are scarce. Especially popular are members of the group Umbelliferae—the parsley family. That group includes dill, fennel, coriander, caraway, and Queen Anne's lace. Beneficial parasitoid wasps in particular like the delicate, lacy flowers for their nectar. Those wasps help keep pests in check by laying their eggs in or on the bodies of other insects. The young develop there, taking nourishment and eventually killing the hosts.

Sally recommends planting seeds for these herbs or just allowing seedlings to stick around the garden. "The trick," she says, "is to recognize a Queen Anne's lace or dill seedling when it is one-half inch tall and not to weed it out."

Delight the dragonflies. Dragonflies eat a whole host of nuisance insects, including beetles, moths, flies, and termites. Dragonflies live around water, so the easiest way to attract them is to live near a pond or lake. Many times, though, setting up any water source, such as a birdbath, is enough.

Know your beetles. Everybody knows that ladybird beetles—aka ladybugs—are good to have around the garden because they eat aphids. In fact, a single beetle can consume more than 5,000 aphids during its lifetime. But take heed: You may be reducing your garden's ladybug population without even realizing it. See that little bluish black and orange, six-legged, alligator-shaped insect hiding out under the leaf of your tomato plant? It's probably a ladybird beetle larva. Most people don't recognize the immature, or larval stage of this otherwise easy-to-identify garden

Ladybird beetle larva

denizen and destroy the larvae. But those larvae are just as hungry as their older brothers and sisters. And not only do adult and larval ladybugs feed on aphids, but they also eat scale insects, mealybugs, spider mites, and the small egg masses of other insects.

Love your lacewing larvae. The lacewing, named for its gauzy green or brown wings, is another terrific insect to have hanging around the garden. The adult insect feeds on aphids, caterpillar eggs, leafhopper nymphs, mealybugs, scales, spider mites, thrips, and whiteflies (whew!), and its larvae devour aphids. In fact, the lacewing larvae are called aphid lions for their ferocious appetites. They're grayish brown and about $\frac{3}{8}$ inch long, and they have sharp, curved jaws that extend beyond their heads.

Lacewing larva

pests, diseases, and
w e e d s

YES, WE KNOW THAT EVERYTHING IN NATURE IS BEAUTIFUL (thank you, Ray Stevens), but that doesn't necessarily mean that you want it all in your backyard—or your garden or attic, for that matter. For instance, as graceful as deer are to watch, they can severely damage your flower and vegetable gardens. Those adorable, fuzzy moles can chew up your lawn. And dandelion greens are delicious on a salad, but they can take over your lawn and turn it into a weed patch.

So how can you discourage these pesky pests from venturing

350

where you don't want them? You'll learn some ingenious ways in this chapter. We'll start with birds, work our way through four-footed pests large and small, and then tackle creepy crawlers and weeds. Along the way, you'll meet experts such as wildlife biologist Tom Moore from Suwanee, Georgia, who explains why purple martins are your ally in repelling mosquitoes; master gardener Joanne Tanner from Orchard Park, New York, who shares her recipe for a whitefly repellent; and biologist John Scott from Sandwich, Massachusetts, who offers tips for repelling deer and rodents. The best part? They do it all without using harmful chemicals.

Warding Off Winged Marauders

Before you start using complicated ways to keep starlings and house sparrows from nesting on your property, you may want to do a little simple house maintenance. "People in urban and suburban neighborhoods can discourage starlings and house sparrows from nesting by fixing loose siding and roofing and plugging holes in exterior fixtures and building surfaces, especially under the eaves," says wildlife biologist Carol Foss of Penacook, New Hampshire.

So what's the big problem with those species? "They're not indigenous to North America and are detrimental to native birds," Carol says. "Not only do they compete for nesting sites, but they also tend to roost in flocks and create a considerable mess with their droppings."

So don't be afraid to wield hammer and nails or to plug gaps with whatever is available. Some home owners swear by balled-up aluminum foil molded to fit into tiny gaps. Here are some other clever ways to discourage birds you'd rather not have around.

Foil those woodpeckers. Woodpeckers are colorful, but that's about the only good thing you can say about them when one

FIRST THINGS FIRST

Before you take any measures to rid your yard or garden of pests, especially animal ones, look around your house and property. "The first step in controlling nuisance wildlife is to find out why the critter is there," says John Scott. "Then you need to determine whether there is anything you can do to make your home and yard less attractive to it."

What about the garbage can (empty or full) that sits outside overnight? Or the bowl of dog food near the doghouse or dog pen? Do you leave the lid off the barbecue grill when it's not in use? Do you clean the grill regularly? Each of these items gives off a crucial scent: food. And each is an open invitation—no RSVP required—to deer, squirrels, raccoons, chipmunks, even a roaming bear or two. So put a lid on it—literally. Make sure you stash all of your trash in a securely covered plastic or metal can, and store the can in the basement, an outdoor shed, or the garage until trash day. (Of course, close all doors at night.) Clean and close your barbecue grill after cooking, and bring in all pet food dishes at night.

is pecking away at the wood siding on your house. Not only do they make a racket, but they also cause serious damage to one of your biggest investments. But John Scott offers two ingenious and inexpensive ways to discourage those home wreckers.

1. Hang strips of aluminum foil on short strings along the side of the house, John advises. The simplest way to do that is to secure a length of string between two thumbtacks that you've put up on either side of the area affected by the woodpeckers. Cut strips of aluminum foil about 2 inches wide and 10 to 12 inches long, then fold the strips over the string, creasing them tightly and smoothing them flat against the siding of the house. Not only will the birds back off from the shiny reflection, but when their beaks hit the foil, they'll recoil—and head for a tasty tree trunk instead. (Hope it belongs to one of the neighbors.)

2. Or try pie plates. Hang a few aluminum pie plates from a string along the affected area of the house. Woodpeckers will back away from the reflected sunlight that flashes off the metal.

PROTECT YOUR FRUIT

Fruit-growing guides are chock-full of recommendations for keeping birds from eating your cherries, plums, raspberries, and strawberries. Garden centers are loaded with netting and scare devices. But our home gardeners have come up with ingenious ways to accomplish the same goal with homemade tools and home-grown tricks.

Turn on the radio. Gardening experts advise turning on loud rock or country music or an animated talk radio station as a bird alarm. As with any other scare tactic, the sound should be intermittent, coming on and turning off at different times throughout the day. Of course, this technique works only if your neighbors' homes aren't too close to yours.

Hang up a hawk. Despite what you may have heard, that cute cat or owl garden sculpture probably doesn't mean much to the birds who snack on your fruit. It just sits there like the lifeless object that it is. Here's the solution. Get some old x-ray film (ask your doctor or check your own

annals of ingenuity

HISTORY IN A BOTTLE

early Americans had to deal with the same annoying insects that we do—mosquitoes, gnats, flies, and the like. But they didn't have high-powered chemical pesticides. Instead, they had birds. To encourse insect-eating birds such as martins and wrens to make their homes nearby, the colonists hung small pottery bottles or pitchers beneath the eaves of their houses, barns, shops, and other buildings. The birds would then take up residence in these bottles. Today garden centers and gardening catalogs sell similar versions of these bottle birdhouses.

WHATSIT?

Q: This ingenious object is made from wood and brass, and it spins around and around. It's about a foot long. Is it an old-time party noisemaker?

A: Not quite—it's a bird scarer. In England and early America, boys had the lonesome job of bird scaring. One boy with a scarer like this could protect many acres of corn—for only pennies a day (that's ingenious and frugal). Scarecrows were used then, too, but the best kind of bird scarer was this clapper, with its toothed wheel that clicked on a springy strip of beech.

medical records) and cut it in the shape of a hawk or owl. Hanged the winged silhouette on or near your fruit. Unlike the statuary, your cutout will blow around realistically in the breeze, and that just might be enough to fool those little birds and cause them to think twice about making a meal of your fruit.

Expose your berries. Birds feel more comfortable when their feeders and baths are sited near trees. The trees provide a convenient escape route in case a hawk flies overhead or a cat or other predator attacks. Conversely, birds will likely steer clear of berry rows or cherry trees that are completely exposed and sited far from the safety of a hedgerow or shade tree. If the birds do come to snack on your fruit, they probably won't stay very long.

Net more berries. If you grow blueberries or raspberries, then you know the heartbreak of birds—even if you love those little winged creatures. A flock of birds can decimate a berry bush long before you get to pick a peck for yourself. But here's some good news: You can bird-proof your berry patch simply and inexpensively with tulle, the fine netting that's normally used to make ballerinas' tutus. You'll find it at most fabric stores, and it's less expensive and sturdier than much of the netting you'll find in garden centers.

Buy the tulle as wide as you can (probably 60 inches) and drape it over a row of bushes. You may have to sew two pieces together, depending on the height of your plants. Drape the tulle over tall stakes or fencing. The fabric doesn't tear easily, but just to be sure, place upside-down flowerpots over the stakes before you drape the netting. Another nice thing about the netting is that it's usually white or pale pink, which makes it more inconspicuous than most garden netting. It's almost tulle good to be true.

MAKE it **LAST**

Garlic repels more than vampires

DURING ROUNDTABLE DISCUSSIONS at meetings of the Northeast Organic Farming and Gardening Association of New York State, organic growers often compare notes about repelling insects and other animals from the garden. Garlic always comes up as an effective repellent, whether for keeping rabbits from munching the lettuce or Japanese beetles away from any foliage plant. Here are three ways to use garlic to make your garden last longer than a week.

1. Plant it in several rows around the perimeter of the garden. While the garlic plants are small, grind up some garlic in a blender with water, then sprinkle the mixture around that area. Animals won't develop the habit of dining there.

2. Soak rags or ropes in garlic juice (made in a blender or pail) and lay them around the rows or sections of targeted plants. This is too much work to do for a massive planting, but it works for home gardeners. A couple of rainfalls seem to invigorate the scent, but after a while, you will need to resoak the material.

3. Plant garlic cloves in the fall in the corners of raised beds. Fall is the best time to start garlic for actual use, and the plants will have a head start as pest repellents as well. (This works anywhere you have a permanently mulched area that does not require tilling.)

Take care to fasten the bottom edges of your netting to the ground. Otherwise, a hungry explorer might get caught under the net, and that could be traumatic for both of you. U-shaped pins are sold for this purpose, but rocks or boards will do the trick, too.

Plant a trap crop. Vegetable gardeners often use so-called trap crops, which lure pest insects away from more valuable plants. This works with fruit trees and birds, too. Most birds like mulberries more than almost any fruit, so fruit growers often plant mulberry trees at the edge of a field away from their orchards to protect their cherries or plums. The birds will be happy to have the mulberries and will establish a pattern of dining on those white or purple fruits and never even think about your favorites.

Discouraging Deer

To city folks, spotting a deer can be like seeing some exotic animal: It's big, beautiful, and graceful. But to many jaded country dwellers, deer are nothing more than slow-moving obstacles on a dark road or the creatures that eat everything in the garden. Here are several ways to repel those dear deer without harming them.

Hang soap. Deer don't like the scent of deodorant soap. So head to the supermarket and pick up a few bars. (You may have to experiment to see which brands work best on your herd.) At home, slice each bar into several pieces, then place each piece inside an old nylon stocking or an onion mesh bag. Hang the soap bags from tree or bush branches in and near your garden. The soap actually works best when it's wet (maybe that's when it releases the most scent), so if you're not scheduled to get any rain, dip the bag or stocking containing the soap in water before you hang it up. Some folks just pop whole bars of soap, wrapper and all, inside the bags; that way, the bars last longer.

distract deer with apples

MANY GARDENERS KEEP themselves busy trying to repel, fence out, and otherwise thwart the deer that dine on their landscapes and gardens. Not Beth and David Buckley of Ashford Hollow, New York. Beth and David, who've observed one herd of deer for some 30 years, offer up one of their fruit trees to those four-footed creatures.

"There are right ways and wrong ways to deal with deer," Beth explains. If you like deer and want to help them, don't just put out corn and hay. Deer don't digest those high-protein foods well, so they'll just snack on your home landscape anyway. Instead, leave some apple trees on your land just for them, and they'll leave the rest of your greenery and fruit alone.

Beth and David recommend pruning the trees to keep up production. "A scrub apple tree doesn't have to be a work of art, but it's important to prune back the higher branches," David says. "That encourages the lower, accessible branches to fruit and lets lots of light into the tree. Also, during the winter, take a hike and prune the trees with a good saw while they're still dormant. To encourage the best fruiting (and make the tree more attractive to deer), clear the other brush or competing shrubs from around that tree, too."

Scatter hair. You might think that your hair is simply gorgeous, but believe us, deer don't think so. It's nothing personal—they just don't like the scent of human hair, says John Scott. He suggests that the next time you visit your barber or hairdresser, you collect the clippings from your cut (and everybody else's) in a plastic bag. At home, cut the legs off some old panty hose, put a handful or two of hair into the feet, and hang each foot from a tree

PLANT A DEER-RESISTANT GARDEN

Sometimes the best way to cope with Mother Nature is to go along with her. (Remember trying to argue with *your* mother?) So if the neighborhood herd of deer has decided that your garden is the place to be, try to relax. Rather than battling the problem with repellents, begin to change the flowers, bushes, and trees in the garden, choosing ones that the deer don't like. We admit that planting a deer-resistant garden is not an exact science, but there are some favorites among gardeners that are not-so-favorites among deer.

Deer tend to shy away from fragrant plants, particularly herbs such as basil, lavender, thyme, and yarrow. They also avoid plants with fuzzy foliage, such as black-eyed Susans, lamb's ears, and rose campion. And they certainly don't want to chomp on thorns, needles, or prickles, such as those found on junipers, pines, spruces, and all types of holly. Here's a list of more trees, shrubs, and other plants that deer are likely to avoid.

1. Trees: bitternut hickory, English hawthorn, paper birch

2. Shrubs: butterfly bush, common boxwood, Japanese andromeda

3. Other plants: columbine, lady's mantle, lily of the valley, periwinkle

branch or stake near your garden. (Hang as many panty hose pouches as you can fill with hair.) Replace the hair in each pouch the next time you get a haircut, and you'll notice that the deer aren't as interested in your garden as they once were.

Set out a meal of blood. Dried bloodmeal—plain or mixed with water—repels deer, says John Scott. You'll find bloodmeal at most garden centers, or you can order it from a gardening catalog. Follow the instructions on the package, then sprinkle the meal over the ground around your plants, or mix it with water and spray it directly on the plants. Reapply the bloodmeal weekly and after heavy rain.

Wrap your trees in foil. Deer love to munch on the new bark of young trees, but you can discourage that nasty behavior. Just wrap the base of the tree in heavy-duty aluminum foil, up to a height of about 3 feet. The foil not only will discourage deer, but it also will repel gypsy moths, which can damage many types of trees.

Repelling Furry Foes

You've worked hard on your garden, and you really don't want small rodents such as mice, moles, and chipmunks to destroy it. Here are some ingenious ways to protect your hard work.

Let dead trees stand. If there's a dead tree near your garden, you may have help with your rodent problem. Instead of cutting down the tree, leave it standing, says John Scott. "It can be used by hawks or owls from which to hunt," he explains. "Leaving such a tree standing, or even planting a garden near a dead tree, may encourage hawks or owls and discourage small rodents."

Try an (Or)kestrel arrangement. American kestrels, are predatory birds that hunt small rodents such as mice and chipmunks. That means you can discourage those pests by inviting kestrels to your yard. All you need is the right birdhouse near your garden, says John Scott.

When you shop for a kestrel condo, choose one with a base that's roughly 8 inches square and a house that is 12 to 15 inches tall, with the entrance hole in the top third of the front panel. The hole should be about 3 inches in diameter. (If you're handy, you could just build a birdhouse with those dimensions.) Hang the house 10 to 30 feet high, on either a tree trunk or a pole. Keep in mind that it may take a season or two for the kestrels to settle in.

Kestrel house

Mark your territory. Critters such as groundhogs and moles don't really appreciate the scent of human urine, says Jim Ouellet. So if you have the stomach for it, pour a little in the entrance to the den of any animal you'd like to shoo away. The creature will get the message quickly and move on.

Close the squirrel branch office. Before you drive yourself crazy creating elaborate Rube Goldberg measures to keep squirrels out of your bird feeder, watch how they are gaining access to it. In many cases, squirrels leap from a spot above the feeder, such as an overhanging tree branch. And they can jump much farther than you might suspect. Once you determine which branches the squirrels are using, get out your pruning saw and cut the branches back so the squirrels can't reach the feeder. They'll get frustrated and move on to another source of food—and the birds will thank you.

CLOSE THE KITTY LATRINE

One of the most common pest complaints gardeners have is that cats use their garden beds as litter boxes. Here's a three-step way to prevent strays (or your own outdoor cats) from using your garden as a public toilet.

1. Open a new bathroom. One way to keep cats from "going" in your garden is to give them another option. Leave an area of soft sand or uncovered soil that would make a desirable litter spot. If the cats don't catch on right away, add some commercial cat litter.

2. Make it smell like home. Add a little of the soil where the culprits previously sprayed or littered to the new bathroom. Animals tend to return to the scene of an accident.

3. Close the old bathroom. Use one of the commercial products designed to keep pets away from greenery anywhere you don't want cats.

GET MOLES MOVING

A re moles driving you crazy? You can drive them away with a little castor oil, says Bill Winter, a lawn specialist at Russell's Garden Center in Wayland, Massachusetts.

Just spray the ground above their tunnels with castor oil, which is available in spray-top containers at garden centers. "The castor oil won't hurt the lawn," Bill says, "but moles don't like it. They don't like the taste of it when it gets on their food, and they don't like getting it on their fur." Although moles are bad for your lawn because their tunneling damages the roots, they do feed on grubs—as long as the grubs aren't covered with castor oil.

Conquering Creepy Crawlers

According to the pros who know, there are more than 1 million species of insects in the world, and about 90,000 of them live in North America. If you're a gardener, you're probably thinking that they're all living in your vegetable patch. We can't promise to get rid of all 90,000 of them, but we do have some ingenious ways to get rid of some of the peskiest.

Shoo slugs. Slugs just may be the ickiest garden pest known to gardeners. Here are two ingenious ways to get rid of them.

1. Pour them a beer. Slugs are attracted to beer, so in the evening, place a shallow dish (such as the plastic lid from an empty butter tub or coffee can) containing a few tablespoons of beer in your garden. The following morning, you'll probably find several tipsy—or drowned—drinkers in the dish. Dispose of the entire contents and repeat the following evening.

2. Sow seashells. Mulch your garden with crushed seashells, which you can obtain at a garden center or on your own if you live near a beach. Slugs have sensitive skin and don't like to crawl over

---

FOUR BIRDS, ONE STONE

Skunks love to eat grubs," says Jim Ouellet. "So to get rid of skunks, you need to get rid of any grubs in your lawn." Grubs are the tiny, white, soft larvae of various insects that live in the earth under grass. "Skunks can hear the grubs underground and will dig up patches in your lawn during the night," Jim explains. Moles love grubs, too, and will tunnel underground, chomping the grubs as they go and leaving little hills of dirt in their wake.

"The best way to get rid of these guys—and rejuvenate your lawn in the process—is to adopt a lawn care program that includes a biological grub-control agent, which you can find at any garden center," Jim says. By zapping the grubs, you'll be solving four problems at once: skunks, moles, unwanted insects, and a torn-up lawn.

---

the sharp edges of the shells, so there's a good chance they'll find another garden to settle in.

Attract martins. If you don't want to spray your yard or garden with chemical repellents, try getting rid of bugs by attracting purple martins. They're insect eaters whose favorite meal is mosquitoes. "Purple martins migrate from North America to South America and back each year," says biologist Tom Moore. "And they like to return to the same place." Here are three of Tom's favorite tips for attracting martins.

1. Go for the gourd. One trick is to build a house that catches the martins' attention. "Purple martins like to nest in gourd houses," Tom says. "They also prefer open areas near fields or meadows." So pick up a few gourds at the supermarket, produce stand, or garden center. Cut a 3-inch hole in the widest side of each gourd, hollow it out, and let it dry for several days. Hang your gourd house by its neck from a tree branch. And don't worry: Tom assures us that martins don't need perches in front of their houses.

2. Choose early spring. It's best to put up your gourd houses in late March or early April, when the birds are returning from South America. Be patient. Purple martins are choosy and don't readily change their habitats, so it may take a season or two before they notice the new houses. But once they select a home, they're likely to return year after year.

3. Do a little housekeeping. Be sure to clean the gourds between seasons, advises Tom. You'll enjoy years of relatively mosquito-free living along with the companionship of these beautiful birds.

that's • ingenious!

brew up whitefly tea

MASTER GARDENER Joanne Tanner knows a thing or two about keeping pests away from plants. Not only that, but she's also invented a homemade spray, called Joanne's Herbal Concoction, that repels whiteflies. Those pests are especially prevalent in greenhouses and indoor plant collections, but outdoor plants—fuchsias, begonias, geraniums, chrysanthemums, dahlias, and some vegetables, including tomatoes—are also susceptible.

To make her concoction, add 1 teaspoon each dried rosemary, basil, and thyme to 1 quart boiling water. Simmer for 10 minutes. Let the mixture cool, then strain and pour it into a spray bottle.

To use Joanne's Herbal Concoction, rinse the whiteflies from the plant with some water. Then spray the tops and bottoms of the leaves with the mixture. "I spray the soil, too," Joanne says. "And I guarantee that whiteflies are deterred by the smell of this concoction. In fact, it also seems to deter fungus gnats when applied to the soil. Make sure to reapply after rain."

stir things up

PEOPLE THESE DAYS are concerned about mosquito larvae and the risk of West Nile virus—and rightly so—not to mention plain old mosquito bites. Standing water—in puddles and pools, as well as in discarded tires, buckets, and cans—is the culprit. It's where mosquitoes breed. Once you disturb the water, you disturb the larvae.

Each time you water your garden, use high pressure to rinse out buckets, barrels, birdbaths, and any other vessels that hold water. If you're catching water for your garden, use it up regularly. If you see small wiggling things in the rain barrel, use the water or dump it, because the mosquitoes will be arriving shortly.

Don't let fear of mosquitoes or the nasty diseases they might carry prevent you from keeping water around the garden. Just be smart about it!

Make the grubs go away. Grubs—the larvae of Japanese beetles, oriental beetles, or chafers—are a common lawn care problem. An early warning sign of their presence, even before your lawn turns brown, are sightings of grub-eating animals such as moles, crows, or skunks. To be sure, dig up some square-foot patches of your lawn and count how many grubs you find in each patch. More than nine or so indicates a problem. If grubs are bugging you, try these two tips for sending them on their way.

1. Nematodes are nice. Invite what are known as beneficial nematodes to dine on the grubs that are destroying your lawn. You can buy the microscopic worms that feed on grubs from most garden centers or mail-order outlets. The nematodes available from garden centers aren't very aggressive, but they're good to use as a preventive measure. The more aggressive seek-and-destroy type of nematodes are available by mail. (Their life span is only 3 to 4 days, so garden centers don't stock them.) During their short but productive lives, they'll do a good job of clearing out a grub hot spot.

2. Don the sandals of death. Also available at some garden centers are the "sandals of death," aerating sandals with spikes attached to the soles. Those spikes, which break up compacted soil, also stab and kill grubs.

Weeding Out Weeds

What do we hate about weeds? Is it the fact that if you don't keep up with them, they'll choke your garden? Is it because no matter what you do, they always seem to come back? Maybe it's because most of them are just plain ugly. Although weeds can be tough to get under control, don't lose hope. Whacking weeds takes persistence and a little ingenious know-how.

Don't stir things up. The trouble with tilling your garden before you plant is that stirring up the soil actually encourages weeds to grow. Weed seeds can sit dormant in the soil for decades waiting for just the right conditions to sprout. Usually, that means light and moisture. When you till, you bring new seeds to the surface, where they can germinate much faster than your vegetables or flowers. Do yourself (and your back) a favor by not tilling the ground before you plant. Dig only where you're going to plant your seeds, and leave the soil between rows untouched. Chances are the weed seeds near the surface have already sprouted and been pulled. Let those seeds sitting a few inches underground stay dormant for one more season.

Wait to weed. If you're one of those gardeners who runs around the yard pulling up dandelions and other flowering weeds as soon as they sprout, you may be wasting your time, says Bill Winter. "It's better to wait until the weed has flowered," he notes. "The dandelion will have used up its energy reserves to put the flower out, and it won't be able to recover."

weed by the light of the moon

TILLING YOUR GARDEN can encourage weed growth. That's because tilling stirs up the soil and exposes the weed seeds to light, which is all they need to germinate. One solution is to till only where you're going to plant. Another is to till several weeks before you're ready to plant. You can still outwit those pesky weeds by letting them grow for a couple of weeks, then cutting them down at night, when they're most vulnerable.

It's true: Weeds need light to germinate. If you can wait until dark to hoe down the weed seeds that have already sprouted and plant your garden, then you'll be one step ahead of the weeds. Be careful, though, to keep yard lights, night-lights, flashlights, and even tiki torches doused while you do this gardening. Those pesky weed seeds will sprout under any source of light.

Block weeds with black. If you plan to lay plastic around your plants to keep out windblown weed seeds (and to keep in moisture and warmth), make sure it's black, not clear. If you use clear plastic, the seeds that blew in before you had a chance to cover the soil will still get enough light to germinate.

Hoe, hoe, hoe. One of the most effective ways to control annual weeds is to hoe frequently, especially on hot, dry days. The weeds will dry up and die. Hoeing won't totally eliminate weeds, but it will significantly reduce their numbers in your garden.

Boil 'em. Trying to pry weeds from between paving stones is backbreaking, blister-inducing work. But there's an easier way. Just pour a little boiling water onto the weeds (watch your toes), and they'll die posthaste.

CHAPTER 1 • **Teresa Black** is a daycare provider from Seymour, Tennessee; **Nancy Byrd** is a marketing manager from Indianapolis, Indiana; Nine-year-old **Frances Hall** lives in Knoxville, Tennessee; Librarian **Joanne Kennedy**, from Toano Virginia, is the mother of eight; **Lynn Naliboff** is a food editor who lives in Stamford, Connecticut, and works in New York City; **Jim Slate** of Winnsboro, South Carolina, is a retired electrician; **Wade Slate** is a professional handyman from Knoxville, Tennessee; **Keyne and Rob Stanford** live in Tampa, Florida, where Keyne teaches kindergarten and Rob works as an executive chef; **Judy Van Wyk** is an assistant professor of sociology and criminology at the University of Rhode Island; **Amy Witsil** is a mechanical engineer from Chapel Hill, North Carolina.

CHAPTER 2 • **Penny Bosch** is a grandmother from Orange, California; **Todd Graham** owns the Totally Clean! housekeeping service in San Francisco; **Donna Liangis,** of Dearborn, Michigan, owns the House Ka-Teers cleaning company; **Robert F. Maiolo,** known as The Friendly Plumber, lives in San Francisco; **Jonni McCoy,** of Colorado Springs, Colorado, is the author of *Miserly Moms: Living on One Income in a Two Income Economy*; **Marcie Ness,** of Tulsa, Oklahoma, owns Marcie's Housecleaning Service; **Karl Smith,** a retired Naval warrant officer, lives in Newark, Delaware; **Bobby Wright** is assistant manager at the Sierra Club's Clair Tappaan Lodge in Norden, California.

CHAPTER 3 • **Bob Grimac,** of Knoxville, Tennessee, writes and edits an environmental newsletter; **Marie Hofer** is a horticulturist in Knoxville, Tennessee; **Wade Slate,** a professional handyman, lives in Knoxville, Tennessee; **Chad Speerly** is the supervisor and buyer for a natural foods co-op in Knoxville, Tennessee; **Francie Stull,** of College, Station, Texas, runs flea products business; **Amy Witsil** is a mechanical engineer in Chapel Hill, North Carolina; **Robin Woodruff** is a graphic designer from Concord, Tennessee.

CHAPTER 4 • **Rosella Campion** of Medford, Massachusetts, has worked in the clothing industry for many years; **Colleen L. Jones** owns the Fancy Threads School of Custom Sewing in Newton, New Hampshire; **Nancy Kimball** is a professional seamstress from Exeter, New Hampshire; **Mario Ponte** owns Exeter Jewelers in Exeter, New Hampshire; **Kate Ross** is a professional milliner and co-owner of the Head Over Heels hat and shoe shop in Exeter, New Hampshire; **Jan Russell** is co-owner of Head Over Heels.

CHAPTER 5 • **Peter Alexson** is a professional upholsterer in Framingham, Massachusetts; **Kevin Bianchi** is a furniture restorer from Framingham, Massachusetts; **Phoebe Davidson** is a professional decorator in Natick, Massachusetts; **Karen Krowne** is a professional decorator in Wayland, Massachusetts; **John Lawrence,** of Wayland, Massachusetts, is a professional furniture restorer; **Bruce Sweeney,** of Wayland, Massachusetts, is an antique lightning expert; **Wayne Towle** is a furniture and woodwork restorer in Needham, Massachusetts.

CHAPTER 6 • **Larry Bean** is a writer and editor who lives in Natick, Massachusetts; **Rob Dixon** is a contractor from Monticello, Illinois; **Jim Gapinski,** of Des Plaines, Illinois, is a professional handyman; **Bill Keller** is a home improvement enthusiast and handyman from Lemont, Illinois; **Wayne Towle** is a furniture and woodwork restorer in Needham, Massachusetts; **T. J. Wilson,** from Monticello, Illinois, is an amateur handyman.

CHAPTER 7 • **Julie Amato** manages an automotive store in Knoxville, Tennessee; **Bunni Hood** manages a greenhouse in Knoxville, Tennessee; **Michele Karl** is a collectibles expert from Seymour, Tennessee; **Jim Slate** from Winnsboro, South Carolina, is a retired electrician; **Wade Slate** is a professional handyman in Knoxville, Tennessee.

CHAPTER 8 • **Curt Bohlmann,** from Des Plaines, Illinois, is an experienced handyman; **Brian Cannaday** of Hinsdale, Illinois, is a professional window cleaner; **Jim Gapinski,** of Des Plaines, Illinois, is a professional handyman; **Greg Jasinski,** of Lockport, Illinois, is a professional painter; **Dwight Martino** operates his family's construction business, D. Martino Construction Company, in Worth, Illinois.

CHAPTER 9 • **Larry Bean** is a writer and editor who lives in Natick, Massachusetts; **Barbara Falla,** a former nurse and social worker, lives in Natick, Massachusetts; **Donald Ingram** is a fire inspector in Needham, Massachusetts; Lieutenant **Nick Mabardy,** from Natick, Massachusetts, is a police officer; **Terry Marshall** is Director of Emergency Management in Adams County, Nebraska; **Michael Melchiorri,** of Natick, Massachusetts, is a building commissioner; **Daniel Walsh** is a building inspector from Needham, Massachusetts.

CHAPTER 10 • **Karen Bates** is a personal chef from Kansas City, Kansas; World War II veteran **Ed Jensen** of Hastings, Nebraska, was a chef in the service and later ran a bakery and café; **Lynn Naliboff,** of Stanford, Connecticut, works in New York City as a food editor; Personal chef **Sandy Phillips** is from Medfield, Massachusetts; Chef **Tim Rodgers** is associate dean at the Culinary Institute of America in Hyde Park, New York; **Karl Ronhave,** of Portland, Maine, has worked in restaurants as a professional chef for more than 10 years; **Nancy Seaton** is an enthusiastic home cook in Hastings, Nebraska; **T. J. Wilson** of Monticello, Illinois, is an enthusiastic football fan.

CHAPTER 11 • **Colleen Donahue-Bean** is a mom who lives in Winchester, Massachusetts; **Norma Hansen,** from Hastings, Nebraska, is an expert entertainer; **Susan**

Lane is a professional caterer in Weston, Massachusetts; **Lynn Naliboff** is a food editor who lives in Stamford, Connecticut, and works in New York City.

CHAPTER 12 • **Susan Baker** is an aesthetician and herbalist from Atlantis, Florida; **Sally Cadwallader** is a licensed cosmetologist from Costa Mesa, California; **Jonni McCoy,** of Colorado Springs, Colorado, is the author of *Miserly Moms: Living on One Income in a Two Income Economy*; **Angela Stengler,** N.D., and **Mark Stengler,** N.D., are husband-and-wife naturopathic physicians from La Jolla, California; **Stephanie Tourles** is a licensed aesthetician from West Hyannisport, Massachusetts.

CHAPTER 13 • **Dale Anderson,** M.D, FACS, DABHM (Diplomat American Board of Holistic Medicine) is a clinical assistant professor at the University of Minnesota Medical School in Minneapolis and resides in Roseville, Minnesota; **Karen Cichocki** is a retired emergency room nurse from Dyer, Indiana; **William Forgey,** M.D., is president of the Wilderness Medical Society in Gary, Indiana; **Victoria Hamman,** N.D., of San Francicso, is a naturopathic physician; **Dan Hamner,** M.D., is a sports medicine physician and visiting professor of rehabilitation medicine at the New York Hospital-Cornell Medical Center in New York City; **Jerry Huber** is a certified massage therapist in San Francisco; **Doug Levy** is a retired emergency medical technician in San Francisco; **Tiffany Medlin Osborn,** M.D. is an emergency medicine and critical care physician and spokesperson for the American College of Emergency Physicians; **Mark Stengler,** N.D., of La Jolla, California, is a naturopathic physician.

CHAPTER 14 • **Bob Byrd** is a retired high school tennis coach in Indianapolis, Indiana; Master league bowler **Lisa Fine** is from Sevierville, Tennessee; Attorney and fishing expert **Mike Finley** is from North Hills, California; **Margy Floyd,** an avid camper and hiker, manages an indoor rock-climbing gym in Costa Mesa, California; **Chuck Kennedy** is an attorney in Watchung, New Jersey; **Trish McCollum** is an elementary school art instructor in Fountain City, Tennessee; **Lisa Price** edits a sewing and craft Web site in Knoxville, Tennessee; Softball gold medal winner and orthopedic surgeon **Dot Richardson,** M.D. lives in Orlando, Florida; **Tom Russell** of Knoxville, Tennessee, is a program guide art director for a cable television house and garden network; Veteran Little League coach **Wade Slate** is from Knoxville, Tennessee; **Bubba Teeters,** of Lake Worth, Florida, is a softball coach.

CHAPTER 15 • **Bill Brewer,** of Brewster, Massachusetts, is a retired home builder; **Kevin MacIntyre** is a retired contractor from North Reading, Massachusetts; **Linda Mansfield** lives in Stow, Massachusetts; **Joe Murphy** is former masonry professional who worked for many years in Philadelphia; **Roger Neal** lives in Tewksbury, Massachusetts; **Steph Sickles** is a landscaper who lives and works in Arlington, Massachusetts; **Bill Underhill** is the aquatic department manager at Hyannis Country Garden in Hyannis, Massachusetts.

CHAPTER 16 • Groundskeeper **Nick Caggiano** handles field maintenance for Holman Stadium in Nashua, New Hampshire, which hosts the Nashua Pride's minor league baseball games; **Sally Cunningham** is a Cooperative Extension agent and organic gardener from East Aurora, New York; **Bob Dembek** is the golf course superintendent at Stow Acres Country Club in Stow, Massachusetts; **Peggy Giermek** owns Nature Calls Landscaping in East Aurora, New York; Landscaper **Jim Ouellet** is from Exeter, New Hampshire; **Rochelle Smith** is a horticulture/agriculture educator with the Orleans County Cornell Cooperative Extension; **Bill Winter** is a lawn care expert from Wayland, Massachusetts.

CHAPTER 17 • **Danny Papadatos** lived and worked in Buffalo, New York; **Marian Prezyna,** a beekeeper, herbalist, and Master Gardener, is from Marilla, New York; **Joanne Tanner** is a Master Gardener from Orchard Park, New York; **Craig Vogel,** of Eden, New York, is a builder and gardener.

CHAPTER 18 • **Sally Cunningham,** from East Aurora, New York, is a gardening writer and County Extension agent; **Steve Grinley** owns Bird Watcher's Supply & Gift in Newburyport, Massachusetts; **Tom Moore** is a wildlife biologist who works in Suwanee, Georgia; **Jim Ouellet** is a retired florist from Exeter, New Hampshire; **Jen Roediger** worked at a birdwatcher's supply store in North Hampton, New Hampshire; **John Scott,** of Sandwich, Massachusetts, is a wildlife biologist who works for an environmental engineering firm.

CHAPTER 19 • **Beth and David Buckley** are homeowners in Ashford Hollow, New York; **Carol Foss** is a wildlife biologist in Penacook, New Hampshire; **Tom Moore** is a wildlife biologist in Suwanee, Georgia; **Jim Ouellet** is a florist in Kensington, New Hampshire; **John Scott** is a wildlife biologist from Sandwich, Massachusetts; **Joanne Tanner** is a Master Gardener from Orchard Park, New York; **Bill Winter** is a lawn specialist at Russell's Garden Center in Wayland, Massachusetts.

RECOMMENDED READING

Proulx, Earl. *Earl Proulx's Yankee Home Hints: From Stains on the Rug to Squirrels in the Attic, over 1,500 Ingenious Solutions to Everyday Household Problems.* Emmaus, PA: Rodale Press, 1993.

_____. *Yankee Magazine's Make It Last: Over 1,000 Ingenious Ways to Extend the Life of Everything You Own.* Emmaus, PA: Rodale Press, 1996.

_____. *Yankee Magazine's Practical Problem Solver: 1,001 Ingenious Solutions to Everyday Dilemmas.* Emmaus, PA: Rodale Press, 1996.

_____. *Yankee Magazine's Vinegar, Duct Tape, Milk Jugs & More.* Emmaus, PA: Rodale Press, 1999.

Yankee Magazine, ed. *Living Well on a Shoestring.* Emmaus, PA: Rodale Press, 2000.

index

Boldface references indicate illustrations.
Underscored page references indicate boxed text.